THE
DATA
GAME

THE
DATA
GAME

Controversies in
Social Science
Statistics

Mark H. Maier

M.E. Sharpe, Inc.
Armonk, New York
London, England

Library of Congress Cataloging-in-Publication Data

Maier, Mark.
The data game : controversies in social science statistics / by
Mark H. Maier.
p. cm.
Includes bibliographies and index.
ISBN 0-87332-588-5 (cloth) — ISBN 0-87332-768-3 (paper)
1. Social sciences—Statistical methods. 2. Social problems—
Statistics. I. Title.
HA29.M236   1991
300′.1′5195—dc20
90-39658
CIP

Printed in the United States of America

∞

MV (c) 10 9 8 7 6 5 4 3 2
MV (p) 10 9 8 7 6 5 4 3 2

Contents

Figures, Tables, and Boxes

Figures

Tables

Boxes

Preface

This book fills the need for a companion text to introductory statistics courses on the collection and use of social science data. It is suitable for undergraduate courses in statistics and research methods, as well as for first courses in statistics offered in many social science graduate programs.

An analysis of statistical source material is readily justified and often called for by social science practitioners. As illustrated throughout this book, many public policy debates arise because of different interpretations of the underlying data. For topics as diverse as the size of the middle class and the crime rate, ambiguities in the data produce statistics that appear to support opposite positions. Cases such as those included here bring statistics to the real world, demonstrating to students the critical role that data play in a wide variety of social issues.

The subject areas in this book include demography, housing, health, education, crime, the national economy, wealth and poverty, labor, business, and government. Students in all disciplines will benefit from this wide coverage because much research involves social statistics that transcend narrow disciplinary confines, and because almost every example teaches a lesson that has relevance for all the social sciences. Several common questions recur across the disciplinary spectrum represented in this book. How do the popular media misinterpret social statistics? Why are some social statistics continually cited, even though they are widely known to be misleading? Why are some data collected in abundance, while much critically needed data are missing? Why are the categories into which data are organized so critical for statistical analysis? In addition, fundamental statistical techniques are reviewed, including the difference between surveys and complete counts, index numbers, the use of means and medians, and the use of absolute and relative measures. These issues are probed further in case study questions at the end of each chapter, and they are summarized in the final chapter.

In brief, this book is an invitation to social science research for students, whether as future practitioners in social science or as enlightened citizens. *The Data Game* demonstrates the excitement, the frustrations, and always the importance of social statistics as an instrument for understanding and changing the world in which we live.

Acknowledgments

I owe profound thanks to the many specialists who offered guidance in their respective fields of expertise. These generous individuals include Randy Albelda, James Campen, Robert Carson, Todd Easton, Matthew Edel, Theodore Joyce, Peter L. Maier, Scott R. Maier, William D. Mosher, Michelle Naples, Robert Pollin, Richard McGahey, Michael Schiller, David Stern, Michael Swerdlow, Robert Untermann, Thomas E. Weisskopf, and Steven White. Many others provided encouragement and professional advice at key points during this project. In particular, I thank David M. Gordon and members of the Greater Los Angeles Political Economy Seminar. The entire project benefited from the assistance of Lou Ferleger who read every chapter. Lou's political acumen and good sense of pedagogy provided sound advice when it was much needed. For library assistance, gratitude is due in particular to Mary Thomas, Marshall Nunn, and Vitalia E. Aguero. At M. E. Sharpe, I thank Barbara Leffel for her enthusiasm during the book's early stages, and Michael Weber, whose persistent care and interest guided the book to completion. The Glendale College Faculty Development Fund provided much-appreciated release time. And finally, thank you to Anne, my life partner, for whom words are not enough.

THE
DATA
GAME

Chapter 1

Introduction

THE PURPOSE OF THIS BOOK

Social statistics can be frustrating. It seems as if there are numbers to prove anything—even entirely opposite points of view. For example, there are statistics to ''prove'' that the average U.S. family is becoming richer *and* that it is becoming poorer; that the crime rate is up *and* the crime rate is down; that illegal immigration is increasing *and* that it is decreasing; and that the traditional family is both disappearing *and* returning.

A quite natural inclination is to reject all statistical results. After all, why trust any number if equally convincing numbers prove precisely the opposite conclusion? This cynical view was summed up by Benjamin Disraeli, who according to Mark Twain listed, in descending order of credibility, ''lies, damn lies, and statistics.'' Indeed, examples abound in which politicians, journalists, and policy makers fit statistics to their preconceived ideas. This book provides hints to alert readers to ways in which statistics can be misused.

But statistics are more than just sophisticated lies. In most cases the source of contradictory numbers is sincere disagreement between experts. If we can find out why the experts reach different conclusions, we will understand much more about the problem being analyzed. Consider, for example, data on cancer.

The National Cancer Institute maintains the United States is winning the war on cancer because of increases in cancer survival rates and a decline in the cancer death rate for all but the elderly. On the other hand, well-respected health statisticians argue that the war on cancer has failed because the overall cancer death rate has not fallen. As described in chapter 4, the statistics each side marshals in its favor are neither right nor wrong, but instead are based on differing assumptions about which cancers should be counted and what should be expected from a population that is getting older on average and thus more likely to suffer such diseases. At stake in this statistical debate are billions of dollars in research funds as well as potentially costly regulations aimed at controlling the incidence of environmentally caused cancers.

Other statistical controversies presented in this book teach a similar lesson. For example, experts disagree about whether the death penalty deters murder, whether rent control causes housing shortages, and whether taxes are becoming more unfair. No book of reasonable length could presuppose to answer these or any of the many other policy questions raised in the following chapters. Instead, the intent here is to show *why* well-respected researchers are able to reach such contradictory results. In some cases such understanding will help us decide which side is correct; often it is less important to decide which side is correct than to uncover the complex measurement problems that underlie the issue.

Another purpose of this book is to help researchers, both students and more experienced practitioners, in using social statistics. Consider the following hapless case:

A social science researcher wanted to study the effect of military spending on jobs. Do communities with large military contractors benefit from increased employment, as advocates of military spending argue, or does military spending create relatively fewer jobs than other types of government spending, as critics of military spending have charged? To answer this question, the researcher obtained records of military contracts from the U.S. Defense Department arranged by the city where the contractor was located. To measure the number of jobs, the researcher obtained publications of the U.S. Labor Department's Bureau of Labor Statistics, listing employment by location. Armed with a microcomputer statistical package and all the latest knowledge about statistical probability, the researcher was ready to punch in the numbers and find the answer to his question.

But suddenly the project stalled: just about everything was wrong. The Defense Department data were unusable because they listed contracts by the year in which they were awarded, which was not necessarily the year in which they were spent. To make matters worse, the location where the contract was awarded was not necessarily the location where people were hired. In fact, many contracts were subcontracted to other companies of unknown locale. There were problems with the employment data as well. When one employer dominated the industry, the data were not available on the grounds that the information would betray that company's trade secrets. Finally, data from the Defense and Labor departments were incompatible because of different definitions of location. The "city" or "metropolitan area" in each survey was not necessarily the same.

I was the ill-informed researcher in this case. But I was not the first researcher whose good idea floundered because of unusable data. It is a recurring complaint in the social sciences that researchers, from the student in training to the advanced scholar, do not know enough about the data they use. By examining the pitfalls encountered by previous researchers, this book will help today's users of social statistics be more aware of which data sources are available and of the limitations of these data. Had I been aware of the problem of Census Bureau confidentiality frequently encountered by research on business corporations (see chapter 10) before undertaking my failed research on military spending, I would not have expected to find employment data for large firms that dominate a single city's industry. Similar examples will serve as cautionary tales for other researchers.

In summary, this book is written for two groups of readers. First, it will help everyone who is confused by statistics that seem to prove everything and anything. By sorting out the reasons behind seemingly contradictory statistics, we can better understand the issues under debate. Second, this book will assist researchers in assessing the problems of the underlying data. Without such knowledge many social science projects will fail, as in the case of my military spending research, or worse, projects will proceed without sufficient caution as to the data's limitations.

HOW TO USE THIS BOOK

Subsequent chapters are each devoted to a single subject: Demography; Housing; Health; Education; Crime; National Economy; Wealth, Income, and Poverty; Labor Statistics; Business Statistics; and Government. While students of a particular field will find the chapter in that area most useful, the book is intended to be read as a whole. Social scientists work within their own narrow specialty at considerable cost. Most projects use data from outside a narrow discipline, and the data may have limitations that are unknown to the researcher. For example, almost every area in social science measures variables on a per-person basis, a calculation that presupposes accurate population data, which is not necessarily a warranted assumption (as is discussed in chapter 2 on demography). Similarly, geographic units such as Metropolitan Statistical Areas (chapter 3) and corrections of price data for inflation (chapter 11) are common throughout social science research. Thus, it is useful for researchers to consult chapters beyond their narrow specialization.

Each chapter opens with a brief overview of the data sources for that area of social science. These sections will acquaint readers with the names of the most important government and private sector data sources, which statistics they publish, and in many cases, an illustrative "data sample." The names and major publications of these data sources are listed in a table at the opening of each chapter.

Following the "Data Sources" section are "Controversies," a series of debates about the use of statistics in each area. No attempt is made to cover every debate in each field. Instead, controversies have been selected primarily because they form the basis of recent public policy disputes. These include controversies "in the news" such as the U.S. Census population undercount, the disappearing middle class, and the number of homeless individuals in the United States. A second criterion for including a controversy was its use as an instructive illustration of a statistical issue. For example, while the rating of individual cities as the best places to live or the lists of the nation's largest corporations are not particularly critical policy questions, debates about these numbers teach important lessons about the use and misuse of ranking in social statistics.

All of the controversies obviously predate the publication of this book in 1991. But readers should resist the temptation to reject the examples from past years as out-of-date. Almost all the debates are ongoing, perhaps with different individuals or institutions, but still involving the same issues. As long as the underlying social and economic system remains the same, controversies based on fundamental measurement problems will stay with us.

Finally, each chapter concludes with "Case Study Questions," which instructors may assign to students as a means for further learning. These questions are designed to stimulate thought about the issues raised in each chapter. In most cases there is no single "correct" answer, but rather, the questions pose problems that are frequently encountered by researchers. In many instances citations are given for those who want to explore the question in greater depth.

Finally, readers should not overlook the Notes section. There may be found for each subject area recommended guides to data sources, including both official government handbooks as well as privately published works. For each controversy, references include popular presentations in magazines and newspapers, which are often the most accessible sources and worth consulting to see how the topic was generally understood—or misunderstood. In addition, there are references to summary reviews of each public policy debate that often appear in academic journals, as well as citations for the key technical articles for each controversy.

Chapter 2

Demography

Demography, the scientific study of population, provides some of the most fundamental social statistics. This chapter looks at demographic controversies about the size of the population, the birth rate, the classification of individuals by race and ethnicity, household characteristics, and the trend in marriage and divorce. These controversies have public policy implications for congressional representation, social security financing, affirmative action, and family law. In addition, because demographic data are used in so many areas of social science, the potential problems described here have implications for research outside the field of demography itself.

In the United States, the major source of demographic data is the U.S. Census, an attempt made every ten years to count each individual, citizen or noncitizen, with or without legal documentation, who resides in the country. Less well known but similarly comprehensive are U.S. Vital Statistics that tabulate most births, deaths, marriages, and divorces. Researchers accustomed to surveys and the problem of sampling error, might wonder how there can be controversies about statistics based on complete data. This chapter identifies four major problems: (1) despite valiant efforts to be inclusive, not everyone is counted; (2) the categories used to classify race, ethnicity, and type of household are arbitrary, and therefore subject to debate; (3) the most commonly used categories to describe households leave out significant parts of the population; and (4) demographic data on births, marriage, and divorce sometimes lead to misleading predictions.

Where the Numbers Come from

Organizations	Data Sources	Key Publications
Bureau of the Census U.S. Department of Commerce	U.S. Census	*U.S. Census of Population; Statistical Abstract of the United States*
National Center for Health Statistics U.S. Department of Health and Human Services	U.S. Vital Statistics	*Vital Statistics of the United States; Monthly Vital Statistics Report*
Statistics Branch Immigration and Naturalization Service, U.S. Department of Justice	Records of border crossing and naturalization	*Statistical Yearbook of the Immigration and Naturalization Service*

DATA SOURCES

U.S. Census

Collected every ten years since 1790, the U.S. Census is the longest-running consecutive data set in the world. It is also the world's largest data set, compiling information about the sex, age, marital status, and race of nearly every individual residing in the United States. In addition, about one in six households receives a ''long form'' asking forty-five additional questions on such diverse matters as number of motor vehicles owned and level of education. A number of surveys sponsored by the U.S. government use the census as a statistical base, most notably the Current Population Survey (see chapter 9).

> *Data Sample:* In the 1980 U.S. Census for Hazard, Kentucky, of 5,377 inhabitants, 1,839 listed English as their single ancestry group, 34 listed Hungarian, and 14 listed Greek.

Vital Statistics

Most countries have a system for recording births, deaths, marriages, and divorces, called vital statistics. These data were among the first ever collected and thus are used by historians to estimate population for time periods before governments began national censuses. For the United States, Vital Statistics are more recent, and in some cases still incomplete. Data are collected by individual counties and states, and assembled on a national basis by the U.S. National Center for Health Statistics. Hospital records and doctors' reports provide a nearly complete count of births and deaths. (Death rates are discussed in chapter 4 on health.) Local information provides a count of marriages and divorces for the entire nation. However, because of inadequate records in some states, as of 1989 the official Marriage Registration Area omitted eight states, while the Divorce Registration Area omitted nineteen states, including California where one-eighth of all divorces occur.

> *Data Sample:* In 1987, U.S. Vital Statistics recorded 3,809,394 live births, for which 1,375 mothers reported their age to be between 45 and 49 years.

CONTROVERSIES

The Population Undercount

Since 1960, the U.S. Census has relied on self-enumeration, that is, voluntary completion of forms mailed to individual households. Finding those who fail to do so is the Census Bureau's major expense, involving nearly half a million employees recruited for the 1990 census. The homeless, migrants, and transients were counted in a "shelter and street night" visit to inexpensive hotels, shelters, parks, train stations, and abandoned buildings.

For all its efforts, the Census Bureau admits that it misses some individuals. For 1980, the shortfall was estimated at about 3.5 million individuals, or just under 2 percent of the population. Although this error seems small, it was unevenly divided across the country. The undercount was estimated to be four times as high for blacks as for whites, and nine times as high for inner-city residents as for the general population. This bias has important implications for congressional representation and dispersal of government funds. According to New York City officials, the 1980 undercount cost the city one lost congressional representative and a $50 million reduction in federal funds for

---

Box 2.1. **Undercount in History**

Concern about census undercount dates back to 1790 when 3,929,326 individuals were counted but, as Thomas Jefferson wrote to George Washington, the omissions were "very great," and "we are certainly above four million." Following the 1870 census, New York City and Philadelphia successfully demanded recounts, increasing their census population by just over 2 percent. Indianapolis, home of powerful Senator Oliver Morton, obtained a recount based on land annexed *after* the census date so that the city could reach the prestigious 50,000 level. Subsequent research suggests that the biggest error in the 1870 census went uncorrected, an undercount by 10 percent of recently freed Southern blacks.

---

each year. When New York and other large cities filed a lawsuit to force adjustment of the 1990 census, the Census Bureau agreed to an experimental recount in some areas, but only after bitter dispute; uncertainty about how well it will work continues.

During the mid-1980s, census officials devised a plan to survey an additional 300,000 housing units and then compare the data with the original census. The proportion of individuals in this sample that was missed in the original census could be used to provide a minimum estimate of the entire census undercount. However, in late 1987, U.S. Department of Commerce officials who oversee the Census Bureau canceled the plan on the grounds that any manipulation of the numbers would undermine public confidence in the census. Many experts objected strenuously to the decision not to correct the census. Barbara Bailar, the head of Census Bureau statistical research, resigned in protest, charging that "the decision was politically motivated because Republicans would lose from an adjustment." Stephen Feinberg, chair of a National Academy of Sciences panel appointed to study the issue, agreed that the "[Department of] Commerce canned the project" because it "will mean more funds and more votes in areas heavily black and urban."

In July 1989, the census Bureau reached a compromise with civil rights groups and representatives of state and local governments. An additional 150,000 households were to be surveyed, but there was no specific commitment about how this information will be used. As this book went to press, there was renewed discussion of lawsuits to force the Census Bureau to make adjustments in its official reports.

Implications   No population count will ever be completely accurate. When the undercount is higher for some part of the population than for others, there can be significant error in electoral misrepresentation. The 1990 census provides the first test case to see whether it is technically possible to make an accurate adjustment for the undercount—and whether that adjustment will be accepted by all the political groups involved.

For researchers, the problem of the undercount presents a major challenge. Official population data may be misleading, in particular for research that focuses on minority groups or inner-city residents who are most likely to be undercounted. For example, in 1987 sociologists Reynolds Farley and Walter R. Allen recomputed census data to take into account the maximum effect the undercount might have on important social and economic variables for black men aged twenty to thirty-four. This change eliminated the apparent shortage of men relative to women, and, according to Farley and Allen, disproved the thesis that black women remain single because there are relatively few black men in their age group.

Farley and Allen found that other important social statistics were affected in a less dramatic manner. The pay gap between young white men and young black men, measured at 36 percent with traditional statistics, increased only slightly to 39 percent, assuming uncounted black men had extremely low earnings. Similarly, the difference in unemployment rates between black and white men, measured at 5.6 percent, increased to 7.1 percent, assuming the uncounted have very high unemployment rates. Thus, correcting for the undercount caused only a small increase in the measurement of the already severe economic deprivation for young black men.

The lesson for researchers is that population data should be analyzed for the effect of the potential population undercount. Even if the correction is relatively minor, as in the case of income and unemployment, such adjustment adds credibility to research results. Farley and Allen calculated their own estimates of the potential undercount. The availability of official Census Bureau adjustments will simplify the task for researchers, although debate will likely continue about the accuracy of the revised numbers as well.

Undocumented Immigrants

How many immigrants enter the United States without legal status? No one knows for certain. At stake is political representation of areas with large numbers of undocumented immigrant populations. Even though noncitizens cannot vote, they are counted in the U.S. Census and therefore contribute to the apportionment of congressional representation. In 1988, a lobbying group called the Federation for American Immigration Reform, joined by forty members of Congress and the states of Pennsylvania and Kansas, filed a lawsuit to exclude illegal aliens from the U.S. Census. Executive director of the federation Roger L. Conner compared the current system to counting "an army of Russian troops in Oregon." Critics of this position point out that the U.S. Constitution specifically mandates a complete count of all inhabitants, including all nonvoting residents, as the basis for representation.

One problem in the debate about apportionment is that there is wide disagreement about the number of undocumented aliens, who, not surprisingly, are reluctant to report their status to survey takers. In 1975 the U.S. Immigration and Naturalization Service commissioned a survey of experts about the number of illegal aliens; the consensus was approximately 8 million, though the estimates ranged as high as 12 million. These estimates, however, were criticized as "little more than guesses," in a strongly worded 1985 report by the private National Research Council, who suggested a likely range of 1.5 to 3.5 million for the number of undocumented aliens resident in 1980.

In 1990, the U.S. Census Bureau continued its effort to count all residents, documented or not. An arrangement was made with the Immigration and Naturalization Service to postpone arrests during the census period in order to decrease fear of government officials. And it appeared unlikely that representation laws would be changed because of undocumented immigration. But there still was no accurate estimate for the number of undocumented immigrants residing in the United States, so its effect on apportionment remains unknown.

A Birth Dearth?

According to Ben J. Wattenberg of the American Enterprise Institute, the United States will face a population shortage during the next century. Today's low birth rate will produce too few young workers to pay for the elderly's pensions and medical care when the relative size of what he calls the "Western Community" shrinks from its current 15 percent of the world population to 5 percent in the year 2085. Wattenberg asks: "Is it possible that the spread of democratic values may be slowed? Or stopped? Or reversed?" Wattenberg's argument received front-cover attention in national magazines and newspapers, and was adopted by 1988 Republican presidential hopefuls Jack Kemp and Pat Robertson.

Critics charge that Wattenberg's vision is subtly racist because the fast-growing nations he is afraid will dominate the United States are primarily nonwhite. In addition, others argue that it is impossible to predict future populations as accurately as Wattenberg claims. Past experience demonstrates the difficulty in making such projections. For example, after World War II most demographers failed to predict the U.S. baby boom. In 1945, the U.S. Census Bureau underestimated by more than 25 percent the population growth for the following twenty-five years. Demographer Nathan Keyfitz, who studied the error in 1,000 population growth predictions using modern methods, concludes: "We know virtually nothing about the population fifty years from now. We could not risk better than two to one odds on any range narrower than 285 million to 380 million for the year 2030." In other words, the margin of error encompasses both Wattenberg's scenario of too few Americans as well as those who argue that the United States will suffer from *over*population. Keyfitz advises researchers to be modest. Rather than attempting to predict population size far into the future, Keyfitz would like to see social scientists study problems for the population *already* born. For example, schools need assistance in planning for enrollments, which can be easily anticipated on the basis of the current birth rate, which is seldom used in education planning.

Will You Still Feed Me?

Declining births and increasing longevity (see chapter 4) combine to create an aging U.S. population. With more people retired, and proportionately fewer people working, some policy advisers warn that the United States faces a social security funding crisis. Today more than three workers contribute to the social security fund for every beneficiary; by the year 2030, there will be fewer than two workers for every beneficiary. Former presidential economic adviser Paul Craig Roberts fears that we face the choice of curtailing future benefits or raising taxes to "prohibitive levels." Michael Boskin, chief economic adviser to President Bush, argues in his book, *Too Many Promises: The Uncertain Future of Social Security*, that we should begin now to phase out benefits for the well-to-do, and place greater reliance on individually financed pension programs.

Other social scientists are much less pessimistic about the ability of tomorrow's workers to support the elderly. No one disputes the unavoidable reality of an increasingly older population, but it is also likely that the pyramid will shrink at the bottom at the same time that it grows at the top. Most demographers also anticipate continued low birth rates so that the working population will support a smaller number of young people. The total population dependent on those of working age includes both the elderly *and* children, a fraction that Merton Bernstein, principal consultant to the National Commission on Social Security Reform, estimates to rise to about 72 percent in 2040 from its 1980 level of 63 percent. But this will still be well below the 80 percent dependent proportion that existed in 1960. Based on such evidence, economist Frank Ackerman concludes, "If we could afford to live through the childhood of the baby boom generation, we can afford to live through its retirement."

Those who are more worried about the future of social security respond that *federal* expenditures for children are only about one-sixth the amount currently spent on adults. Thus, there will be no easy transfer of funds from one purpose to another, in particular because, as Phillip Longman observes, "we must consider the harsh reality that most parents derive far more satisfaction and reward in spending money on their own children than in paying taxes to support the elderly in general." On the other side, some policy makers favor the use of general federal tax revenues to pay for social security. Such programs already exist in Western Europe to support relatively generous retirement programs for elderly populations already nearly as large on a percentage basis as the United States will experience during the next century.

The debate about the future of social security is complicated because it combines two issues, one demographic and one political. On one hand there is a demographic estimate for the future population profile. All researchers agree that the number of elderly will increase dramatically; retirees for the problem years around 2030 are already born. We are uncertain about the future number of young working people and children, but barring a radical change in the birth rate, their numbers will be proportionately less than at present. The second issue is political: How will the smaller sized working population pay for the increased number of retirees during the next century? It is important for researchers not to confuse the two issues. Politicians may prefer to use demographic certainty to defend policies they favor for other reasons. Good social science can ascertain how much demography in fact will constrain future policy, and how much political leeway we have in funding programs such as those for the elderly.

Race and Ethnicity

The fourth question of the 1990 U.S. Census read:

Fill ONE circle for the race that the person considers himself/herself to be:

__White __Black or Negro __Indian (Amer.)
(Print the name of the enrolled or principle tribe)_____
__Eskimo __Aleut
Asian or Pacific Islander (API)
__Chinese __Japanese __Filipino __Asian Indian __Hawaiian __Samoan
__Korean __Guamanian __Vietnamese __Other API_____
(If Other Asian or Pacific Islander (API) print one group, for example, Hmong, Fijan, Thai, Tongan, Pakistani, Cambodian, and so on)_____
If Other race, print race_____

Many respondents answered without difficulty; the question is common in student surveys, affirmative action programs, and other questionnaires where policy makers want to assess racial and ethnic populations. But, in a debate that is already two centuries old, social scientists remain uncertain how to measure race and ethnicity. As the United States becomes an increasingly multiethnic nation, such classification will be even more difficult. Recent controversy raises three questions: who is black, who is Asian, and who is Hispanic?

Who Is Black? Enumeration by race dates back to the first U.S. Census in 1790, when black slaves were enumerated separately so that

---

Box 2.2. **Black "Insanity": An Argument for Slavery**

When the 1840 U.S. Census counted the "insane and idiots," they measured an extraordinarily high rate of 1 in 162 for Northern free blacks (and 1 in 6.7 in Maine), compared to only 1 in 1,558 in the South. Proslavery advocates cited these census results to argue that "free negroes of the northern states are the most vicious persons on this continent." This curious statistical result was not fully explained until the 1980s when historian Patricia Cohen looked at the original census forms. Apparently many census takers miscoded as black, older senile whites, who were considered idiots in common parlance. The mistake was easy to make because the two items were close together on an unwieldy eighty-column form.

---

they could be counted as three-fifths of a person in congressional apportionment. For free individuals, tabulation by race presented problems that continue to the present day. The Census Bureau follows the commonplace North American social definition of race by which a person is classified as "black" if one parent is black, or pushing the definition back one generation, an individual also is black if one grandparent is black, even if three grandparents are white. Responses different from the standard black-white dichotomy, such as mulatto, Creole, African, or Afro-American, are automatically recoded as black. This practice is also used in official U.S. Vital Statistics where instructions read: "When the husband is white and wife is not, the child is assigned the wife's race. When the husband is not white, the child is assigned to the husband's race."

Such a definition of race by ancestry is not universal; Central and South Americans define race more commonly by skin color. North American racial categories likely derive from the time when the offspring of white masters and black slaves were classified as slaves. During the 1800s, the U.S. Census experimented with expanded categories for mulattos, quadroons, and octoroons. But this was abandoned because census takers, who were supposed to classify individuals on sight, could not consistently allocate individuals to these categories. In the modern census, race is self-determined, but most often on the principle that any degree of nonwhite background causes an individual to be nonwhite.

Who Is Asian? Since 1870, the U.S. Census question about race included choices of countries of origins for Asian-Americans. Originally only Chinese or Indian, the choice was expanded by 1930 to include Japanese, Filipino, Hindu, Korean, and "other." When later immigration included significant numbers from other countries as well, the Census Bureau intended for respondents to use the "other" category. Instead, however, some Thais and Cambodians wrote in their background, usually in place of Vietnamese, causing the computer to misread their forms. In addition, some respondents used the "other" category to report themselves as Taiwanese (instead of Chinese as the census intended), or Greek (instead of white as the census intended).

To avoid these problems, and to save space in the form, the Census Bureau proposed that all Asian-Americans write in their background for the 1990 census. Census officials were eager to abandon the Asian "race question" because it took so much space in proportion to the number of respondents affected. Representatives of Asian communities protested that the procedure would cause a serious undercount, because Asian-Americans with poor English-language skills would be unable to write in their background. At stake were social programs such as English education that are sometimes allocated based on census data. Census officials rejected attempts to reinstate the check-off for Asian background, compromising only as far as a promise to publish Asian-American data without the five-year delay that followed the 1980 census.

Who Is Hispanic? Debate about how to count U.S. residents from Spanish-speaking countries (except Spain) is now several decades old—but still unresolved. The census has changed how it counts Hispanics in nearly every census since 1930, beginning with answers to the race question: "other nonwhite" (1930), "persons of Spanish mother tongue" (1940), "white persons of Spanish surname" (1950 and 1960), and "persons of both Spanish surname and Spanish mother tongue" (1970), and finally, differentiation of Hispanics in a separate question (1980 and 1990).

Each of these designations created confusion for respondents. Reinterviews following the 1970 census showed that more than 20 percent of those with Spanish background changed their answer to the same question, with an approximately equal number shifting themselves from "non-Spanish" to "Spanish" as from "Spanish" to "non-Spanish." And, aside from errors in the original data, researchers do not have a consistently defined population to compare over time.

Dissatisfaction with such uncertain data, coupled with growing political power among Hispanics, resulted in a new question for the 1980 census:

> Is this person of Spanish/Hispanic origin or descent? No (not Spanish/Hispanic); Yes, Mexican, Mexican-Amer., Chicano; Yes, Puerto Rican; Yes, Cuban; Yes, Other Spanish/Hispanic.

Although separation of the race and Hispanic ethnicity questions eliminates one source of ambiguity in the census, other problems remain. Jamaicans and other West Indians are still often confused about how to classify themselves. As non-Hispanics, and nonnative blacks, they often list their background in the "other" category, which, as noted above, was intended by the Census Bureau for Asian-Americans only. In addition, West Coast Hispanics, primarily of Mexican background, prefer the term "Latino" which does not appear on the census form.

These uncertainties, coupled with nonresponse to the census by illegal immigrants, leads some researchers to conclude that the Hispanic count in the census is far too low. The Census Bureau admits an undercount as high as 5 million, but some researchers claim there are as many as 16 million uncounted Hispanics, double the official number. At stake are programs to increase Hispanic political representation, as for example in a 1989 court order for the Los Angeles City Council to redraw its districts in order to increase Hispanic representation.

Implications   At present, the traditional black-white classification is satisfactory for most research purposes. Modern anthropology demonstrates that the human species as a closely inbred group in which there is little genetic variation between so-called racial groups. This newly accumulated evidence weighs in favor of an argument put forward nearly fifty years ago by anthropologist Ashley Montagu that we abandon race altogether as a meaningful scientific category.

Even if it has no *scientific* basis, self-enumeration by race has legitimate *social* validity. In other words, if people describe themselves as black or white, then for most research it makes sense to classify them in that category. Nonetheless, it is important for researchers to be

Box 2.3. **Ethnicity and Race**

Classification of Hispanics by race also changed in recent years. Prior to 1980, respondents who identified themselves as Cuban, Puerto Rican, or Chicano were automatically reclassified as white. When the separate category of Hispanic background was introduced, Hispanics could choose a racial label in addition to their ethnic identification. A majority of Hispanics (about 58 percent) identified themselves as white, only about 3 percent as black, while most of the remainder wrote in a response that was coded as "Spanish race." Nonetheless, race remains important for Hispanics in the United States. In a major study of housing segregation, demographers Nancy A. Denton and Douglas S. Massey found far greater segregation for black Hispanics than for white Hispanics. Denton and Massey conclude, "race . . . is more important than ethnicity in explaining patterns of residential segregation."

aware of social changes that may alter our racial and ethnic perceptions. The shifting nature of race classification is evident in Census Bureau categories for Asian-Americans and Hispanics. Increased political power has enabled these ethnic groups to demand a more accurate census count. But by changing the categories in almost every census, the census has made it difficult for researchers to compare population groups over time. Future censuses likely will introduce new race and ethnic categories, further challenging our research skills. But the changing manner in which we view race is itself a fascinating window on human relations in the United States.

Households and Families

The U.S. Census Bureau uses the terms "household" and "family" differently from everyday usage. The household is defined by the housing unit, not by the social or biological relationship of the individuals. Thus, two families sharing a single home are counted as a single household, as are a family and a lodger, or a group of individuals sharing a home. Households are subdivided between "family households," groups of two or more persons related by birth, marriage, or adoption, and "nonfamily households," including individuals living alone and unrelated individuals residing together.

Table 2.1

Types of Households (1987)

	Percentage of total persons in household type
Family households	87.2
Married-couple family	70.6
With own children under 18	42.8
Without own children under 18	27.8
Male householder, no spouse present	3.0
Female householder, no spouse present	13.5
Nonfamily household	12.8
Living alone	8.9

Source: Statistical Abstract of the United States (Washington, D.C.: U.S. Government Printing Office, 1989), p. 48.

As recently as 1950, nearly 80 percent of all households were married-couple families. By 1988, only 57 percent of households fell in the traditional family household, largely because of an increase in the number of individuals living alone (see Box 2.5). Unfortunately, many research projects are limited only to family households, thereby leaving out a significant proportion of the population. Sociologist Christopher Jencks points out that even the Census Bureau is guilty of this bias in its annual report on income (see chapter 8), which understates the well-being of U.S. households by looking only at family incomes, leaving out the growing number of young, affluent individuals who live on their own.

Even less likely to be included in research projects are individuals who not do not live in households as defined by the Census Bureau. For example, the Current Population Survey, the source for much data on housing, education, income, and employment (see chapters 3, 5, 8, and 9), leaves out most of those who live in group quarter populations such as military barracks, prisons, hospitals, and nursing homes (college dormitory residents are counted with the parents' families).

"Oh No, I Forgot to Get Married!"

"Too late for Prince Charming?: A new study reports that college-educated women who are still single at the age of thirty-five have only

Box 2.4. **Head of Household**

Until 1980, the "head of household" was automatically assigned to a man—even if a woman respondent coded herself as the household head. The procedure was abandoned, in part because it perpetuated sexist stereotyping, but also because the increasing number of nontraditional family arrangements made it difficult to identify the head of the household. Now, one individual of either sex can be designated the "householder"; over 1,600,000 married women out of about 52,000,000 married couples identified themselves as householder in 1980.

a 5 percent chance of ever getting married,'' was the provocative title to *Newsweek*'s cover story for June 2, 1986. This and similar articles were fueled by a single research paper by social scientists Neil Bennett, David Bloom, and Patricia Craig. In addition to frightening well-educated women about their marriage prospects, the research prompted alarm from writers such as Bryce J. Christensen who predicted that the ''flight from marriage'' would cause higher health care costs (because single people are more often ill) and would decrease the future tax base to pay for old-age benefits (because these unmarried women will bear fewer children).

By contrast, a U.S. Census Bureau study only one year later directly contradicted the Bennett-Bloom-Craig conclusions, estimating that college-educated women over thirty-five years old actually had a 32 percent chance of marrying. These data generated relatively little interest, and no news magazine cover stories. The lack of attention to the Census Bureau study is especially remarkable because the Bennett-Bloom-Craig findings were only tentative results, as part of a larger research project on differences between black and white marriages. In fact, when Bennett-Bloom-Craig officially published their research in 1989, the disputed findings about marriage were omitted.

Why did Bennett-Bloom-Craig and the Census Bureau reach such different conclusions? Although both groups used past marriage rates to predict future marriage rates, they differed in the assumptions about how those marriage rates would be distributed across the lifetimes of today's unmarried female population. The Bennett-Bloom-Craig model assumed that today's women would marry over a similar range

---

Box 2.5. **Individuals Living Alone**

Since 1940, the fastest-growing household type was the single individual, increasing from under 8 percent of all households to over 20 percent of households in 1980. Then, abruptly during the mid-1980s, the trend came to a halt. Demographers identified two sources for the change, each adopted as statistical evidence for divergent political viewpoints. Conservatives acclaimed the decline in single-person households as a return to traditional marriage. Liberals pointed to the number of young adults returning to living with their parents because of adverse economic prospects, an alleged legacy of Reagan administration policies. Both factors probably play a role in the decline of single-person households.

---

of years as their mothers. In other words, the marriage rate would peak at age twenty-five and decline quickly thereafter. On the other hand, the census model assumed that women would spread marriage over a broader range of years so that postponing marriage would not mean foregoing marriage.

Data collected since 1980 weigh against the Bennett-Bloom-Craig position. By 1985, the proportion of ever-married women in the age group thirty-five to thirty-nine years had *already* increased above the level predicted in 1980 by Bennett-Bloom-Craig for these women during their *entire lifetimes*. But like the Census Bureau report, such corrections to *Newsweek*'s "Too Late for Prince Charming" have received relatively little publicity.

Divorce

Data on divorce are less accurate than most other family statistics for several reasons. The usually comprehensive Vital Statistics are incomplete for divorce, leaving out several states, including California, where one-eighth of all divorces occur. To make matters worse, statistics from reporting states lack data on race in more than 25 percent of all divorce reports and on age in over 10 percent of divorce reports. Alternative data from the U.S. Census Bureau are unsatisfactory because respondents do not accurately report their marital history: men report more than 10 percent fewer divorces than women (although the number should be nearly precisely equal). Even the more accurate women's answers measure a divorce rate substantially less than must have occurred based on legal records counted in U.S. Vital Statistics.

Despite these problems in divorce statistics, the trend in the U.S. divorce rate is unmistakable: it more than doubled during the 1960s and 1970s, and declined slightly during the 1980s. The recent trend away from divorce prompted speculation by the popular media about the return to traditional values, and rejection of divorce as a solution to marital problems. Pollster Louis Harris reported in 1987 that "The prophets of doom could not be any more wrong. The American family is surviving." On the other hand, demographers Teresa Castro Martin and Larry L. Bumpass argue that "it would be foolish" to jump to the conclusion that marital life has become more stable.

These contrasting assessments occur because no one knows for certain what the future holds. Harris anticipates continued decline in the divorce rate on the basis of survey results showing 89 percent of married respondents satisfied with their relationship. Martin and Bumpass estimate that two-thirds of all current marriages will fail, including marriages ended by separation without divorce, a category not included in official statistics.

Census Bureau researchers Arthur J. Norton and Jeanne E. Moorman take a middle position. They concur that recent marriages appear to have a lower divorce rate—but only slightly. The projected rate of divorce for women 25 to 29 years old in 1985 was 53.6 percent, only 2 percent lower than the projected 55.5 percent total divorce rate for women 35 to 39 years old, and far greater than the 36.4 rate for women 45 to 49 years old. These data suggest to Norton and Moorman that the divorce rate is highest for baby boomers (women 35 to 39 years old in 1985), but the general rate of divorce will remain high for those born afterward.

Few social science studies cause such furor as estimates for the trend in marriage and divorce. Questions about family appear to raise doubts about both our individual futures, as well as our society's well-being. On the individual level, it is important to apply overall statistics with caution. The chance of marriage and divorce depends as much on individual circumstances as on social averages. For example, the divorce rate for couples who marry late in life is far lower than for those who marry young. On the societal level, we should remember that estimates for future marriage and divorce rates depend critically on what assumptions we make. Already the low marriage rates for older women estimated in 1986 appear to be inaccurate. Predictions about the divorce rate vary tremendously; we must wait to see what actually will occur.

SUMMARY

The demographic controversies described in this chapter serve as an introduction to problems researchers find in all social science statistics.

First, we never have complete data. Even when our source attempts universal sampling, as in the U.S. Census and Vital Statistics, some of the population will be missed. There is no secret to this lack of completeness. Census Bureau researchers are at the forefront in identifying the extent of the undercount, and developing methods to correct it. Similarly, shortcomings in the Vital Statistics, primarily nonreporting states, are a matter of public record. Responsibility lies with researchers to explicitly recognize the possible implications of less-than-complete data.

Second, all studies are limited by the categories in which the data are classified. This chapter summarizes U.S. experience in racial and ethnic categories. Classification that seemed "natural" in the past is today considered hopelessly naive. Researchers need to remember that today's categories, based on today's social biases, will change with new developments in race and ethnic relations. Official use of the terms "household" and "family" also demonstrate the importance of careful attention to classification. In this case, not only are official definitions different from everyday usage, but the changing characteristics of U.S. living situations mean that research on traditional "family households" will leave out increasing numbers of individuals.

Third, studies of marriage, divorce, and social security demonstrate the hazard of predicting the future. Even when our knowledge about past trends is relatively accurate, estimates for the future must involve debatable assumptions. We do not know if past trends will continue, or new trends will arise, as indeed occurred in recent marriage and divorce rates. Although such uncertainties plague all predictive social science research, popular media coverage rarely warns readers about the problem. Moreover, in the case of marriage predictions for older women, the media were selective in emphasizing the projection of large numbers of presumably unhappy unmarried older women, but not the rejoinder from the Census Bureau that found far more flexibility in the choices for older women. Predicting the future of social security was more complicated because it involved not only assumptions about the future, but also dispute about which statistic is most relevant. Again, the popular media emphasized only frightening prospects—too many retirees—without reporting the possibly countervailing trend of fewer children.

The overall lesson is one of cautious activism. We have much to learn from demography. It would be a mistake to throw up our hands and reject all research using demographic statistics just because no data are perfect. Instead, the controversies imply a constant struggle to understand the world. By learning about limitations in the data and biases on the part of data users, we can better evaluate the policy implications of current research.

CASE STUDY QUESTIONS

1. In a survey using Census Bureau race and ethnic categories, 20 percent of California college students left the question blank. How might these omissions affect research projects on enrollment, financial aid, or graduation rates?

2. About one-half of all Americans who married during the early 1980s lived with someone of the opposite sex before their first marriage, four times the percentage a decade earlier. How does cohabitation affect the marriage rate? The divorce rate?

3. There are conflicting measures of the U.S. divorce rate. In the U.S. Census, men report 10 percent fewer divorces than women. Vital Statistics measure more divorces than reported by women or men to the census. Explain these discrepancies.

4. Space for questions in the 3.5-square-feet of the Census Bureau's long form is extremely limited. Lobby groups campaign hard for the addition of new questions. In 1990, the successful contenders included questions about access to different types of transportation and the presence of stepchildren in the household. Losers included questions about home heating and the number of pets. What arguments would you make in favor of or against each of these questions?

5. The 1924 "National Origins Act" severely restricted immigration based on the proportion of national backgrounds already in the current population. Estimates of ethnicity were derived from surveys of family names in which Mueller might indicate German background, O'Leary might indicate Irish background, and Miller or Leary might represent English background. German and Irish lobbyists challenged the numbers, and gained an increase in their quotas. Why?

6. The U.S. Census counts 20 percent more black men marrying non-Hispanic white women than the U.S. Vital Statistics. Many factors probably are involved, including racial self-identification, incomplete coverage in the Vital Statistics, previous marriages not counted in the census, and cohabitation reported as marriage. Why did each of these factors lead to discrepancy between the census and Vital Statistics?

7. In Brazil and most Caribbean islands, race is a graduated category, with approximately twenty subtle classifications depending on skin tone and physical features, not necessarily correlated with the racial designation assigned to one's parents. Nonetheless, researchers document discrimination in the social status and pay levels of white versus dark-skinned workers. How would you design a survey form to measure "race?" in these countries? How would it differ from the U.S. Census classification described in this chapter?

Chapter 3

Housing

Housing is the largest single component of U.S. household budgets, comprising more than 40 percent of expenditures as measured by the Bureau of Labor Statistics (see chapter 9). In national income accounts, residential construction is the largest component of investment, averaging about $200 billion per year. Thus, housing statistics warrant separate and detailed attention.

This chapter first looks at two major U.S. housing statistical debates: Have housing standards improved? And is housing less affordable? These two factors are the source of most controversy about the role of government housing programs and the efficacy of private-sector housing. Next, this chapter reviews debate about the number of homeless, an interesting case study of problems that occur when policy makers focus on a single difficult-to-measure statistic. The final section of this chapter looks at geographic divisions used in social science research, most of which are based on place of residence. Researchers need to know how changes in geographic units affect the definition of urban, metropolitan, and rural areas. Two studies based on geographic divisions are summarized: the trend in racial segregation, and comparison of the desirability of different urban areas.

DATA SOURCES

U.S. Census

Although the U.S. Census is best known as a population count, it is officially a "Census of Population *and Housing.*" Impetus for a na-

Where the Numbers Come from

Organizations	Data Sources	Key Publications
Bureau of the Census U.S. Department of Commerce	U.S. Census	*U.S. Census of Housing*
U.S. Department of Housing and Urban Development Bureau of the Census, U.S. Department of Commerce	American Housing Survey; Census of Construction	*Current Housing Reports; Current Construction Reports*
Bureau of Labor Statistics, U.S. Department of Labor	Consumer Expenditure Survey	*Monthly Labor Review*

tional housing survey came during the Great Depression of the 1930s in order to determine the degree of inadequate housing, and to assess how new housing construction would stimulate the economy. When these surveys proved successful, the U.S. census added housing to its 1940 population count. By 1990, the housing section of the census grew to six out of fourteen questions on the short form (administered to all households) and nineteen out of fifty-nine questions on the long form (completed by a sample of nearly 20,000,000 households).

Census housing data provide the most comprehensive statistics. The major drawback to the census is timeliness; the mobile-home data cited below were published in October 1984, more than four years after the census.

> *Data Sample:* In the 1980 census, there were 3,874,236 households living in mobile homes, of which 36,851 moved into the home before 1960. On the local level, there were 158 mobile-home households in New Orleans with incomes reported over $50,000.

Box 3.1. **U.S. Census versus AHS**

One might expect that the U.S. Census and American Housing Survey would yield similar results. But in 1980 about 200,000 more units were counted in the census; homeownership was approximately one percentage point less; multiple units were 3 percent more common; and 3 percent more houses had been built in the last decade than were counted in the AHS. Several factors are thought to account for these differences:
• Sampling error—as a survey, the AHS is subject to uncertainty because of the random choice of respondents. This error can be calculated precisely and is published in AHS reports.
• Coverage error—both programs have identified weaknesses: the AHS tended to miss new buildings because recent permits were not added to the sample; the census was not effective in finding conversion units.

American Housing Survey

The American Housing Survey (AHS), called the Annual Housing Survey until 1984, provides data on a speedier and more frequent basis than the census. Conducted by the Census Bureau for the Department of Housing and Urban Development every year since 1973, the AHS samples households across the country on a staggered basis, providing data on the size and quality of housing, neighborhood characteristics, home financing, and recently moved households.

> *Data Sample:* In 1984, the Housing Survey estimated 290,600 households in Cleveland had dishwashers, while 265,100 had in-sink disposal units.

Other Census Surveys

Census Bureau economic surveys provide data on the housing industry. Most closely watched are "housing starts," a key measure of the economy's overall health, and one component of the Index of Leading Economic Indicators (see chapter 7). In addition, extensive local data in the economic surveys on vacancies, mortgages, and rents are used by the housing industry for planning purposes.

Data Samples: The October 1988 *Current Construction Report* shows permits for forty-three structures with five or more units in Orlando, Florida, in August 1988. In *Characteristics of New Housing* we learn that 58 percent of new 1986 houses had fireplaces, up from 50 percent in 1982.

Other Price Data

The Department of Labor's Bureau of Labor Statistics monitors housing costs in the Shelter Index, a part of the Consumer Price Index (see chapter 11). The Shelter Index provides a single statistic for the cost of rents, new home prices, mortgage rates, and home upkeep for the United States and selected geographic areas. Widely reported statistics on new and existing home prices, including the "Affordability Index" described below, are assembled by the National Association of Realtors and the National Association of Home Builders based on a combination of census data and their own surveys.

CONTROVERSIES

Housing Quality

Is there a crisis in U.S. housing standards? Housing experts disagree. In one view, the quality of U.S. housing has improved dramatically since World War II, testimony to the success of the private-sector housing market. Another view argues that serious problems in housing quality remain, requiring an expanded public role in housing markets. These opposite conclusions occur in part because data in the U.S. Census tell a quite different story from data in the American Housing Survey.

By traditional U.S. Census housing statistics, housing quality problems have almost disappeared. Severe overcrowding, more than 1.5 persons per room, at one time associated with health problems such as tuberculosis, fell from 9 percent of housing units in 1940 to only 1 percent in 1980. Similarly, a second key statistic, lack of complete plumbing, dropped from 45 percent of housing in 1940 to about 2 percent in 1980. The Census Bureau's overall indication of dilapidation declined from 18 percent of all housing units in 1940 to only 3.7 percent of housing in 1970. (This measure was dropped after 1970 because subjective judgments about what constituted "dilapidation" varied so greatly from one census enumerator to another.) Such remarkable improvements in U.S. housing quality are hailed by some policy advisers as evidence that the United States has solved housing problems better than many people realize.

Other researchers maintain that census data focus on limited, outdated indicators of housing quality. Since 1973, far greater detail has been available in the American Housing Survey, which covers more than twenty-five deficiencies including leaky roofs, rat infestations, and neighborhood problems such as crime. For rental units, these three deficiencies worsened during the first eight years of the AHS. (There was a slight improvement for owner-occupied housing.) On this basis, some policy makers argue in favor of activist government housing programs, most importantly to assist low-income renters.

Those opposed to new government housing programs complain that a "moving target" is being applied to the housing problem. In other words, when housing was no longer overcrowded or dilapidated, government program supporters changed the definition of decent housing to the much broader criteria in the AHS. In this view, the housing crisis can never be solved if we keep changing our goals to ever-higher standards, when in fact existing housing policy, relying on the private market, has solved the major housing problems.

Implications For researchers, expanded data in the AHS are clearly an improvement over U.S. Census housing statistics, if only because the housing quality problems measured by the census now apply to so few houses. However, the wide scope of the AHS requires researchers to make decisions about which quality issues are relevant. Because some quality measures usually improve in any given year, while others decline, the overall trend depends upon which factors are selected. Researchers should consider using widely accepted indexes of housing quality that combine different variables in the American Housing Survey. Such indexes are available from the U.S. Department of Housing and Urban Development, the Congressional Budget Office, or the U.S. Office of Management and Budget.

Is There an Affordability Crisis?

Beginning in the late 1970s, the most contentious housing policy debates shifted away from the issue of substandard housing toward the problem of reasonably priced housing regardless of quality.

Proportion Spent on Housing   According to most household budget experts, housing costs should comprise no more than 25 percent of household income. But in recent years a majority of renters broke the 25 percent rule and 34 percent paid 35 percent or more of their income for housing. For homeowners with mortgages, 31 percent broke the 25 percent rule, and 21 percent paid 35 percent or more. (Those with paid-off mortgages, primarily the elderly, have much lower housing costs.) These data are cited frequently as evidence for a housing crisis. In fact, given the reality of housing costs, some consumer experts have shifted to 33 percent as a more realistic expectation for housing costs as a proportion of income.

Other experts question this pessimistic view of housing affordability on the grounds that homeowners have chosen improved housing quality in return for higher costs. Not surprisingly, better housing absorbs a greater proportion of household budgets. But the measurement of quality is tricky. The Census Bureau estimates a "new housing price index," taking into account quality changes. By this statistic, over one-half of price increases during the early 1980s resulted from larger houses with more amenities. But new houses are only a small part of the housing market, in particular for low-income families. The U.S. Labor Department's Bureau of Labor Statistics estimates costs for all homeowners (adjusted for quality changes) in its "Shelter Index." On this basis, housing costs increased significantly faster than the overall cost of living. (See chapter 11 on controversy about the Shelter Index in the overall inflation rate.)

Proportion Able to Afford the Median-priced Home   The National Association of Realtors calculates a housing "affordability" index based on the income needed to qualify for the median-priced resale home, assuming mortgages should comprise no more than 25 percent of income. In May 1982, the index reached a low of 65.2 percent, meaning the typical, "median" family had less than two-thirds the income necessary to purchase the typical home. As interest rates declined, this affordability index improved steadily during the 1980s, rising nationwide above 100 percent in 1986 (the median family could afford the median house).

Two problems have complicated interpretation of this index. First, despite apparent unaffordable housing, more people are buying houses.

At the height of the affordability crisis in 1980, more married couples under thirty-five owned their own home than ever before, increasing to 62 percent in 1980 from 49 percent in 1970. Based on such shortcomings, American Enterprise Institute researcher Ben Wattenberg assails as a myth the popular conception of "we-just-can't-seem-to-afford-a-house." Political columnist Warren T. Brookes adds that rising incomes during the 1980s further improved the homeowning prospects of first-time buyers.

However, a second problem with the affordability index questions these rosy assessments. Improved homebuying circumstances on the *average* combine falling home prices in some areas with skyrocketing home prices in precisely those areas where the job market attracted new residents. Thus, low median 1988 prices in Des Moines, Iowa ($54,800), and Lansing, Michigan ($56,700), are no solace to someone with a job in a fast-growing area with high median housing prices such as Los Angeles ($191,200) and San Diego ($157,200). In addition, housing availability is not evenly distributed across price ranges. Sociologist James D. Wright measures a "housing squeeze" in which the number of low-income households increased faster than the number of low-priced housing units, in his view a critical factor in the 1980s rise in homelessness (see below).

Implications The debate about housing costs illustrates the pitfalls of looking at only a single statistic. By itself, national housing data may misrepresent changing housing quality as well as differences in the housing market faced by households in varying regions and income groups. Similarly, a single time period can mislead, as for example the late 1970s when home prices increased, or the mid-1980s when prices moderated. To fully appreciate the housing market, researchers need to look at a variety of statistics.

Government in the Housing Market?

Should governments become involved in housing, either with rent controls or public housing projects? Or should housing be left to unregulated private industry? Those researchers who measure problems in housing quality and affordability tend to argue in favor of government programs, while those who measure improved housing quality and less of an affordability problem argue for the private market. A second difference between these two groups is their assessment of past government programs, in particular rent control and public housing.

Rent Control   No housing policy is more heatedly debated than rent control, especially in view of its relatively minor importance in U.S. housing markets. The most frequently cited example of rent control is an actual freeze on rents imposed in New York City after World War II, even though such restrictions have been enforced practically no where else. And, after 1970 in New York City, as well as in the few other cities with rent control, landlords were allowed to increase most rents in line with rising operating and maintenance costs. Despite rent control's limited coverage, housing experts have engaged in an extended debate about its impact.

The argument against rent control is straightforward: low rents cause landlords to abandon housing as a profitable investment, in terms of both maintaining existing structures and building new ones. Not surprisingly, much evidence for this view comes from New York City where indeed low-cost private-sector housing declined dramatically after World War II. Data also have been collected elsewhere, for example in New Jersey cities where apartment construction fell by over 50 percent after rent control was introduced.

Defenders of rent control argue that the decline of low-cost housing is a complicated process that cannot be blamed on a single policy. As evidence they point to New Jersey cities *without* rent control where there was an even faster drop in construction than in the rent control cities. Federal housing surveys document housing abandonment not only in rent controlled New York City, but also in Cleveland, St. Louis, and Oakland, and other major cities where there was no rent control.

An additional argument against rent control is that it does not benefit those in need. For example, Hudson Institute researcher B. Bruce-Briggs cites Census Bureau data showing a sizable proportion of New York City rent control households paying less than 20 percent of their income in rent. (Briggs also points out that Census Bureau data leave out 30 percent of tenants for whom there are no income or rent data, so perhaps even more allegedly undeserving tenants benefit from rent control.) Once again, however, New York City's now-defunct rent freeze is the target; according to rent control advocates, nationwide there are large numbers of low- and moderate-income households who would benefit from rent control.

Public Housing or Trickle Down?   Direct government provision of public housing is a second major policy controversy that is out of proportion to its actual importance. Again, the argument is about the effect of government programs on the private housing market. Opponents of public housing point to studies measuring little improvement in the housing market in cities with public housing. To the critics this is evidence that public housing simply substitutes for private housing that would have been built in any case. As an alternative to public housing, these housing experts argue for letting the private market provide all new housing—even if housing is built for the well-to-do. In this view, new high-income housing causes *all* families to move up the housing ladder, eventually benefiting the poor by lifting them out of the worst housing.

Those in favor of government assistance argue that existing public housing, comprising only 11 percent of the total U.S. rental housing market, far less than in many Western European countries, is insufficient to affect the overall housing market, particularly in cities with massive economic problems. Moreover, the alleged advantages of the private sector have been difficult to prove. As of the late 1980s there were no large-scale data on the same housing stock over a long period of time. Indirect evidence from data comparing differences in housing between cities shows modest evidence of the trickle-down benefits of high-cost housing. But supporters of public housing point to rising housing costs for low-income groups as better evidence that increased high-income housing displaces the poor rather than improving the quality and quantity of housing available to them.

Implications   The debate about how to create low-income housing demonstrates an imbalance in the availability of data. Data are relatively abundant on government programs such as rent control and public housing, the effectiveness of which is the source of ongoing debate. On the other hand, the impact of high-income housing on the overall housing market is not as well analyzed. Housing experts believe this is a fertile area for research; even though fewer data are available, we have much to learn about the housing process with existing data in the U.S. Census and American Housing Survey.

The Homeless

During the 1980s, the issue of homelessness suddenly emerged as a matter of national concern. Although everyone agreed there had always been homeless people in the United States, the general impression was that the problem had recently become worse. Media reports, however, suggested that social scientists were hopelessly in disagreement about the number of homeless, with estimates ranging from 250,000 to 3,000,000. This more than tenfold range proved unhelpful in determining the appropriate policy response, but it is illustrative of how media coverage rarely asks *why* statistics appear so inaccurate. In this case, the specific count of homeless was less informative than careful research about the origins of less-than-adequate housing.

250,000?   The low estimate derives from a 1984 report by the U.S. Department of Housing and Urban Development (HUD), "Report to the Secretary on the Homeless and Emergency Shelters." Although the number was reported as an official government statistic, officials responsible for the estimate recognized likely errors in their count, an aspect seldom mentioned in the media. The HUD estimate actually was a range from 192,000 to 586,000, of which 250,000 was determined to be the "most reliable" lower limit. But, debate focused instead on the assertion that the HUD report was slanted in an effort by the Reagan administration to downplay the housing issue, an interpretation so widely accepted that in 1985 the Federal Emergency Management Agency refused to use the disputed HUD findings in its disbursement of federal funds for the homeless.

3,000,000?   The high estimate has been traced to an off-the-cuff remark by homeless activist, Mitch Snyder, who told a congressional committee: "How many nationally [are homeless]? Millions. Of that we are certain. Precisely how many? Who knows?" In subsequent written testimony for the committee, Snyder's group, Communities for Creative Non-Violence, conducted a telephone survey, suggesting 2.2 million homeless, a figure that was later rounded up to 3 million and widely quoted in newspaper and magazine reports.

What Do We Mean by Homeless?   In actual fact the HUD report and Communities for Creative Non-Violence agreed far more than was commonly recognized. With the exception of Chicago, a single anomaly in the Communities' data later revised downward by a factor of ten, the city-by-city count was nearly identical. Thus, the overall count in both studies was about 250,000, confirming an independent 1983 study by Harvard economist Richard Freeman.

But according to many housing experts, the effort to pin down a specific number for the homeless deflected attention from underlying housing problems. In this view, the homeless are only the most visible of the inadequately housed. Traditional homeless statistics overlook the fact that most people who leave their homes do not move permanently to the street or shelters, so estimates of homelessness on a single night greatly understates the overall problem. A Rand Corporation study estimated the number who were homeless during any part of one year was as much as four times higher than the traditional statistic of homelessness on a single night.

Eventually many of the homeless find shelter with relatives or friends, causing ''doubling up,'' found among 10 percent of low-income families in a 1983 New York City survey. If the research goal is to measure the shortfall of adequate housing, then these displaced people should be included. A 1987 study by the Neighborhood Reinvestment Corporation, a nonprofit group funded by Congress, projects a shortfall of more than 18 million low-rent housing units by the year 2003. Although these individuals may not be homeless, displacement is a reasonable measure of housing needs and the basis for policy debate about increasing the number of low-cost homes.

This case study demonstrates the shortcomings of media attention on the single ''correct'' number of homeless. A ''ballpark'' estimate, approximating the number of individuals who live in temporary shelters or on the street, certainly is useful. And for such purposes, Freeman's 250,000 estimate appears to be reasonable. However, far more helpful for public policy is careful attention to the overall state of the housing market, of which homelessness is only one severe consequence.

Geographic Units

Housing location is used to designate geographic area, a common research variable. Although seemingly easy to define, geographic designation often presents research headaches and, in some cases, requires intervention by the president's Office of Management and Budget.

The smallest geographic classifications are census blocks. For the 1990 census, the United States was divided into about 7.5 million of these units, corresponding in urban areas to city blocks. They were subdivisions of 49,000 census tracts, the statistical unit for many research projects such as the studies of segregation described below.

What is a city? What is a rural area? These are obviously subjective questions, complicated by the growth of neither-urban-nor-rural suburbia. Not surprisingly, the division between city and country involves arbitrary classification, and categories that change over time. Beginning in 1910, the census defined any incorporated place with more than 2,500 residents as urban. The standard shifted slowly, so that by 1980, urban areas required a population of 50,000 and "built-up" characteristics. This changing definition caused the measured urban population to rise slightly during the 1970s to 73.7 percent, although under the old definition the urban population actually declined slightly.

Since 1949, the Bureau of Budget (now the Office of Management and Budget, OMB) has attempted to create useful boundaries for urban areas called Metropolitan Statistical Areas (MSAs). Approximately 300 MSAs are now used in most U.S. government data, including the U.S. Census and American Housing Survey. Nonetheless, problems remain for researchers. For example, some MSAs are eliminated, while others are newly created. In 1980, Rapid City, South Dakota, lost its metropolitan status because of population loss, while thirty-five new areas were established in 1981 based on the previous year's census.

The boundaries of MSAs also can present research problems. Some MSAs include entire counties (or cities, in New England) that have close social and economic relationships with the central urban area. Because some western counties are so large, the resulting MSA is geographically huge, stretching over fifty miles into the Cascade Mountains in the case of Seattle, Washington, while Los Angeles County extends twenty-five miles into the Mojave desert. In both cases the outer reaches of the MSA are entirely unpopulated. Nationwide in 1980, more than 15 percent of MSA housing units were in rural ares. Widespread urban areas encompassing different political boundaries create special problems for defining MSAs. For example, Nassau and Suffolk counties of New York's Long Island are designated a separate MSA, even though both counties are closely tied to the New York MSA, which includes New York City and counties to the north.

What can be done about these problems? First, consult your data source. Government publications typically comment in detail about these geographic issues. In addition, government officials often can help assess the significance of boundary problems. Alternative statistics may compensate for disappearing cities; urban area data may correct for rural parts of MSAs; Standard *Consolidated* Statistical Areas combine data for adjacent MSAs.

Segregation

In 1968 the National Advisory Commission on Civil Disorders warned: "Our Nation is moving toward two societies, one black, one white—separate and unequal." Has this prediction come true? Data on segregation were considered so sensitive by the Nixon administration that studies by the Census Bureau were blocked during the 1970s out of fear that evidence of continued segregation would be politically explosive. Many more studies were conducted during the 1980s, sometimes with contradictory findings because of difficulties in measuring segregation.

The first problem confronting researchers is the relevant geographic scale. On the level of MSAs, the United States became more integrated during past decades in the sense that many cities have more diverse populations. But segregation is still present because, within those cities, racial groups live in separate neighborhoods. Consequently, most research on segregation looks at census tracts, for which total counts by racial group are available in each census. (See chapter 2 on problems in defining racial groups.) But even on this small-scale level there are different types of segregation indexes, about which there is a vast literature, and at times, seemingly contradictory trends. For example, between 1970 and 1980 black-white segregation appeared to decline based on one index that measured whether blacks were evenly distributed among communities, while another index measured greater segregation based on the proportion of blacks in individual communities. These opposite conclusions occurred because of black migration from inner cities to traditionally black suburbs, thus causing more even distribution of the black population, but an increased proportion of blacks in segregated suburban communities.

Recognizing such problems with segregation measures, sociologists Douglas Massey and Nancy Denton surveyed nineteen different ways to measure segregation in their important 1987 study of residential segregation for blacks, Hispanics, and Asians during the 1970s. Some sociologists had anticipated a decline in segregation because of fair housing legislation, more tolerant attitudes by whites, and a growing black middle class. Instead, Massey and Denton found: "most blacks continue to reside in predominantly black neighborhoods . . . race continues to be a fundamental cleavage in American society." Moreover, segregation is as high for blacks with income over $50,000 and graduate degrees as it is for blacks with low incomes and a fourth-grade education.

On a positive note, Massey and Denton point out that there was slight lessening of segregation in small and mid-sized cities that included relatively few blacks at the time. Thus, the long-term trend is not yet determined and further study of racial segregation is in order. In addition, investigators of the issue would like to know more about trends in segregation for groups other than blacks and whites. But because of changing categories used by the census, compatible historical data are not yet available (see chapter 2).

Is Seattle the Best Place to Live?

What is the overall desirability of a city, or more technically, an MSA? Obviously, such a statistic must combine a great variety of data. Two contrasting methods for making MSA comparisons illustrate the relative advantages of different summary statistics, one quite simple, the other complex.

Ratings   In 1989 newspapers lauded Seattle, Washington, as the best place to live based on *Places Rated Almanac*, a compendium of living costs, climate, crime, and other attributes of 333 U.S. cities (Pine Bluff, Arkansas, was the worst). Despite widespread reporting on this study, its results should be interpreted with caution because a simple, but potentially misleading, method was used to capture the effect of many variables. In fairness to the authors of the *Almanac*, we should note that they caution against use of the overall ratings; a short list of "winners" appears late in the book, on page 392, and the losers are not highlighted. But press reports focused on precisely this aspect of their study.

The problem is one of "weighting," that is, how much importance to give each variable? Should crime count more than rain? The *Almanac* simply added up each city's ranking on a list of attributes ranging from employment to recreation. Although Pine Bluff ranked best in the country in living costs, this advantage was quickly swamped by other categories such as poor access to arts that were valued equally with living costs. Moreover, within a category, the authors make assumptions about what constitutes quality. Seattle's high overall rating was helped by a good score on climate, twelfth best in the country, because Seattle's moderate temperatures were valued highly, while incessant winter rains caused no significant penalty.

Hedonic Index   A more sophisticated estimate for the quality of life measures how willing individuals are to accept higher housing costs and lower wages in exchange for amenities such as good weather and good schools. Using this method, called hedonic pricing, economists Glenn C. Blomquist, Mark C. Berger, and John P. Hoehn estimated that residents of Pueblo, Colorado, "traded" $3,289 in higher costs to live in this highest-ranked city, while residents of St. Louis, Missouri, enjoyed $1,857 compensation for their lowest-ranked city. Although this technique avoids the subjective judgments of the *Almanac*, it assumes there is a fluid marketplace for housing. If some desirable cities are inaccessible because of job and family ties, then the hedonic method will not accurately measure a city's "value."

For many social science topics there are relatively simple statistics such as the "Places Rated" index, as well as complex statistics such as the hedonic index. Comparison of the two methods for rating cities illustrates drawbacks for each approach. Simple indexes are arbitrary in the sense that another researcher might attach different importance to each variable, for example, counting rain as a greater disadvantage for Seattle. On the other hand, the hedonic index and many similar measurements assume a well-functioning economic market in which individuals freely make informed judgments. Because of the complexity of statistics such as the hedonic index, users may not be aware of the underlying assumptions it requires. Researchers can learn from both approaches, borrowing the easy-to-use characteristics of "Places Rated," along with the more subtle insights of the hedonic index.

SUMMARY

The issues reviewed in this chapter underscore the ambiguity of social statistics. Attempts to measure housing cost and quality suggested contradictory trends: housing quality improved and deteriorated; housing affordability rose and fell; the homeless are fewer than 200,000, or over 3,000,000—or cannot be meaningfully counted. Such discrepancies were the source of media debates. Less often reported was what researchers actually know about housing. For example, on an overall basis, there is evidence of improvement in U.S. housing quality and affordability based on Census Bureau surveys and data on housing costs as a proportion of income. On the other hand, analysis of specific housing problems such as rat infestation, or specific markets such as low-income rentals, or local data on affordability reveals considerable problems in housing markets. The lesson for researchers is to specify carefully the research goal before choosing between the nationwide or more specific data.

The debate about the number of homeless illustrates a situation where considerable effort was spent attempting to measure a social problem that could not be summarized in a single number. Statistics on displacement and the effect of high-cost housing on the overall housing market are more likely to give insight into underlying housing problems, as well as the need for government programs such as rent control and public housing. Unfortunately, such statistics are lacking, although some experts believe they can be constructed from existing data.

The choice of geographic units is a common step in research projects. Although the federal government attempts carefully to standardize its data along common geographic boundaries, the definition of urban versus rural areas and the designation of Standard Metropolitan Areas can pose problems for some research projects. For example, analysis of racial segregation requires attention to population shifts within neighborhoods as well as within larger-scale units such as MSAs. Finally, on a less serious level, the "places rated" debate reinforces the lesson that the underlying method for combining disparate data into a single, usable statistic can predetermine the outcome.

CASE STUDY QUESTIONS

1. Between 1974 and 1981, the Annual Housing Survey measured the numbers of dwellings with deficiencies, as shown on the following page.

During this time period, the number of occupied structures increased by about 17 percent. How might these data on deficiencies be used to measure improved, stable, and declining housing quality?

Condition present in neighborhood	1974	1981
Crime	12,115,000	18,371,000
Streets in need of repair	13,741,000	14,399,000
Odors	7,240,000	6,640,000

2. Just as there is an underground economy (see chapter 7), there are unreported and often illegal housing units. In particular, illegal conversions are estimated to account for the largest proportion of new housing units for some locales, but they are often missed in the census and the AHS. How might these missing housing units affect measurement of housing quality?

3. The number of new-home sales changes dramatically from month to month. For example, in 1989, July sales rose by 14 percent, August sales were stable, September sales fell by more than 11 percent, October sales were stable, while November sales rose by 10 percent. These data are adjusted for seasonal variation—that is, they take into account typical month-by-month changes during past years. What other factors might cause such erratic month-to-month variation?

4. Average down payments for houses rose from 24.1 percent in 1981 to 27.2 percent in 1987. Columnist Warren Brookes cites this statistic as evidence that families were better able to afford houses in 1987. How might this statistic also indicate the difficulty of homebuying?

5. In 1988, median home prices in Orange County, California, were over three times as high as in Louisville, Kentucky. Nonetheless, housing experts believe this statistic underestimates the actual difference in home prices between the two locations. Why is this likely true?

6. Counts of homeless depend critically on estimates of the ratio of those who live on the streets to those in shelters. For example, Freeman's 1983 study measured a 2.2 to 1 ratio of the unsheltered to sheltered homeless. This estimate was criticized both for being too low and for being too high. Why is this ratio so difficult to measure, and why is it so important?

Chapter 4

Health

Health statistics involve the expertise of many disciplines ranging from economics to medicine. This chapter reviews controversies about a cross-section of these statistics, including infant mortality, life expectancy, cancer, and traffic fatalities. These examples are chosen because in each case there are apparently conflicting statistics, measuring both improvement and decline in health. A final section examines benefit-cost analysis, a commonly used technique for evaluating public health policies that also yields contradictory results. As in the case of other social science statistics, careful examination of the underlying data helps resolve the apparent statistical quandaries. The task is made especially difficult by the varied sources used in health research, but an understanding of the data is a necessary first step for successful evaluation of health care issues.

DATA SOURCES

Some U.S. health statistics are based on complete counts of all relevant individuals. For example, U.S. Vital Statistics attempt to count all births and deaths (see chapter 2), and the U.S. Centers for Disease Control collects as complete a count as possible of many diseases and causes of death. But because it is infeasible to take a complete count for most other health statistics, survey data are used instead. Extensive surveys are compiled by the National Center for Health Statistics in the Vital and Health Statistics publications, known as the ''rainbow series'' because of the vibrant colors used for each subject. These

Where the Numbers Come from

Organizations	Data Sources	Key Publications
National Center for Health Statistics U.S. Department of Health and Human Services	U.S. Vital Statistics; National Survey of Family Growth	*Monthly Vital Statistics Report; Vital Statistics of the United States; Vital and Health Statistics*
Bureau of the Census U.S. Department of Commerce	Current Population Survey	*Current Population Reports* (P–20)
Centers for Disease Control U.S. Department of Health and Human Services	Reports of notifiable diseases	*Morbidity and Mortality Weekly Report*
National Cancer Institute U.S. Department of Health and Human Services	Surveillance, Epidemiology, and End Results	*Annual Cancer Statistics Review*
World Health Organization	Individual country reporting	*World Health Statistics Quarterly; World Health Statistics Annual*
Metropolitan Life Insurance	Private survey	*Statistical Bulletin*

For summary information see *Statistical Abstract of the United States.*

surveys are extraordinarily specific, covering such detail as "Percent of persons 18 years of age and over who ate breakfast every day."

Other U.S. government surveys covering health-related topics include the U.S. Census Bureau's Current Population Survey (see chapter 9), specialized data collected by the Social Security Administration, the Bureau of Indian Affairs, the National Highway Traffic and Safety Administration, and the Food and Drug Administration. Private-sector organizations also assemble health statistics, including health care associations for physicians, nurses, and hospital administrators, voluntary organizations such as the American Heart Association, the American Cancer Association, and the Cystic Fibrosis Foundation, and the insurance industry, most notably the Metropolitan Life Insurance Company surveys of health and medical costs. Because so much health survey data are available, librarians advise researchers to begin with guides to data such as *Facts at Your Fingertips*, the *American Statistics Index*, or *Index Medicus*.

> *Data Sample:* In *Facts at Your Fingertips* under the subject "headaches," the recommended references include Health Statistics Series 10–125, a survey on headaches, and the American Association for the Study of Headaches and its publication, *Headache.* Also listed is the name and telephone number for the contact person at the National Center for Health Statistics (NCHS) responsible for the study of headaches.

For worldwide health statistics, research will likely begin with World Health Organization (WHO) publications, complete and detailed vital statistics, and comparative data on infectious diseases and health care usage. Researchers should be cautious in making comparisons between countries because reporting systems and standards vary widely. The WHO information service will assist researchers in assessing the comparability of data between countries.

> *Data Sample:* In the *World Health Statistics Annual* we learn that there were 7,099 hospital beds for psychiatry in Bulgaria and 397 chicken pox cases in the Faeroe Islands in 1980.

CONTROVERSIES

Infant Mortality

The infant mortality rate is a key health status indicator. Because it is easy to collect data on infant mortality, at least in countries where hospital births prevail, this statistic provides an accurate comparison of

Box 4.1. **Abortion**

Abortion statistics are unusual in that the best data are available from a nongovernmental source. Based on a survey of clinics, hospitals, and doctors' offices, the Alan Guttmacher Institute, a private foundation affiliate of Planned Parenthood, provides the most detailed information on U.S. abortions. (Since 1970 abortion data also have been collected by the Centers for Disease Control from state health departments, but the data are incomplete, averaging about one-sixth less than the Guttmacher estimate.) According to Guttmacher data, the number of abortions in the United States more than doubled between 1973 (when abortion was legalized nationwide) and 1980, but since then has remained at about 1,500,000 per year, or about 3 for every 100 women between the ages of 15 and 44. The data include religion (the rate for Roman Catholic women is measured as nearly identical to the overall rate), age (60 of every 1,000 18-year-olds have had an abortion, double the rate of abortion for English teens, the highest rate in Europe), and race (the abortion rate is 5.3 per 1,000 for nonwhites).

health care in different places and at different times. In addition, the infant mortality rate responds quickly to improvements—or failures—in health care. For example, one of the first signals of problems in Soviet Union health programs was an increase in infant mortality during the 1970s. Controversy about the U.S. infant mortality rate focuses on an apparent slowdown in its improvement during the 1980s, and continued failure of the United States to reduce infant mortality to levels already achieved in other countries.

Infant mortality traditionally is measured in deaths per 1,000 live births. A 1912 Federal Children's Bureau survey estimated this death rate at more than 100 of every 1,000. Since then there has been nearly constant improvement, so that by 1988 the death rate was 9.9 per 1,000. Some experts are concerned, however, that the *rate* of improvement has slowed down, from 4.5 percent per year improvement during the 1970s to 2.7 percent per year during the first half of the 1980s. The Children's Defense Fund blamed the slowdown in improvement on reductions in health care funding during the cutbacks in the Reagan administration. However, medical researcher Harry Schwartz responded that the Children's Defense Fund is unnecessarily pessimistic. According to Schwartz, it is to be expected that social programs will show less dramatic effects over time so that we should celebrate the continued decline in infant mortality, even if it is falling at a slower rate.

Whatever the reasons for the change, U.S. infant mortality exceeds that of many other countries, including such relatively poor nations as East Germany, Ireland, Spain, and Singapore. Sweden and Japan have the lowest infant morality of all, less than 6 per 1,000, 40 percent better than the United States. In one study, the *worst* infant mortality of any Swedish province was lower than infant mortality in Utah, which had the lowest of any U.S. state.

Again, researcher Harry Schwartz objects to comparisons of infant mortality in the United States with infant mortality in ethnically homogeneous countries such as Sweden and Japan. Indeed, infant mortality for U.S. blacks is nearly twice as high as the rate for whites. Moreover, during the 1980s white infant mortality declined at a faster rate than black infant mortality. Research at the National Center for Health Statistics and Stanford University has suggested that high infant mortality persists even for blacks with favorable economic circumstances and access to prepaid health care. But these results may be social in origin, perhaps caused by transportation and child-care problems, inflexible employment schedules, or lower satisfaction with health care providers. In one study, prenatal care alone reduced low birth weight for blacks, a major cause of infant mortality, at almost double the improvement measured for whites. As a result of such findings, many policy makers question whether the United States should accept high infant mortality rates because of a heterogeneous population. In this view, endorsed by the *Journal of the American Medical Association*, the United States can achieve the low infant mortality already achieved elsewhere. For example, if black infant mortality had been reduced to the rate for U.S. whites, more than 5,000 infants would have been saved in 1980.

Infant mortality is an example of a social statistic in which the same numbers are interpreted differently by policy analysts. The level of U.S. infant mortality is alternatively a measure of success and failure, and the higher rate for some groups is either an explanation of the relatively high overall infant mortality, or an illustration of the failure of U.S. health care. Whichever interpretation one accepts, it is necessary for researchers to be aware of alternative viewpoints.

Are We Living Longer?

It is difficult not to feel a little cheered when one reads about increases in average life expectancy. For example, in 1987, overall U.S. average life expectancy at birth reached 75 years for the first time. But few readers understand the limitations of this statistic.

Blacks' Life Expectancy   Life expectancy is not the same for all groups. There is a troublesome divergence between life expectancy for whites in the United States, which reached a new high of 75.6 in 1987, and for blacks, who experienced declining life expectancy during the mid-1980s to 69.4 years in 1986 and 1987. Homicide, accident rates, and AIDS are likely the cause of higher death rates among blacks and may indicate a more severe decline in economic conditions for some blacks than is measured by traditional economic variables (see chapter 8).

The Very Elderly   Life expectancy data may also be unreliable for the very elderly because many individuals do not truthfully report their ages in the U.S. Census. Those under 21 years tend to exaggerate their age and adults 21 through 70 report their ages relatively accurately, while the largest misreporting occurs for the extremely elderly who tend to exaggerate their age, which results in a tendency for life expectancy for the elderly also to be exaggerated. The reason is that age at death is more likely to be accurately reported on death certificates. Thus, there are too many people claiming to be of advanced age in the census, but fewer who actually die at those ages, causing an exaggerated survival rate. According to researchers at the University of Pennsylvania in 1980 this problem caused significant underestimation of the death rate for nonwhites and misrepresentation of the trend in the cancer death rate for all persons over 85 years of age.

Mean and Median Life Expectancy   A third problem with longevity statistics is confusion about the meaning of mean and median life expectancy. In 1982, noted paleontologist Stephen Jay Gould was diagnosed with mesothelioma, a serious cancer, for which he learned the *median* life expectancy is only eight months after discovery. Gould recounts how his knowledge of statistics gave him hope, a sense of optimism he credits with helping him overcome the disease (and remain in sound health as of 1990). What Gould knew was that life expectancy for mesothelioma was pulled down by a large number of patients who die soon after the cancer is discovered—that is, one-half are dead within eight months, but an equal number of individuals survive longer, many far longer. Consequently, the *mean*, or average, life expectancy is much greater than the median. Thus, those who survive beyond eight months need not expect to die momentarily, having already lived longer than most who have the cancer. Some individuals will live for years, increasing the value of the mean, but leaving the median at eight months. Being young and receiving the best treatment, Gould thought he would fall in this longer-lived group, an outlook that itself may have helped him fight the disease.

The difference between the mean and the median applies to life expectancy for the population as a whole. For example, mean life expectancy in 1980 was 76.6 years for men who were 40 years old. But median life expectancy was higher because more than one-half of all men will survive longer. Early deaths for a few individuals pull the mean below the median. For health researchers the mean provides a reasonable measure of longevity. But for individuals who want to know a typical lifespan, leaving out the possibility of a very early death, then the higher median life expectancy is the most representative statistics.

Can We Predict Future Longevity?   Although few individuals can resist the temptation to calculate their own expected lifetimes based on life expectancy statistics, in fact actual longevity may be quite different. The reason is that today's life expectancy calculations assume that today's death rates will continue into the future. In fact, it is not unreasonable to assume that most age groups will have lower death rates in the future, and that life expectancies will rise slightly, as they have in past years. By projecting past improvements into the future, the journal *American Demographics* estimates that men will live to nearly 100 by the year 2100. One oddity in this technique is that it anticipates women will average only 93 years. Although women currently live longer than men, the extrapolation method predicts shorter women's lifetimes because the current *rate* of improvement in women's life expectancy is lower than for men.

It is possible that there will be extraordinary scientific breakthroughs, extending life expectancy at a faster rate than in the past. Physician-writer Roy Walford suggests that genetic engineering will increase lifetimes to more than 140 years for both men and women.

Box 4.2. The Oldest Person on Earth

Although the number of aged is growing, reports of extreme ages often prove to be false. Reports of yogurt-eating Russian Caucasus villagers living to mid-100 years old lack documentation. Even cases with written records sometimes prove inaccurate, as in the celebrated example of American Charlie Smith, who claimed to be 137 years old based on records of his sale into slavery in 1854. A subsequently discovered marriage certificate showed he was a hearty but much younger 104 when he died. Similarly, another American claiming to be 130 was proved to have used his father's documents to avoid army service in World War I. The oldest U.S. resident with fully acceptable credentials was Californian Fanny Thomas who died in 1980 at age 113.

However, the likelihood of life-extending medical benefits is by no means certain; in fact, unexpected effects of war or environmental destruction could turn death rates sharply upward. More serious scientific inquiry attempts to understand why longevity increased in the past.

Why Are We Living Longer? Is modern medicine responsible for longer lives? Historians and epidemiologists give a mixed diagnosis. The best long-term data come from Great Britain where health statistics cover several centuries. Historian Talbot Griffith concludes that increased use of drugs, inoculations, midwives, and hospitals significantly reduced British mortality after the eighteenth century. But physician T. McKeown responds in his 1976 book, *The Role of Medicine: Dream, Mirage or Nemesis*, that nutrition, not medical care, was the single most important reason for longer lives. For the period prior to 1900 McKeown makes the strong claim, "Therapy made no contributions," and "the effect of immunization was restricted to smallpox which accounted for only about one-twentieth of the reduction of the death rate." For the twentieth century McKeown allows that immunization has had a greater effect, but one that is far less easily demonstrated and less important than nutrition and hygiene, to which he attributes about two-thirds of the mortality decline.

In summary, life expectancies have strict definitions that are slightly different from everyday usage. They are useful research tools for appraising the overall health of a population, but they can be misleading when used as estimates for individual longevity. Projections of future life expectancy are even more problematic, dependent on the unknown effect of medical and environmental change.

Cancer

On December 23, 1971, President Richard Nixon signed the National Cancer Act, calling for a war on cancer of the ''same kind of concentrated effort that split the atom and took man to the moon.'' Initially hopes were raised that massive funding could find a cure for cancer by the 1976 bicentennial. Nearly two decades and hundreds of billions of dollars later, critics point out that cancer death rates have increased. Are we losing the war on cancer?

Recent statistical debate about cancer pitted the National Cancer Institute (NCI), the conduit for National Cancer Act funding, against outside epidemiologists. NCI representatives conceded that no cure for cancer appears close at hand. Instead, the institute targets halving of the U.S. cancer mortality rate by the year 2000. Critics admitted that cancer research has produced some important life-extending treatments for a few types of cancer. But overall, more people were getting cancer, and, in total, cancer patient life expectancy had not increased.

Advocates of the effectiveness of the war on cancer pointed to improvements in cancer survival rates. Although this statistic received much publicity, epidemiologists question its validity. Better record keeping in recent years means that more cancer survivors are retained in the data files, thereby pushing up the measured survival rate. Also, because cancer now is detected earlier, cancer patients appear to live longer. A second statistic used to defend the war on cancer is a decline in the cancer death rate—at least the cancer death rate for the young and for cancers excluding lung cancer. The cancer death rate for those under fifty-five years old fell, in part because of remarkable progress in treating childhood leukemia. But critics point out that those under fifty-five years old account for less than 25 percent of all cancers. Because cancer death rates are increasing for those over fifty-five years old, the overall cancer death rate is up.

Almost all increased cancer mortality since 1950 is attributable to lung cancer. Thus, not surprisingly, the cancer death rate falls if lung cancer deaths are excluded, a statistic used by some NCI officials to argue that the war on cancer has been successful. In this view, increased lung cancer deaths (caused by cigarette smoking) could not be prevented by medical research. Epidemiologist and NCI critic John Bailar III argues that the same logic could be used to exclude stomach cancers, for which early detection, rather than NCI-sponsored research, reduced the death rate. Excluding both lung and stomach cancers removes the apparent progress against cancer.

Few epidemiologists expect medical research to achieve the war on cancer goal of halving cancer mortality by the year 2000. The policy question is whether to continue funding cancer treatment in an effort to raise the survival rate, a goal already partially met according to NCI officials. Critics, including John Bailar, advocate reallocation of resources toward cancer prevention as a more effective means of reducing cancer deaths. But, in part because of emphasis on survival rate statistics, of the nearly $1.5 billion National Cancer Institute 1988 budget, only $74 million was allocated for prevention and control.

Cancer Incidence   In addition to the cancer death rate, researchers would also like to know the prevalence of cancer among the living, or what epidemiologists call the incidence rate. The problem is that this statistic measures not only changes in the number of people who have cancer, but also changing rates of cancer detection. For example, there was an unprecedented increase in reported breast cancer in 1974 when public disclosure of the disease by the wives of the U.S. president and vice-president prompted more women to have their breasts examined. As a result, more borderline lesions were discovered and reported to the NCI, although the cancer mortality rate was not affected in subsequent years.

Similarly, the male prostate cancer rate varies, depending upon the level of examination. Prostate surgery and autopsy uncovers prostate cancer in as many as 25 percent of the men examined. But since the overall incidence for prostate cancer is no more than 1 percent, even for the most susceptible elderly, it appears that lesions discovered incidentally during surgery or autopsy are not malignant, or are so slowly so that they do not qualify according to traditional definitions of cancer. A similar problem exists for skin cancer and *in situ* cervical cancer, both relatively frequent cancers in need of treatment, but uncommonly fatal. The inclusion of such cancers in incidence reports

Box 4.3. **Likelihood of Breast Cancer**

U.S. Department of Health and Human Services Secretary Margaret M. Heckler asserted in 1985 that "one out of every 11 women in this country will develop breast cancer." Although often cited, this statistic does not actually measure the average likelihood for breast cancer among women, but is based on an error similar to misinterpretation of "your chance of marrying after age 35" (see chapter 2). The one out of every 11 cancer likelihood is derived from the sum of current age-specific rates for ages 1 to 85. Because most women will not live to age 85, and because future cancer incidence rates may change, this figure does not measure the actual likelihood of cancer (although the statistic is useful for epidemiologists in assessing various cancer risks). Physician Richard Love calculates that the actual risk of breast cancer is about 1 in 30 during the fifth and sixth decades of life, the time when breast cancer is most worrisome, and a time period most women can expect to survive.

would cause the cancer rate to vary with the detection rate of these common but less severe cancers.

Because of these problems, the overall cancer incidence rate often excludes superficial skin cancers. Most researchers, however, prefer to look at the incidence rates for specific cancer sites, taking into account possible changes in cancer detection rates.

AIDS

Accurate data on AIDS or its apparent cause, HIV infection, are critical for policy making. Is the epidemic worsening? Who has contracted the disease? And what policies will prevent its spread? Although the Centers for Disease Control attempts to gain a complete record of AIDS cases (1,649 new AIDS cases in January 1989, one in North Dakota, and 334 in New York State), an estimated 10 to 30 percent of AIDS cases are not reported. The undercount is particularly high for intravenous drug abusers who enter the health care system only when they are near death and there is no need to perform an AIDS test.

Even more difficult to estimate is the rate of HIV infection. As of 1989, no nationwide survey had been conducted, although Congress had been asked to fund a 50,000-person sample, large enough to track the growth in HIV infection. Meanwhile, preliminary estimates were mere guesses, ranging from 500,000 to 2 million HIV-infected individuals. These estimates are based on the proportion of at-risk groups estimated to be infected (about 20 percent of drug users to 50 percent of gay men in urban centers), multiplied by the number of individuals thought to be in each group (about 2.5 million gay men, over 1 million intravenous drug users nationwide). Such high rates of infection, combined with the long incubation period of the disease, mean that AIDS will reach epidemic proportions during the 1990s. But without an accurate measure of HIV infection, we cannot tell how many people AIDS will strike, and thus what level of medical resources will be needed, or whether public health measures have been effective in reducing the spread of the disease.

Is Slower Safer?

Speed limits are a health policy issue because traffic fatalities are the number one cause of death for many age groups. Recent controversy has focused on an unintended consequence of a 1974 government regulation to conserve fuel by lowering the nationwide speed limit to 55 miles per hour. Afterward there was an abrupt 15 percent drop in highway fatalities. When Congress agreed to raise the speed limit on rural interstate highways to 65 MPH in 1987, some safety experts feared that there would be an increase in fatalities. Specifically, the National Research Council estimated that the higher speed limit would result in an increase of 500 highway deaths per year. But the effect of this change has been difficult to measure, leading to considerable controversy about the relationship between speed limits and highway safety.

The problem is that highway fatality data have not followed an easy-to-understand pattern. Data collected by the U.S. Transportation Department show that highway fatalities continued to drop long after the lower speed limit was introduced, even though average speeds increased well above the legal 55 MPH limit. When the 65 MPH speed limit was introduced there was a noticeable jump in the death rate, seemingly confirming the National Research Council prediction. However, in defense of the higher speed limit, Transportation Secretary Jim Burnley pointed out that there was an even greater increase in deaths on interstates maintaining the 55 MPH limit. Critics answered that tolerance of high speeds on these highways, well over the ostensible 55

MPH speed limit, caused the fatality increase. In this view, the Transportation Department could have enforced the 55 MPH speed limit by denying funds to states that did not reduce their average highway speeds.

Traffic experts are still trying to sort out the effect of speed limits. One intriguing possibility put forward by economist Charles A. Lave points to variance in speeds as the critical factor. In other words, different speeds on the same highway may contribute to serious accidents. But other researchers disagree, maintaining that speed is still the critical variable; in one study, variation in speed *upward*, that is, higher speeds, caused fatalities, whereas *lower* speeds did not. Better data, examining individual roads, are needed to fully explain the relationship between speed limits and fatalities.

The speed limit debate is a good example of how public policy making desperately needs good statistics, but often must make do with ambiguous results. It seems likely that the 65 MPH speed limit will be extended, providing additional data, although if the critics are correct, at the expense of lost lives.

Benefit-Cost Analysis

Is government regulation necessary to protect the nation's health? In answering this question, policy makers often use benefit-cost analysis, a method developed by economists to measure the relative advantages (benefits) and disadvantages (costs) of a proposed program. Although seemingly straightforward common sense, benefit-cost analysis is controversial because of problems in putting a dollar value on all benefits and costs.

Value of Human Life   Full accounting within the benefit-cost framework requires putting a dollar value on human lives. Although the idea often shocks the general public, valuing human life is well-established practice among economists who maintain that trade-offs between money and human life are implicit in everyday life. In this view, whenever we buy a less than perfectly safe car, accept a dangerous job, or even cross the street, we trade a risk of death—albeit slight—in return for measurable financial gain. The proportion between these risks and the gain (see Box 4.4) is called the "willingness to pay" by an individual for his or her own life.

A major problem with the willingness-to-pay technique is that it yields widely varying estimates for the value of life. Risky jobs such as mining and elephant keeping imply values as low as $300,000 per life, whereas surveys about the willingness to pay for environmental safeguards measure values more than $8 million per life. As an alternative method, some researchers advocate the use of estimates of lost earnings. The advantage to this method is that it yields relatively consistent estimates, but it suffers from the shortcoming of severe inequity. For example, in one study an eighty-five-year-old black woman was "valued" at $128, an unacceptable measure for most analysis. The variation in values for human lives makes it difficult to derive policy advice from benefit-cost analysis. Projects judged wasteful with one measure may be quite worthwhile if human lives are more highly valued. For example, in opposing a safety standard for construction workers who handle concrete, the U.S. Office of Management and Budget advocated valuing these workers at $1 million per life rather than $3.5 million as proposed by the Occupational Safety and Health Administration.

One technique that avoids the problems of valuing human life is "cost effectiveness." For example, in evaluating different methods of reducing infant mortality, researchers measure the cost per infant life, then compare which technique saves the most lives without putting a dollar value on the lives saved. In a similar manner, Ralph Nader's associate, Mark Green, advocates separate accounts for human lives and dollar benefits. By this method, Green calculates that many health and safety programs cut by the Reagan administration had been value-effective in terms of decreased medical care, lost work time, and other benefits measurable in money— even without placing a dollar value on human life.

Risk Assessment   A second controversial assumption in benefit-cost analysis is the measurement of the probability of unlikely events, a calculation called risk assessment. Some policy makers argue that these risks are far less than is commonly assumed. In this view, the public consistently overestimates the risk associated with nuclear power plants, acid rain, and other environmental hazards targeted by proregulation activists. For example, in a series of advertisements, the Mobil Oil Corporation observed that most people accept the potential risks of lawn mowers, vacuum cleaners, bathtubs, stairs, and other everyday necessities that are responsible for over one million yearly

Box 4.4. **Cost of Tamper-proof Closures**

Mathematically, the value of human life is calculated by dividing the financial gain by the likelihood of death. For example, Paul MacAvoy, a member of President Reagan's Council of Economic Advisors, calculated that tamper-proof closures, introduced after the 1982 Tylenol poisonings, implied the value of human life equal to $2 million: $.02 (the cost of the closures) divided by 1 in 100,000,000 (the chance of a single bottle containing poison based on historical record). MacAvoy opposed the tamper-proof closures on the grounds that $2 million per human life was greater than the "actual" value of a human life measured in willingness-to-pay studies. Neither drug companies nor government regulators followed MacAvoy's advice.

accidents because benefits outweigh the risks. Mobil would like the same logic applied to the risks of oil exploration compared to the benefits derived from the use of oil. Nuclear power plants are defended on similar grounds, because the worst accident to date at Chernobyl in 1985 is expected to cause at most about 17,000 additional cancer deaths worldwide. Based on this kind of risk assessment, rational public policy would pay more attention to the 500 *million* cancer deaths from other causes than to the alleged dangers of nuclear power.

Critics of risk assessment agree that why people worry about certain risks more than others is an interesting puzzle, but such apparent confusion about risk may not be irrational. Sociologist William R. Freudenberg points out that the experts are often wrong, as demonstrated by the explosion of the space shuttle Challenger. NASA rejected its own studies indicating a failure rate as frequent as 1 in 70 space shuttle boosters, in favor of a study measuring only a 1 in 100,000 risk. The historical track record suggested a 1 in 25 failure rate, which proved sadly but coincidentally correct when the shuttle exploded on its twenty-fifth launch. The "uninformed" consensus of the public, evaluating the risk of new technologies such as nuclear power and off-shore oil drilling, may be more accurate than expert estimates which have traditionally proved too optimistic.

Implications   Measurement problems for the value of human life and risk assessment seriously undermine the usefulness of benefit-cost accounting for policy-making purposes. As illustrated by the space shut-tle tragedy, erroneous assumptions can produce seemingly precise, but wildly erroneous results. Similarly, different values for human life can cause completely different evaluations of public policies. At a mini-mum, it is good research practice to use "sensitivity analysis" for all assumptions, that is, the use of different values for human life and risk assessment to see how such substitution alters the results. By demon-strating that results do not depend on arbitrary assumptions in any of these controversial measures, researchers can broaden the influence of their findings beyond the already convinced.

Alternatively, researchers should consider whether benefit-cost analysis or risk assessment are the most appropriate techniques. As described above, cost effectiveness measurement may provide useful policy advice without encumbering the analysis with unwarranted as-sumptions about the value of life. In the case of risk assessment, policy adviser Langdon Winner warns that traditional technique biases the analysis in favor of the status quo by imposing an unnecessary burden of proof on those who would like to see alternatives to unsafe technol-ogy. For example, in evaluating genetic engineering, Winner believes that risk assessment is nearly impossible, and that attempts to make this tricky estimate have caused policy makers to sidestep the more critical moral debate about direct control of human evolution. In such cases, discussion of a wider scope may provide better guidance, even if it does not appear as mathematically precise as the calculations in benefit-cost analysis.

SUMMARY

Each of the controversies reviewed in this chapter occurs because of statistical ambiguities. There is uncertainty about the trend in infant mortality and the reason for its remarkably high level in the United States. There is disagreement about the reason for the increase in life expectancy as well as about its future trend. Experts debate vigorously about the success of the war on cancer. And there are conflicting interpretations of the effect of the 55 MPH speed limit. Even attempts to state explicitly the costs and benefits of government policies are controversial because of assumptions about the value of life and risk assessment.

However, most especially in the case of health policy, there is little opportunity for social scientists to take a wait-and-see attitude. Decisions must be made about the allocation of health care resources, even if the statistics or decision-making techniques are less than perfect. But at least these decisions can be made based on understanding of the data's limitations. For example, in the debate about the war on cancer, critics have been able to warn us that statistics emphasized by the National Cancer Institute overstate the success of existing health policies. Similarly, careful analysis of life expectancy statistics provided insights about the uncertain effect of modern medicine, and potential shortcomings in health care for black Americans. The analysis of benefit-cost analysis and risk assessment shows that researchers must look critically at official studies that "prove" the efficacy or failure of government regulations. Overall, these examples prove the usefulness of health statistics—but only with careful attention to their limitations.

CASE STUDY QUESTIONS

1. Between 1950 and 1967, NCHS data show a 32 percent *increase* in the number of low-weight births among blacks, greater than the low-weight increase measured for war-ravaged Holland and Leningrad during the food shortages of World War II. At the same time, the percentage of out-of-hospital births declined for nonwhites from 42 percent in 1950 to 7 percent in 1967. How might the decline in out-of-hospital births explain the unusual—but likely overestimated—increase in low-weight births?

2. Fertility rates are a critical issue in developing countries. A 12 percent decline in Pakistani fertility between 1960 and 1975 was quite noteworthy. But follow-up research by demographers from Pakistan and the East-West Population Institute claimed that Pakistani fertility actually *increased* for this period from just below seven children per woman to above seven children per woman. According to these researchers, survey respondents often rounded up the ages of children under six years of age. For example, a nine-month-old infant would be reported as one year old and a three-and-a-half-year-old would be reported as a four-year-old. How did this simple bias cause a major error in estimating the Pakistani fertility rate?

3. Life expectancy for whites increased during the 1980s to a new high of 75.6 years in 1987. At the same time, life expectancy for

blacks declined to 69.4 years. Why do many social scientists consider this statistic a more accurate—and worrisome—measure of black economic problems than traditional economic variables such as unemployment or income?

4. The state of Utah has an extremely low death rate from heart disease, a benefit sometimes ascribed to Mormon abstinence from tea, coffee, alcohol, and cigarettes. But, based on *age-adjusted* death rates—that is, taking into account the relative young age of Utah's population—Utah's heart disease death rate is higher than its neighboring mountain states. On the other hand, Utah's liver cirrhosis and lung cancer rates are lower, even in the age-adjusted data. What implications can you infer about the benefits of life-styles prevalent in Utah?

5. During the late 1980s, the Federal Aviation Administration (FAA) used benefit-cost analysis to analyze the need for safety seats on airlines for children under two years old. Because young children usually ride in their parents' laps, the primary cost of providing such safety is the additional regular airline seats, estimated to cost $56 million per year. On average, five infants die per year in U.S. commercial airline accidents. The Federal Aviation Authority valued infant lives at $500,000 each. Based on benefit-cost analysis, what did the FAA decide? How would you evaluate this decision-making method?

Chapter 5

Education

Education is widely perceived as a critical issue for the United States. In order to develop sound education policies, we need a wide variety of data about schools, students, and educational outcomes. Indeed, much data are collected, but according to many experts, existing education data are poor, especially in comparison to the extensive statistical programs for other social science statistics. This shortcoming is the first controversy discussed below. In addition, this chapter summarizes debates about other educational issues including dropout rates, illiteracy, black educational progress, school desegregation, teacher shortage, and class size. Although newspapers and magazines cover these issues extensively, there has been little assessment of the weaknesses and strengths in the underlying education data.

DATA SOURCES

National Center for Education Statistics

The U.S. Department of Education's National Center for Education Statistics (NCES) is the conduit for most U.S. education data. State and local agencies report to NCES data on enrollment, number of teachers, expenditures, and characteristics of public elementary and secondary schools. In addition, the NCES conducts its own surveys for data on private schools and higher education.

> *Data Sample:* NCES survey data show that the number of students studying Russian in high school fell from an estimated 27,000 in 1965 to only 6,000 in 1982.

Where the Numbers Come from

Organizations	Data Sources	Key Publications
National Center for Education Statistics U.S. Department of Education	Common Core of Data; High School and Beyond; National Assessment of Educational Progress; surveys of private schools, colleges, and universities, and recent college graduates	*Digest of Education Statistics; The Condition of Education*
Office for Civil Rights U.S. Department of Education	Reporting in compliance with Civil Rights Act	"Civil Rights Survey of Elementary and Secondary Schools"
Bureau of the Census U.S. Department of Commerce	Current Population Survey	*Current Population Reports* (Series P–20)
National Education Association	Private survey	*Estimates of School Statistics*

U.S. Census Bureau

Data on school enrollment and educational attainment are correlated with other individual characteristics every ten years in the U.S. Census (see chapter 2), annually in the Current Population Survey (see chapter 9), and occasionally in the Survey of Income and Program Participation (see chapter 8).

> *Data Sample:* In the 1980 U.S. Census, the proportion of the population over 25 years of age with a college degree varied from 10.4 percent in West Virginia to 23 percent in Colorado.

Other Surveys

Much debate about school desegregation is based on data collected by the Office of Civil Rights in the U.S. Education Department. In the private sector, the National Education Association, an organization of teachers and school administrators, conducts its own survey of state education data, often published in advance of NCES data. Finally, there are sources of longitudinal data, that is, studies of individual students over periods of time. Such data have been collected by the U.S. Education Department in an every-other-year survey since 1980 called "High School and Beyond," the National Longitudinal Survey, following 1972 high school seniors, and several university-sponsored surveys.

CONTROVERSIES

Poor Data

Although the U.S. government has collected educational data since 1869, their quality has lagged far behind comparable statistics for other areas of study. Prior to the 1950s, each state reported information to the federal government as it saw fit, and sometimes not at all. The Office of Education's handbooks, first published in 1954, attempted to remedy some of these obvious flaws, but truly national data were not collected until the 1977–78 school year in what is called the Common Core of Data. Originally the Common Core was an ambitious project in which educational statistics would be gathered in a speedy and comprehensive manner, similar to the National Center for Health Statistics or the Bureau of Labor Statistics. However, lack of funding and resistance by state officials and other federal agencies to relinquish their power over educational data resulted in a much-scaled-back project, focusing on enrollment, attendance, revenues, and expenditures.

During the 1980s, the National Center for Education Statistics suffered reduction in budgets more than triple the cutbacks for other federal statistical agencies. Forty percent of the items not dealing with funding were eliminated from the federal data base between 1981 and 1983, including questions about critical policy issues such as school busing and the gender mix of teachers. Researchers identify three overall problems with NCES data: delay; nonstandardization; and irrelevance.

The NCES data often are published so long after collection, that they cannot be used for policy making. In order to maintain a reasonably current public record, the U.S. Education Department's chief statistics publication, *Digest of Education Statistics*, relies on data collected by private organizations such as the National Educational Association because their data are available before the department's own official figures.

Unlike the Uniform Crime Survey (see chapter 6), there has not been a successful federal effort to create uniform reporting procedures for educational statistics. As a result, it is difficult for researchers to compare data between states. For example, variations in how states adjust for absent students make it difficult to compare public school enrollment.

According to its critics, the Common Core of Data too often focuses on easily measured items such as numbers of students and dollar expenditures, avoiding sensitive and timely issues such as inequality and student performance. As a result, even the Department of Education itself cannot rely on Common Core data; their own publication, for example, *A Nation at Risk: The Imperative for Educational Reform*, cited other data sources for all but one educational risk indicator.

With resurgent interest in education during the 1990s, it is likely that efforts will be made to improve the quality of educational statistics. Nonetheless, the stinginess of previous decades will hamper research efforts because there will be no long-standing data base for making historical comparisons.

High School Dropouts

One example of an educational statistic that is poorly measured is the high school dropout rate. It has been particularly contentious in New York City, where, according to critics, more than one-half of all youths fail to finish high school. During the 1984 mayoral campaign, incumbent Ed Koch claimed that the dropout rate was only 11 percent, based on the percentage of the entire high school enrollment who dropped out in one year. More conventionally, dropout rates are measured as the percentage of ninth graders who fail to graduate four years later. On this basis, New York City school administrators reported the city's dropout rate at only 30 percent in 1987. But subsequent investigation revealed that the city minimized the number of dropouts by not counting chronic truants or those who dropped out during the summer. According to the Education Priorities Panel, a private watch-dog group, the true dropout rate was in excess of 50 percent.

New York City's dropout rate is not unusual; similarly high dropout rates have been measured in Los Angeles, Chicago, Detroit, Washington, Pittsburgh, Cleveland, and Philadelphia. In these cities, however, and for the country as a whole, there are also problems in measuring the dropout rate. The U.S. Education Department measures the "attrition rate," the proportion of a given entering high school class that does not graduate four years later. On this basis the dropout rate was about 30 percent during the mid-1980s.

A much lower dropout rate, about 15 percent, was measured by the U.S. Census Bureau based on the proportion of 18- and 19-year-olds who were not enrolled in school and had not completed high school. There are several explanations for the discrepancy between the Census Bureau figure and the Department of Education figure. One important factor is that increasing numbers of dropouts are earning high school diplomas through equivalency examinations, as many as 40 percent in one study. These individuals are counted as high school graduates in Census Bureau data, but not by the Education Department criteria. Much of the remaining discrepancy arises because of errors in each survey. The Census Bureau data are taken from the Current Population Survey (see chapter 9), and the respondent may be unwilling to tell survey takers about lack of education in their households. The Education Department data suffer from the lack of good data tracking individual students over long periods of time. Data collected at single points in time from school districts are likely to misrepresent the status of students who change schools or are transient, as in the case of migrant labor children.

Without consensus among researchers about how to measure the dropout rate, it is not surprising that there is disagreement about the trend in the dropout rate. Both Census Bureau and Education Department dropout rates measured short-term changes during the 1970s and 1980s, but no significant overall pattern up or down. Education researchers Margaret D. LeCompte and Stephen D. Goebel conclude that current U.S. high school dropout rates are useful for only "general identification of what is clearly a major educational issue," not for "evaluation of program effectiveness." In other words, until we have better data, we can use high school dropout rates as an indication that there is continued failure in our school systems, but the statistics are not precise enough to measure differences between school districts or changes over time.

Illiteracy

Educational experts agree there is no single measure of illiteracy; it is a relative concept, dependent on how we define "literacy." Not surprisingly, there is a wide range of measured illiteracy rates, from 0.5 percent based on U.S. Census data for the number of adults who claim not to have finished sixth grade, up to 33 percent based on functional definition estimating the proportion of U.S. adults who could not read simple instructions such as the antidote on a lye bottle.

Such varying definitions helped fuel a 1980s debate about the severity of illiteracy. At that time, U.S. Education Secretary William Bennett defined illiteracy as only 5 percent, those who could only demonstrate the equivalent of a fourth-grade education. On this basis, Bennett concluded, "the United States is not awash in illiteracy," and federal illiteracy programs were cut to less than $100 million per year during the mid-1980s. Advocates of literacy programs argued at least a $5 billion effort was needed.

A 1982 survey by the U.S. Census Bureau for the Education Department measuring about 13 percent illiteracy received a good deal of publicity when it was released in 1986. But critics charged that the survey gave the misleading impression of accurately measuring illiteracy at its estimated range of 17 to 21 million illiterates. Some argued that illiteracy is actually much higher because 20 percent of those surveyed refused to be tested. Others maintained that the Census Bureau measured a peculiar sort of "bureaucratise" literacy because test-takers had to decipher language encountered in government offices such as "you may request a review of the decision made on the application for recertification for assistance and may request a fair hearing concerning any action affecting receipt or termination of assistance." A better-received study by the private Educational Testing Service measured literacy for a variety of tasks. Almost no one failed to find the time of a meeting in a memorandum, but 80 percent could not read a bus schedule accurately, and more than 90 percent could not interpret a four-line poem. This kind of functional illiteracy was emphasized by educator Jonathan Kozol in his 1985 book *Illiterate America*, where he concluded that there were 60 million U.S. adult *functional* illiterates, which is about one-third of the nation.

The lesson for researchers is to be careful in collapsing a complex social issue such as illiteracy into a single variable. The severity of the problem and the amount of government funding needed depend on which type of illiteracy we consider to be relevant.

Black Educational Progress

During the last fifty years, black educational attainment changed dramatically. School enrollment rates, once much lower for black youth, by 1980 were indistinguishable from whites, at about 93 percent. Similarly, the median number of years of schooling completed by blacks more than doubled between 1940 and 1980 to twelve years, near the white figure of 12.5 years of schooling.

But such a positive view of black educational progress is challenged on two grounds. First, as sociologists Walter Farley and Walter R. Allen point out in their book, *The Color Line*, schooling received by blacks, while equal in number of years, is likely to be inferior in quality. For example, whites are twice as likely as blacks to attend private schools. Economists Bennett Harrison and Lucy Gorham measure vastly different outcomes from a college education for blacks and whites. In 1987, one in three black college-educated men earned less than $12,000 (the poverty line for a family of four), while only one in six white college-educated white men earned under that amount. Worse still, nearly one-half of college-educated black women had incomes below this poverty line.

A second objection to the optimistic view of black educational progress is a reversal during the 1980s. While total higher education enrollment grew by 6 percent between 1980 and 1986, the number of black college and university students fell by 30,000 from its 1980 high. The percentage of college degrees awarded to blacks fell to 5.7 percent in 1987, down from 6.4 percent in 1976. There was some evidence for improvement in black college enrollment during the late 1980s, but even so, by 1988, non-Hispanic black college enrollment was only slightly higher than its previous high in 1980.

Finally, many observers are troubled by data showing that all of the college enrollment decline was among black men. One consequence of lower college enrollment is less earning ability for black men. Harrison measured a decline by 28,000 in the number of college-educated black men earning $36,000 or more (measured in 1987 buying power) between 1979 and 1987. William Julius Wilson, 1989 president of the American Sociological Association, fears that less education for black men will decrease their ability to support families. In this view, cutbacks in financial aid during the 1980s not only exacerbate income inequality between blacks and whites, but also further disrupt black families by increasing, in Wilson's words, "social distance and hostility between men and women."

Longer-term data are needed to assess whether the 1980s were a temporary period of setbacks in black educational progress. In addition, these statistics illustrate the limitation of the aggregate statistic, median years of schooling completed, as a measure of black educational status. It obscures comparisons between blacks and whites in college enrollment and economic benefits gained from additional schooling, as well as the different experience of black men and black women.

School Desegregation: What Has Happened?

Recent debate about attempts to enforce school desegregation during the 1980s illustrates the difficulty faced by social scientists in studying a complex issue in the face of intensive political controversy. At the start of the decade, the U.S. Commission on Civil Rights, a target of civil rights groups for allegedly lax enforcement, initiated a study of the effect of federal programs such as mandatory busing on school desegregation. The effort was plagued by political turmoil from the start. The director, Finis Welch, was challenged when he admitted little experience in studying desegregation. In 1985, a key member of the study, Gary Orfield of the University of Chicago, resigned on the grounds that the project was biased against busing programs, and pursued his own separately funded research effort. Finally, in 1987, when the Civil Rights Commission's report was released, three members refused to vote on accepting the study because it allegedly wasted its limited budget repeating already published findings.

To complicate matters further, there were problems with the methods used to analyze desegregation. Finis Welch and his critics debated how to take into account the fact that white enrollment was dropping before desegregation programs were introduced. In other words, it was necessary to estimate whether school attendance patterns would have changed regardless of the desegregation plans. Also, there were debates about the long-run effect on enrollment—did white enrollment stay low?—and on the effect of different types of desegregation programs. These issues caused additional controversy, although this debate took place in academic journals, rather than in newspapers.

It is not surprising that the Civil Rights Commission and Orfield studies reached opposing policy conclusions. According to Welch, director of the Civil Rights Commission study, the evidence convinced him that "we have spent far too many resources trying to see that our children attend similar schools or some racial balance is attained." On the other hand, Orfield and his colleagues opposed efforts by the Reagan administration to curb school integration; they applauded the courts, which had "not followed the election returns." Other research efforts led to similarly conflicting results, so that as of the late 1980s there was little consensus about the effectiveness of school desegregation efforts.

Franklin Wilson, a major contributor to research on this issue, argued that much more sophisticated studies were needed in order to assess school integration programs. In particular, he called for long-term studies of strategies used by school districts, and studies of the broader question of the effect of school programs on residential segregation. However, the existing intense feelings about busing, complicated by ambiguous results, meant that social science research was contributing little to public policy debate.

Teacher Shortage?

Will there be enough teachers in the future? Media attention to the issue was prompted by a 1985 Metropolitan Life survey finding that over one-half of U.S. teachers "seriously considered" leaving the profession. But according to one respected private research group, the National Center for Education Information, there was no teacher shortage during the 1980s, and there was unlikely to be one in the foreseeable future. In a 1986 report, *Teacher Crisis: Myth or Reality*, the NCEI predicted there would be a slow increase in school enrollments during the 1990s that could be met by new hiring. Other researchers disagreed, most notably representatives of the major U.S. teacher unions. For example, representatives of the National Education Association argued that hiring kept pace with demand only because of emergency credentials, allegedly causing "massive hiring of unqualified individuals." In response, the National Center for Education Information maintained that many emergency credentialed teachers were in fact qualified because this credential did not actually measure teaching competence.

Both the National Center for Education Information and its critics agreed there were potential shortages in subjects such as mathematics and a troublesome decline in the number of men teachers as well as teachers from minority groups during the 1980s. It remains to be seen, however, if there will be an overall shortage of qualified teachers.

Class Size

Recent debate about class size is illustrative of the shortcomings of education statistics, as well as of the absence of large-scale experiments that would test the effect of new programs.

The National Center for Economic Statistics publishes a statistic called "pupil-teacher ratio" that is often interpreted as a measure of class size. In fact, these statistics measure student enrollment divided by the number of teachers, with part-time instructors counted as a fraction of their full-time equivalents. For many decades this number fell, from over thirty pupils per teacher for elementary schools classes during the early 1950s, to about fifteen pupils per teacher by the mid- and late 1980s. However, a poll of teachers by the largest representative group for teachers, the National Education Association, estimated class size in 1983 as much as one-third higher than the NCES student-teacher ratio. In part the discrepancy occurs because of specialist teachers working in conjunction with regular classroom teachers; they cause the pupil-teacher ratio measured by the National Center to be lower than the actual number of students in a classroom.

Whatever the trend in class size, some researchers question whether small classes improve educational performance, prompting a bitter debate about this issue during the 1980s. A review of studies by University of Colorado education researcher Gene V. Glass and colleagues claimed to "establish clearly that reduced class size can be expected to improve academic achievement." However, in a strongly worded response, the Education Research Service, a nonprofit group providing information to schools, argued that the effect was irrelevant for education policy because improvement only occurred in extremely small classes; there was no significant improvement for reduction of class size within the 20- to 40-student range. Subsequent classroom experiments confirmed the positive effect of major reductions to less than 20 students per class, but such experiments are expensive; more often reduced-size classes still have more than 20 students, a size for which the effects are debatable.

SUMMARY

The fundamental problem with education statistics is poor data. More timely and standardized data will assist researchers, as will increased willingness by the National Center for Education Statistics to tackle controversial issues. In addition, better-quality longitudinal data will provide better information on dropout rates and the effect of different schooling on the future careers of students.

For several of the issues covered in this chapter, including illiteracy, teacher shortages, desegregation, and class size, relatively adequate data exist. Controversies arose because of different interpretation of the numbers. How many adults are illiterate? Is there a teacher shortage? What are the differences in educational opportunities for blacks and whites? Does desegregation cause lower white enrollment? Does lower class size improve school performance? Media accounts of these disputes rarely explain the origins of the statistical discrepancies, focusing instead on the different policies that researchers recommended. In each case, closer examination of the statistics reveals important information about education. For example, hidden within the debate about the precise illiteracy rate is the more critical issue about what level of literacy is required for functioning in the United States. And even though there are insufficient data to measure the high school dropout rate accurately, we are certain it is so high as to severely handicap a large proportion of urban youth. Although much educational data remain uncollected, and many research questions remain unanswered, there is still much to be learned from careful attention to the data.

CASE STUDY QUESTIONS

1. A higher percentage of U.S. students attend college than in any country in the world. In 1987, over 44 percent of Americans 18 to 24

years old were in higher education, more than double the rate for European nations. What effect do you think this much greater attendance rate has on international comparison of college test scores? On college graduation rates? And on unemployment rates for college graduates?

2. According to a 1988 study of state education departments, *all* claimed their students performed above the national average. This mathematical impossibility was termed the "Lake Wobegon effect" after Garrison Keillor's mythical Minnesota town where "all the children are above average." Technically, the national average is a median, meaning one-half of tested students score below and one-half score above, but that isn't the source of the paradox. The standard was set in the early 1980s. Why were all the children "above average"?

3. In 1990, the Census Bureau changed its question about education attainment from "What is the highest grade (or year) . . . attended?" to the "highest level completed or degree received." Why do you think this change was necessary?

4. In a survey of Illinois high school seniors, 80 percent of respondents reported they had taken a geometry course. Yet, high school transcripts showed that 25 percent of students statewide were never enrolled in a geometry class. What might explain this discrepancy?

Chapter 6

Crime

Researchers new to the criminal justice field may be surprised at the amount of data available, including nearly complete records of arrests and crimes reported to police, and a survey of crime victims almost as large in sample size as the Current Population Survey (see chapter 9). These data are the source of a number of controversies about crime, each with important public policy consequences. This chapter reviews several debates in criminology, including: the accuracy of crime statistics; the chances that an individual will be a crime victim; the age of most criminals; the effect of poverty on crime; the relationship between crime and race; the deterrence effect of capital punishment; and the importance of white-collar crime.

DATA SOURCES

There are two major sources of crime data: the Uniform Crime Reports, a compilation of police reports by the U.S. Justice Department's Federal Bureau of Investigation; and the National Crime Survey of households conducted by the U.S. Census Bureau for the U.S. Department of Justice.

Uniform Crime Reports

When we hear that crime is up or down, the figures usually come from the Uniform Crime Reports (UCR). Since 1930 the Federal Bureau of Investigation (FBI) has collected reports from over 16,000

Where the Numbers Come from

Organizations	Data Sources	Key Publications
Federal Bureau of Investigation U.S. Department of Justice	Uniform Crime Reports	*Crime in the United States*
Statistics Division U.S. Department of Justice	National Crime Survey	*Criminal Victimization in the United States*

police departments across the country. These data include type of crime, time of occurrence, locality, and age, sex, and race of the offender. Crimes included in the UCR, or ''index crimes,'' are: homicide, forcible rape, robbery, aggravated assault (defined as violent crimes); and burglary, larceny over $50, and auto theft (defined as nonviolent crimes). Specifically excluded are petty theft, and so-called victimless crimes such as drug abuse because arrest criteria for these crimes vary from place to place and from year to year.

> *Data Sample:* The 1986 UCR lists 7 homicides and 265 motor vehicle thefts in Muncie, Indiana.

National Crime Survey

The second major data source on crime in the United States comes from crime victims in the National Crime Survey. These data are published annually by the U.S. Justice Department's Bureau of Justice based on a special Census Bureau survey of more than 50,000 households. The survey includes crimes regardless of whether they were reported to the police, but excludes murder, commercial burglary, and robbery, victimless crimes, prostitution, and white-collar crimes such as fraud and embezzlement (see below).

> *Data Sample:* In the 1985 National Crime Survey individuals in families with income under $7,500 said they reported 34 percent of crimes

Box 6.1. **The Crime Index**

The "Crime Index" is a composite number including the total number of index crimes counted in the UCR during a year, calculated per 100,000 inhabitants. As an unweighted index, the Crime Index is dominated by its largest category, property crime, comprising nearly 90 percent of the index, of which more than one-half is larceny-theft. Because the Crime Index is overly responsive to changes in property crimes, it can misrepresent the trend in more serious violent crime. For example, the overall Crime Index showed a 2.2 percent drop between 1982 and 1986, solely on the basis of declines in larceny and burglary. During the same period, violent crime actually rose by over 8 percent. Those who want to emphasize the growing threat of crime typically refer to violent crime, which has increased almost every year since 1977. Those who maintain that crime is under control report the total Crime Index, which shows a downward trend since 1980.

FBI reports feature a "Crime Clock" showing the frequency of index crime, once every two seconds in the UCR index for 1986. Critics charge that such presentation unnecessarily provokes public fear of crime, and not coincidentally argues for higher law enforcement budgets.

to police; individuals in households with incomes over $50,000 said they reported 47 percent of crimes to police.

CONTROVERSIES

How Accurate Are Crime Statistics?

It is generally acknowledged that far more crimes occur than are reported to the police and thus included in the Uniform Crime Reports. Indeed, set side-by-side with the UCR, the National Crime Survey counts about three times as much crime, although, as indicated above, different definitions about what constitutes crime mean that the two data sources are not strictly comparable. The UCR counts crime perpetrators, while the survey counts crime victims. Thus, when a group robs one victim, it is overrepresented in the UCR relative to the survey. On the other hand, when one criminal robs two people at the same time, there are two victims in the survey,

---

Box 6.2. **Rape**

According to a study directed by psychologist Mary P. Koss, both the National Crime Survey and the Uniform Crime Reports may seriously understate the crime of rape. In a survey specifically designed to overcome the fear of respondents to report rape, Koss and her colleagues found that thirty-eight per thousand college-age women reported being raped during the previous six months. This is more than ten times the number of rapes reported for similar age women in the National Crime Survey, which measures more rapes than the Uniform Crime Reports. According to Koss, "It must be concluded that official surveys fail to describe the full extent of sexual victimization."

---

but only one crime in the UCR. Finally, the UCR counts only the most serious crime for each arrest, leaving out other offenses that may have other victims.

Although the National Crime Survey counts more crime, it is not necessarily more accurate for research purposes. As in all household surveys, there are uncertainties about what respondents report. For example, one respondent usually answers for everyone in the household, a practice that leads to underreporting of crimes for other household members, but exaggeration of minor crimes committed against the respondent. To make matters worse, when a person has been the victim of several crimes, he or she tends not to report all of the crimes. Apparently, respondents feel they have been cooperative by reporting a few crimes, and do not want to be bothered to recollect the entire number of crimes. Finally, respondents tend to telescope past events, including in the "past year" crimes experienced more than a year previously.

The Uniform Crime Reports also suffer misrepresentation in their surveys. Most importantly, the data are vulnerable to error at their source, the police departments that report their records to the FBI. There are several documented examples of apparent changes in the crime rate that were later traced to purposeful manipulation by police departments. For many years researchers omitted New York City crime statistics because they were based on individual precincts, where it was common practice for police to underreport crime in order to protect the reputation of their service neighborhoods. When New York

City shifted to a centralized reporting system, burglary reports increased more than fourteenfold in three years. During the 1970s, when President Nixon launched a law-and-order campaign for the District of Columbia, police officials met their quotas for less crime by downgrading the seriousness of crimes so that they would not appear in the UCR. Subsequent investigation by a newspaper reporter revealed that stolen goods often were valued at $49, just under the threshold for grand larceny, the lowest-level crime included in the UCR. A similar strategy to "fight" crime was used in Indianapolis during the mid-1970s, where the police department achieved lower crime rates by tripling the number of crime reports determined to be "without merit" and thus unreported in the UCR.

Implications Although there are drawbacks to both the UCR and the National Crime Survey, no major alternative data source exists. Consequently, the challenge for researchers is to choose the data for which inaccuracies are least likely to affect the issue being studied. For some purposes the choice is readily apparent: the UCR more accurately designates types of crime because it uses standard legal definitions. On the other hand, the National Crime Survey gives a better estimate of the total number of crimes, including those not reported to police.

For measuring the overall crime rate, the choice between these two crime measures is less clear-cut, and unfortunately is sometimes based on political convenience. For example, in 1981 the attorney general's Task Force on Violent Crime cited an increase in UCR-measured robbery rates as an argument in favor of new crime-fighting measures, including the use of trial evidence acquired in violation of constitutional prohibitions. In opposition, the National Council on Crime and Delinquency pointed to a *decline* in robberies measured in the National Crime Survey. Such opposing trends in the two crime statistics occur frequently, in particular for the trend in crime over the short span of a year. In fact, one noted criminologist argues that these changes in the crime rate may occur entirely because of errors in measurement, and thus do not reflect any changes in crime policy for which political leaders can take blame or credit. The lesson for researchers is to be aware of both sets of crime statistics, and to wait for longer-term data to determine the upward or downward trend.

Box 6.3. **A Worldwide Problem?**

U.S. political scientist James Q. Wilson argues that rising crime is a relentless, worldwide problem for which there are few social remedies. Critics point out exceptions to the worldwide crime wave, including countries as different as Japan, Switzerland, Cuba, and the Scandinavian nations. Moreover, in countries like England, where crime increased thirteenfold during this century, it was from such a low base that the English crime rate is still far below the level in the United States. According to critics of Wilson, the United States stands alone with an extraordinarily high rate, especially for serious crimes. To put the matter baldly: the city of Chicago has more burglaries than the entire country of Japan; there are more murders in Detroit than in the more populous and ostensibly violence-plagued Northern Ireland; homicide death rates for U.S. men are more than ten times higher than in Austria, West Germany, Sweden, England, or Denmark.

Will You Be a Crime Victim?

Based on the National Crime Survey, the U.S. Justice Department calculates an individual's chance of becoming a crime victim in his or her lifetime. According to the Justice Department, these statistics are necessary because of a "false sense of security" provided by the apparently low crime rates measured on an annual basis. In this view, the public is misled by statistics measuring only an approximately 5 percent rate for violent crime in a given year, when in fact more than 80 percent of all individuals will be victims of violent crimes over a lifetime. (For blacks, the data are even grimmer: 1 in 30 black men is murdered, compared to 1 out of 133 for all people in the United States.)

The problem with likelihood statistics is that they assume that today's high crime rates will stay constant, which is perhaps an unduly pessimistic view. Most experts agree that the crime rate is likely to fall because there will be fewer young men in the age group most likely to commit crimes. Also, likelihood predictions make the conservative assumption that future social policies will not affect the crime rate, a too-gloomy prognosis according to some critics who argue that employment and income programs could substantially reduce crime.

Thus, "your likelihood to be a crime victim" is another statistic similar to a "woman's likelihood to marry" (see chapter 2). Both estimates will be accurate *only* if past experience is a reasonable guide to the future. Although the statistics can be instructive, as in the high murder rates for black men, the estimates are imperfect predictions of the future unless we make the extremely conservative assumption that social relations will be unchanged either for the better or for the worse.

Are Criminals Getting Younger—Or Older?

Highly publicized stories about "Children Killing Children" suggest that the crime rate stays high because today's youth are more criminally minded, committing acts of unprecedented violence. However, Barry Krisberg, president of the National Council on Crime and Delinquency, points out that each generation characterizes its youth as worse than those of previous years. It may be true that children are being used by adults to commit particularly abhorrent crimes, such as drug murder contracted to youths not subject to adult penalties, but overall the data indicate no worrisome trend. During the early 1980s, the number of youths under eighteen who were arrested grew at a slower rate than the overall crime rate, and the number of fifteen-year-olds arrested actually fell. Moreover, because children often commit crime in groups, the number arrested and thus counted in UCR data is greater than for comparable crimes committed by an adult operating alone.

In a curious twist, reports appeared in 1982 about a crime wave by the elderly. In a manner similar to the youth crime hypothesis, there was unwarranted extrapolation from anecdotal evidence about "over-the-hill criminal gangs." *U.S. News and World Report* headlined: "New Police Worry: Old Lawbreakers." In this case UCR data show a near tripling of the crime rate by older people since 1964, while crimes by younger people only doubled. But the importance of these percentages is disputed by the coordinator of criminal justice services for the American Association of Retired Persons, George Sunderland, who points out that those over sixty-five actually account for less than 1 percent of all arrests. There were, for example, only 151 arrests of the elderly for robbery in 1980 out of 139,476 total robbery arrests. Given such low initial levels, small increases in the number of elderly arrests caused deceptively high percentage increases as reported by the popular media.

Media coverage of "youth" and "elderly" crime demonstrates the pitfall of extrapolating a social trend from a few isolated events. This misinterpretation obscured the well-documented fact that far more individuals are arrested in their youth than in later years. UCR data show the greatest number of arrests among eighteen-year-olds, eight times the rate for forty-five-year-olds. As a result, many crime experts believed the United States would "grow out" of the crime wave when the crest of the baby boom outgrew its high crime years during the 1980s. In fact, the UCR peaked at its highest level ever in 1981. But then contrary to simple demographic theory, the crime rate increased again slightly during the mid-1980s, a shift that is not well understood. As noted above, longer-term data are needed to measure the long-term trend in crime, but most experts believe the crime rate will continue its downward course.

Does Poverty Cause Crime?

It seems obvious that crime is associated with poverty. Basic street sense tells us that poor neighborhoods are more dangerous than wealthy neighborhoods. Superficially, at least, the data support such generalizations. Highland Park, Michigan, a section of inner-city Detroit, suffered twenty-two murders in 1986 according to the UCR. Nearby suburban Grosse Pointe, with a similar population, had no reported murders. Robberies were also disproportionate: 577 in Highland Park; 44 in Grosse Pointe.

However, some social scientists are uncertain about how poverty is related to crime. The problem is that grouped data such as the comparison between Highland Park and Grosse Pointe do not necessarily imply individual differences in the propensity to commit crimes by residents in those neighborhoods. In other words, just because crime is correlated with poverty at the group level (crime is high in poor neighborhoods), it does not necessarily follow that crime is correlated with poverty at the individual level (poor individuals commit more crimes).

Sociologist C.S. Tittle and other researchers argue that low-income Highland Park residents are no more likely to be criminals than high-income residents of Grosse Pointe. Tittle rejects grouped data studies for perpetuating the "myth of social class and criminality" and the "prejudice that lower class people are characterized by pejorative traits such as immorality, inferiority and criminality." In place of grouped data, Tittle suggests we look at self-report studies in which sociologists ask *individuals* about their criminal past. According to Tittle, self-report studies show practically no association between social class and criminal activity.

If economic circumstances are not responsible for crime, then income or job programs are unlikely to lower the crime rate. But those who support these economic solutions to crime take issue with Tittle's reliance on self-report studies. Surprisingly, the rebuttal does not focus on the obvious drawback of obtaining accurate self-incriminating data. Instead, self-report studies are criticized for failing to take into account the seriousness of crimes. It is only by including very minor thefts as crimes that middle-class and upper-class youths have as high a crime rate as lower-class youths. Or, as sociologist Elliott Currie mocks the result, we learned that "American youths of all backgrounds sometimes acted up."

To support the view that the self-report studies overemphasize minor crimes and therefore disguise the relationship between poverty and serious crime, Currie points to 1983 research by the Colorado Behavioral Research Institute showing that the seriousness and frequency of criminal behavior are strongly correlated with social class. Based on such studies, Currie and other criminologists contend that there is sufficient correlation between poverty and crime on an individual level to override the potential pitfall of drawing conclusions from grouped data. However, researchers should keep in mind that there are situations where group data can be misleading.

Why Is the Black Crime Rate So High?

The Uniform Crime Reports tabulate criminal offenders by sex, age, and race. The most obvious observation is that men make up the largest percentage, nearly 90 percent for violent crimes. Second, about one-half of all offenders are under the age of twenty. Third, and most controversial, blacks comprise about 50 percent of those arrested for violent crimes. It is the disproportionate number of young, black men in the criminal justice system that has provoked heated research debate. Part of the difference in crime rates between racial groups depends on what we define as crime. Whites are arrested more frequently for white-collar offenses, a type of crime larger in dollar amount than other crimes (see below), but not included in the UCR. Also, for one of the most common crimes of all, drunk driving, which is also not in the UCR, the arrest rate for blacks is lower than for whites.

Overall, however, blacks comprise 45 percent of those in prison, many times the percentage of blacks in the U.S. population. Sociologist Andrew Hacker ascribes part of this difference to the discriminatory access to crime; that is, black offenders often resort to street robberies, which almost always result in arrest, whereas white offenders are able to operate freely in better-off neighborhoods where they can commit burglaries, a far more profitable and less hazardous occupation. New York State Supreme Court Judge Bruce Wright adds that police discrimination causes blacks to be arrested more frequently, and discrimination by the judicial system causes blacks to receive more frequent and longer prison sentences.

Criminologist Elliott Currie responds that outright bias explains only a small part of the difference in crime rates for blacks and for whites. As evidence, Currie cites homicide data available from the Public Health Service showing that black men from age twenty-five to forty-four are eight times as likely to be murdered as their white age-mates. Because other studies show that most murders are intraracial (black against black), it seems likely that the higher homicide rate for blacks is real and not a result of police or judicial bias. Currie maintains that the eagerness by some researchers to dismiss race as an important factor in crime has distracted policy makers from the task of accounting for what Currie calls the "genuine social disaster wrought by extremes of economic inequality we have tolerated in the United States."

The issue of race and crime has a long, controversial history. Statistics from the Justice Department's Bureau of Justice Statistics show a grisly past in which, for example, blacks have constituted about one-half of those executed by the legal system, including many for crimes other than murder. Researchers need to be aware of the issues raised by Hacker and Wright that cause bias in official statistics, as well as of the complex social factors that Currie urges us to address in understanding the relationship between race and crime.

Does Capital Punishment Deter Murder?

Much recent criminology research focuses on punishment as a determent to crime. At the center of the debate is the efficacy of the death penalty. According to a 1975 study by economist Isaac Ehrlich, approximately eight murders are deterred by every legal execution. In a

1976 brief to the Supreme Court, the U.S. solicitor general quoted Ehrlich's results as "sophisticated" evidence that "execution actually deterred a significant number of murders."

Anti–capital punishment forces take issue with this view. In competing testimony to the Supreme Court, researchers pointed out that Ehrlich's analysis depends crucially on several arbitrary assumptions. Any one of the following changes reduces the deterrence effect measured by Ehrlich: if Vital Statistics replace Ehrlich's FBI crime data; if raw numbers are substituted for the logarithms used by Ehrlich; if the years 1963 through 1969 are removed; if states that never had a penalty are studied separately. Each of these limitations indicates that Ehrlich's results are not robust—that is, he can reach his conclusion only under narrow specifications. Research should ideally be immune to slight changes in the analysis. If changing the data source, the use of logarithms, the years studied, or states included causes the effect of the death penalty to disappear, then it is likely that the original conclusion about the effect of the death penalty was the result of statistical happenstance.

Ehrlich answered his critics with a second study in 1977, comparing murder rates in different states. Again, Ehrlich found a deterrence effect, in this case more than twenty murders were prevented by each execution. But, as in the case of his 1975 study, other researchers challenged Ehrlich's method on the grounds that small changes in the research method would cause the deterrence effect to disappear. In this case, critics argued that the murder rate increased because of factors not considered by Ehrlich, perhaps differences between states in the likelihood of conviction, differences between states in cultural attitudes, or differences between states in the availability of hand guns.

Even if we cannot rule out a deterrent effect to the death penalty, the difficulty in proving that deterrence exists suggests that the deterrence effect is quite small compared with other factors affecting the crime rate. Other social policies, in particular programs to provide jobs and income, have been demonstrated to affect the crime rate strongly. But such social policies are less well studied; as economist Richard McGahey points out, there are exhaustive studies of the death penalty, but no corresponding "spate of articles on . . . 'Murder and Poverty,' or 'The Preventative Effect of Higher Incomes.' "

Box 6.4. **Missing Children—How Serious a Problem?**

"Missing children" became a national obsession during the 1980s, when their pictures appeared on milk cartons, buses, and national TV. Fifty million households watched a fictionalized account of Etan Patz's disappearance in New York City, followed by President Reagan's appeal to find missing children whose pictures were shown to viewers. But are missing children actually as commonplace as the media attention suggests?

According to official FBI statistics, kidnapping is an extremely rare crime. At any one time, fewer than 100 children are listed as kidnapped by strangers and the crime is so infrequent that it is not included in the National Crime Survey because it would show up in the 60,000 household sample an average of once every fifteen years. The total number of missing children is far larger, over one million every year, but most of these children are runaways who return home in a few days and whose disappearance thus is never reported to the FBI. Those who are actually abducted are most often taken by other family members, usually in a custody dispute. Jay Howell, director of the National Center for Missing and Exploited Children, points out that "the most dangerous place for a child in this country is his or her own home."

What about White-Collar Crime?

In 1939, Edwin H. Sutherland used the occasion of his American Sociological Society presidential address to urge study of what he termed "white-collar crime." Sutherland suggested that criminologists previously ignored "upper-world" crime committed in the course of an occupation, offenses he claimed were as important as traditionally defined crime. But measuring the amount of white-collar crime has not been easy.

A few white-collar crimes are counted in national statistics. FBI records counted 5,000 convictions for fraud in 1985, and a lesser number for embezzlement, counterfeiting, and regulatory offenses. As federal crimes they are not included in the UCR, although in any case they would be swamped by the 13 million crimes recorded in 1985. The National Crime Survey also omits white-collar crime because many victims are not aware of the crime.

Many researchers, including Sutherland, have argued for a definition of white-collar crime that would be far broader than the offenses recorded by the FBI. In this view, most white-collar crime is committed by high-status individuals in the course of their work without any arrests, or even a record of a crime. By such a definition, white-collar crime includes violations of antitrust law, safety rules, and environmental standards. As examples the critics often cite egregious cases such as the promotion of Chloromycetin by Parke-Davis pharmaceutical company, and the exploding gas tank in Ford Pinto automobiles. The cost of these crimes can only be estimated; according to Mark Green, former aide to Ralph Nader, price fixing and safety lapses alone caused several hundred billion dollars harm to society.

At stake in the definition of white-collar crime is the allocation of crime prevention resources. Criminologists Harold Pepinsky and Paul Jesilow argue that even the lowest estimates for the value of white-collar crime are still about ten times as high as the total property loss in traditionally defined crime. But crime prevention funds are allocated in just the reverse proportions, with most money spent dealing with non-white-collar criminals. Philosopher David Reiman argues that rational allocation would increase policing of operating rooms and dangerous workplaces where four times more people are killed than in traditionally defined murders.

Most research projects have little choice but to work with existing official definitions of crime; certainly the approach makes sense if one wants to study those who actually are arrested. But if the goal is to study total law breaking or the cost of crime to society, then researchers need to consider a broader approach, taking white-collar crime into account. The problem, of course, is how to measure white-collar crime when few available statistics do so. As a minimal corrective, researchers can acknowledge this shortcoming in the data base.

SUMMARY

Research on crime enjoys relatively complete statistics published in a timely way. Nonetheless, this chapter has illustrated several major problems in the use of crime statistics.

First, crime statistics are unusual in that the same organizations—individual police departments and the FBI—are responsible for carrying out public policy as well as collecting and publishing the most important source of crime data, the Uniform Crime Reports. This conflict of interest sometimes causes inaccuracies in the data, as in the case of police department misrepresentations to the UCR. In addition, critics charge that some statistics such as the Crime Index and the Likelihood of Being a Crime Victim are constructed in a manner that helps the criminal justice system to justify budgets rather than to increase our understanding of crime. A different sort of survey error affects the National Crime Survey in which respondents are not necessarily forthcoming with accurate answers about their experience with crime. Overreporting of crime occurs when respondents exaggerate their own experiences or telescope distant events into the past year being surveyed. Underreporting, however, appears to be the more serious problem, including a severe undercount of the number of rapes, as well as underreporting for other crimes caused by noncooperation or lack of knowledge about crimes involving other household members. All of these measurement problems are well studied. Even if there is no method to "correct" the underlying data for under- or overreporting, the criminal justice literature provides ample evidence of the direction in which survey errors are likely to lie.

Second, there is disagreement in the study of crime about the fundamental question, "What is crime?" The most commonly used crime data, the UCR, include only crimes reported to police, a number that most certainly is much less than the number of crimes committed. A more complete count of crime is available in the National Crime Survey, but it omits some categories such as victimless crime and white-collar crime. This last category is most controversial of all. There is no standard definition for what constitutes white-collar crime, and there are only imprecise estimates about its dollar value. Despite uncertainty about what crime is, most research projects rely on the "official" definition of crime. A single research project will not be able to correct for uncounted crimes. Nonetheless, careful researchers will note these issues, and speculate about the effect they may have on the study of crime. For example, studies of the relationship between race and crime depend critically upon how crime is defined.

Third, as with other social statistics, crime statistics are only as meaningful as the skill of the researcher who uses them. Misinterpretation of official numbers was documented for single-year trends in the crime rate that are too erratic to measure the impact of crime policies, and for the Crime Index, which does not distinguish between different types of crime. In these cases, there are simple corrective guidelines to be followed, involving the use of longer-term data, and indexes that take into account different types of crime. More problematic is the use of crime statistics in a selective manner. The issue arose in two critical matters of social policy: the relationship between race and crime, and the impact of the death penalty. In both cases critics charged that much standard crime analysis focuses too narrowly on the issues of race and the death penalty in isolation, ignoring other social and economic variables that are more important for understanding crime. The choice of variables for analysis crosses over into theoretical issues of criminology that are beyond the scope of this book. At a minimum, however, researchers can be clear about how they have made such choices, making sure their selection of variables has a sound theoretical basis.

CASE STUDY QUESTIONS

1. The total number of offenses in the Uniform Crime Reports rose to 13,210,800 in 1986 from 12,974,400 in 1982. Yet the crime index fell to 5,479.9 from 5,603.6. Explain.

2. Mr. Smith, who profits from "inside" knowledge about the stock market, is robbed by three youths. How many crimes have been committed according to the Uniform Crime Reports? According to the National Crime Survey?

3. In the National Health Survey, a group of individuals known to have visited the doctor within the previous two weeks were asked if they had done so. About 30 percent denied having been to the doctor during that time. Some researchers think this study has implications for the National Crime Survey. What are they?

4. By the year 2000, men aged 15 to 29, responsible for about one-half of all those individuals arrested, will comprise only about 10 percent of the population, down from 13 percent in 1986. Estimate the crime rate in 2000 compared to 1986.

5. Comparison of National Crime Survey with police data on nonfatal gunshot injuries suggests that the survey undercounts these injuries by a factor of three. Why might this occur?

	National Crime Survey	UCR
1977	5,902	475.9
1978	5,941	497.8
1979	6,159	548.9
1980	6.180	596.6
1981	6,582	594.3
1982	6,459	571.1
1983	5,903	537.7
1984	6,021	539.2

6. In 1981, the following headlines appeared in national magazines: "The Curse of Violent Crime" (*Time*), "The Epidemic of Violent Crime" (*Newsweek*), and "Our Losing Battle against Crime" (*U.S. News*). The indexes of violent crime are listed above.

Based on these data, write a more accurate headline and short article on the trend in crime.

Chapter 7

The National Economy

This chapter looks at statistical controversies for national economic statistics including gross national product, productivity measures, savings rates, imports and exports, and international investments. These statistics are very much "in-the-news," but often in contradictory terms, portraying at the same time both the good and the bad health of the economy. In some cases these discrepancies have occurred because of problems with the underlying data; for example, information on imports and exports was collected so haphazardly that some researchers question official trade statistics. More often, U.S. national economic data are considered a model of survey technique, refined over several decades of collection with well-understood limitations. In these cases contradictory statistics arise because of different methods for interpreting the data. Such examples provide constructive case studies of the intersection between economic theory and the construction of economic statistics.

DATA SOURCES

U.S. Commerce Department

National Income and Product Accounts The U.S. Commerce Department's Bureau of Economic Analysis is the single most important agency for statistics on the entire U.S. economy. It is the conduit for data collected throughout the government, consolidated in National Income and Product Accounts, better known by its most comprehen-

Where the Numbers Come from

Organizations	Data Sources	Key Publications
Bureau of Economic Analysis U.S. Department of Commerce	National income and product accounts	*Survey of Current Business*
Bureau of the Census U.S. Department of Commerce	Economic censuses	*Census of Manufacturing* (and other sectors); *Survey of Current Business; U.S. Exports; U.S. Imports*
Bureau of Labor Statistics U.S. Department of Labor	Productivity computations	*Monthly Labor Review*
Board of Governors U.S. Federal Reserve Board	Flow of funds	*Federal Reserve Bulletin*
U.S. Small Business Administration	Small Business Data Source	*State of Small Business; Handbook of Small Business Data*

sive statistic, Gross National Product, or GNP. These data were first collected systematically during the 1930s under the leadership of economist Simon Kuznets, who later won the Nobel Prize in economics for his efforts. At that time, new categories were created that gained worldwide acceptance for the measurement of national economic activity.

In brief, total economic transactions are added up twice. On one side of the ledger, total incomes, including wages, salaries, rents, profits, interest, and taxes are computed from data collected by the Internal Revenue Service, Bureau of Labor Statistics, Social Security Administration, and other government agencies. On the other side of the ledger,

Box 7.1. **The People behind the Numbers**

Take a moment to consider who is responsible for the data we use. For example, U.S. Census Bureau statistics on shoe production are part of the responsibility of six statisticians, assisted by two clerks, comprising the section "Food, tobacco, textiles, apparel, and leather goods." These men and women design the survey forms, tabulate the returns, and review the tables subsequently published in the *Annual Survey of Manufactures* and the *Census of Manufactures*. Multiplied many times in government and private industry, similar groups work largely unrecognized—but willing to talk with interested researchers—to assemble the data we depend on for our research. Thus we learn that U.S.-produced women's dress shoes declined to 46 million pairs in 1982 from 50 million pairs in 1977, data of vital importance to those in the industry, and a stepping stone toward understanding why U.S. manufacturing employment fell by 900,000 and why the overall economy grew by only 7 percent during these five years.

total expenditures are computed based primarily on Census Bureau economic surveys.

> *Data Sample:* Gross National Product reached $1,000 billion in 1970; $2,000 billion in 1978; $3,000 billion in 1981; $4,000 billion in 1985; and $5,000 billion in 1989.

Industry Statistics   Frequently researchers require statistics on parts of the economy, for example on a single industry, or a particular geographic area. Such data are available in U.S. Census Bureau surveys, most notably the economic censuses taken every five years. The Census of Manufactures alone generates eighty-two separate reports on data for groups of industries, as well as geographic and summary data for the entire manufacturing sector. Similar surveys are conducted for retail trade, government, and construction. A useful source of local information is the annual County Business Patterns, with data on employment, payroll, and type of business, for every U.S. state and county.

> *Data Sample:* The 1982 Census of Manufactures estimated $45.4 million receipts in the category, "Standardized tests including both test and answer sheets."

Trade Statistics   The U.S. Commerce Department's Bureau of Economic Analysis publishes many international statistics, based on data collected by other government agencies. Imports and exports are measured from Customs data; military sales are derived from Defense Department reports; foreign investment income comes from Treasury Department data; and travel expenditures are estimated from postcards distributed during one week every three months to travelers at airports and other border crossings.

> *Data Sample:* Trade statistics reports are extraordinary in detail, reporting, for example, $673,000 in pignolia nuts (shelled, blanched, or otherwise prepared) imported from Portugal in 1987.

U.S. Labor Department

Productivity   United States Commerce Department data on production are used by the U.S. Labor Department's Bureau of Labor Statistics to calculate productivity, that is, the relationship between national output and inputs such as labor or capital. Most often productivity is measured in terms of hours of labor, although the Bureau of Labor Statistics has other productivity measures, including a new multifactor productivity statistic that attempts to take into account changes in both labor and capital inputs.

> *Data Sample:* According to the Bureau of Labor Statistics, U.S. business-sector labor productivity grew at a 3.0 percent annual rate between 1947 and 1973, but only 0.9 percent per year between 1974 and 1985.

U.S. Federal Reserve Board

The nation's central government bank, the Federal Reserve, tracks the economy in its own statistical series. Most important for researchers are flow-of-funds data, a quarterly report on the flow of money through the economy. This is a fundamental source on banking, credit, investments, and international capital transactions. In addition, the Federal Reserve Board compiles statistics on industrial production, including the frequently consulted index of capacity utilization, a measure of how different sectors of the economy are using their existing resources. These data are used for Federal Reserve monetary policy decisions. For example, during the Vietnam War, when the Department of Defense underestimated the war's cost to President Johnson's economic advisers, the Federal Reserve took corrective action because of its own data-collection capability.

> *Data Sample:* The Federal Reserve Board of Governors reported residential mortgages advanced by public agencies in 1988 at $104 billion, down from $153.2 billion in 1987.

Private Sector

Private credit-reporting and investment-grading firms also gather economywide data. Among the most often used of these statistics are those from Dun and Bradstreet Corporation on business startups and business failures. Dun and Bradstreet data are also used by the U.S. Small Business Administration as the basis for the Small Business Data Base on the characteristics of different size firms.

> *Data Sample:* Based on Dun and Bradstreet data, the U.S. Small Business Administration reported 793 new liquor store businesses in 1986.

CONTROVERSIES

Which GNP?

Because national economic accounts are so important for policy making, the Commerce Department estimates GNP statistics with as little delay as possible. The first available data are called "preliminary GNP," published fifteen days after the end of the quarter-year being measured. (A "flash" estimate, published fifteen days *before* the end of the quarter was abandoned in 1986 because it proved too inaccurate.) The day before the GNP data are published, they are calculated on a stand-alone computer to which only a select few officials have access. Such secrecy is necessary because an unexpected rise or fall in GNP can affect stocks and other financial markets, creating the possibility of personal profit by those who know GNP data before the general public. In 1985, two government employees were dismissed for such activity; since then, security has been improved.

Preliminary GNP estimates are almost always revised as more data

---

Box 7.2. **Been Down So Long It Looks Like Up**

Economic growth rates almost always are expressed as percent change. For example, less than 2 percent change in GNP is called a "growth recession" because the economy is growing, but not fast enough to maintain expanding employment levels. However, comparisons of growth rates between years can be misleading, as in 1984 when GNP grew by 6.8 percent (taking inflation into account), the highest level of the decade. This expansion, signaling the end of the recession of the early 1980s, assisted President Reagan in his reelection bid.

But the success of 1984 depended in part on low GNP in previous years. In other words, just as a failing student can dramatically improve a test score on a large percentage basis, such improvement does not mean that this student is doing better than a student who initially performed well. The fastest peacetime U.S. growth rates all occurred when the economy rebounded from a downturn. Slower but sustained growth rates, as achieved during the late 1980s, indicate a healthier economy than one, to quote Richard Fariña, that has "been down so long, it looks like up."

---

become available. For example, a study by the Commerce Department showed that the ranges of quarterly GNP revisions were nearly as great as the average growth rate itself. In other words, a reported typical 3 percent growth rate, when correct, could be as low as 0 percent, or as high as 6 percent. Experts recommend that researchers wait for final revisions a year later, or even more preferably, look at annual rates of change rather than the volatile and potentially misleading quarterly reports.

Often researchers cannot afford to wait for revised GNP estimates. However, such haste can cause erroneous economic policy, as occurred in 1965, when the original GNP growth estimates were almost 3 percent too low, and therefore failed to warn President Johnson's economic advisers that the Vietnam War had overheated the economy. More recently, GNP growth was overstated at an annual rate by more than 3 percent in the final quarter of 1984, causing the Federal Reserve Board to take steps that slowed an economy they mistakenly thought was growing too fast. Finally, a major revision introduced during the late 1980s to take into account the improved quality of computers, caused a nearly $100 billion increase in the measured 1988 GNP,

Table 7.1

GNP Revisions (real GNP growth for January–March 1988)

Preliminary estimate (April 1988)	2.3 percent
First revision (May 1988)	3.9 percent
Second revision (June 1988)	3.6 percent
Annual revision (July 1988)	3.4 percent
Annual revision (July 1989)	4.0 percent

Source: U.S. Department of Commerce, *Survey of Current Business.*

raising the estimated growth between 1982 and 1988 from 3.8 to 4.1 percent.

These changing estimates underscore the tentative nature of GNP accounts. Because national income and product statistics rely on survey data, adjusted to take into account new trends such as improved quality of computers, there will never be a final "correct" statistic. For researchers, the revisions can be an inconvenience, as for example when results must be recalculated because of newly released data. Fortunately, national income account data are compiled frequently in the Commerce Department publication *Survey of Current Business*, along with comprehensive discussion of revisions to the original numbers.

Problems with GNP

Gross National Product statistics, both preliminary numbers and subsequent revisions, are estimated according to a set of accounting rules developed by the Commerce Department in consultation with the economics profession. But the standard accounting method is not universally accepted. In recent years several potential problems have led researchers to propose alternative statistics to those officially published.

In designing the original GNP accounts, Simon Kuznets deliberately chose to include all production regardless of moral or aesthetic considerations. Thus, it was considered better to add together all production, including cigarettes and the health costs they incur, rather than to create different GNP accounts based on the subjective values as-

---

Box 7.3. **Forecasting**

The business "cycle" is irregular, so a major task of economic researchers is to forecast future GNP. The most well known predictor, called the Index of Leading Economic Indicators, is published by the U.S. Department of Commerce. Other indexes and economic forecasts are calculated by business magazines and university research centers, including McGraw-Hill publishers, the National Industrial Conference Board, and computer models at the Wharton School of Business, Chase Econometrics, Data Resources, and Townsend-Greenspan.

None of these methods for predicting the future are perfect, nor do they appear to be improving. A study by Geoffrey H. Moore of Columbia University's Center for International Business Cycle Research measured an error rate of 1.8 percent for private forecasters during the mid-1980s, less than the 2.9 percent error rate for government projections but still more than double the previous decade's error rate. In recognition of this issue, the National Bureau for Economic Research and the U.S. Federal Reserve Board calculate the *likelihood* of a recession, predicting, for example, a 6 percent chance of a recession in the six months following December 1989 according to the National Bureau, and 20 percent according to the Federal Reserve. As indicated by differences in these two estimates, this method is also not without uncertainty.

---

signed by each economist. Increased environmental awareness during the 1960s prompted many economists to reassess GNP as a measure of actual well-being. E.J. Mishan, Kenneth Boulding, and others questioned whether *any* GNP growth was desirable if it polluted the environment and depleted scarce resources.

Noted economists William Nordhaus and James Tobin attempted to correct GNP for measurable "economic bads" in a 1972 study, "Is Growth Obsolete?" Their Measure of Economic Welfare computed 35 percent less economic growth between 1925 and 1965 than was measured by traditional GNP. According to Nordhaus and Tobin, this new statistic was a "challenge to economists to produce relevant welfare-oriented measures." But two decades later, their call is largely unheeded; although the Measure of Economic Welfare is mentioned in most economics textbooks, it has not been incorporated into mainstream economic research.

Closely related to the problem of environmental destruction is the issue of resource depletion, which also may accompany an increase in GNP. Robert Repetto, director of the Program in Economics and Institutions at the World Resources Institute, points out that it is possible for a country to increase its income by exploiting its resource base, resulting in short-term gains in income at the expense of permanent loss in wealth. Just as a business keeps track of its assets, Repetto believes National Income Accounts should keep track of its resources. In a 1989 study of Indonesia, Repetto calculated that production rose only about 4 percent per year between 1971 and 1984, far less than the officially reported 7.1 percent. According to Repetto, sufficient data on fuels, timber, minerals, and water resources are available for many countries in order to calculate resource depletion as a part of national income accounts. As of 1990, however, only a few countries, most notably France and Norway, had experimented during the 1980s with accounting of natural resource stocks. At the same time, the United States discontinued research on the topic.

Some economic transactions are not reported to the government, either because the activity is illegal, or because those involved want to avoid taxation. Together these transactions comprise the underground economy, a difficult-to-measure entity that may cause underestimation of total economic activity, and according to some economists, also may cause overestimation of the poverty rate (see chapter 8) and the unemployment rate (see chapter 9). One of the most frequently cited researchers on the subject, economist Peter Gutmann, estimated the underground economy at about 10 percent of GNP in 1977 based on increased circulation of cash used primarily for illegal or tax-avoiding transactions. However, economist Edgar Feige estimated an underground of over one-quarter of GNP, while U.S. Commerce Department officials maintained that a much smaller amount goes uncounted in GNP.

Given all the problems in measuring what people want to conceal, it is unlikely that we will ever know the precise size of the underground economy. For researchers, however, the important question is not the actual size of unreported transactions, but instead their effect on key research variables. For example, the U.S. Commerce Department's main criticism of Gutmann's studies is that he mistakenly assumed all unmeasured activity would be counted in GNP. In fact, many underground transactions are simply transfers of money that do not involve production, and thus would not be counted in GNP. (Some transactions such as theft may not be voluntary, but they are transfers nonetheless.) For this reason, economist Edward Denison argues that official measures of economic growth are accurate, and not underestimated as Gutmann claims.

A final problem with traditional GNP accounting is that it focuses narrowly on production that can be readily measured. For example, almost all housework is left out of GNP, even though the market value of child care and home maintenance is estimated at about one-third of GNP, or more than $1,700 billion in 1990. However, as with the Nordhaus-Tobin Measure of Economic Welfare, these necessarily imprecise adjustments to GNP are little used in policy making or research.

Implications Although professional economists recognize each of these problems in GNP accounting, few corrections are ever made in actual research practice. The major difficulty is that even if adjustments can be justified on logical grounds, the alternative data require many poorly understood assumptions. Researchers do not want their results to depend on data that are not widely credible. Nonetheless, researchers and other users of national economic statistics should be alert to situations where traditional data can be misleading, for example, in comparing the national economies of different countries.

Intercountry Comparisons

Gross National Product (GNP), or its near relative Gross Domestic Product (GDP), is the most common variable for comparing the economic size of nations. The absolute level of GNP measures a country's overall economic size, while GNP per capita (per person) measures a country's production level, corrected for population size. Technically, most research purposes require the use of *real* GNP or *real* GDP, taking into account the effect of inflation (see chapter 11). On the basis of these numbers, countries often are designated ''low income'' or ''less developed.'' For example, the 1989 World Bank *World Development Report* classifies 42 low-income economies, with 1987 per capita incomes below $480, ranging from Ethiopia at $130 to Liberia and Indonesia at $450. (Per capita GNP could not be measured for Afghanistan, Burma, Guinea, Kampuchea, and Vietnam.) But these statistics can be misleading for several of the same reasons that cause error in U.S. statistics.

Unreported transactions are especially significant in Third World countries, including underground activity described above, and also nonmarket production such as home-grown food, family help in medical care, and community construction of homes. These activities, largely unreported in GNP accounts, make it possible for a resident of Ethiopia to live on $130 per year, an income on which survival would be impossible in the United States. To complicate matters further, some countries' GNP measures are subject to revisions even greater than the multibillion dollar revisions noted above for the United States. In countries without sophisticated data networks, new products or services may go unrecognized for years, requiring substantial changes in existing statistics. Major revisions of this sort have taken place for national economic data of Malaysia, Bangladesh, and Egypt.

Uncounted items may cause a bias in highly developed countries as well. For example, residents of many Western European countries enjoy superior vacation and holiday benefits (nearly seven weeks total per year in Sweden). Such benefits contribute in a major way to well-being, but they are not accounted for in traditional GNP accounting. In summary, although there are few alternatives to GNP for comparisons between countries, researchers need to be aware of the many factors that cause GNP to be an imperfect measure of economic development.

Measuring Productivity

For the United States, recent economic controversy has focused on changes in GNP, most especially a measured downward trend in U.S. economic growth since about 1970. One of the most frequently cited indications of this slowdown is the decline in productivity as estimated by the U.S. Labor Department's Bureau of Labor Statistics. Technically, productivity can be measured in many ways, but the most common statistic, and the one regarded as most reliable, is labor productivity measured as output per hour of labor. There appears to be a definite downward trend in this statistic during recent decades, which has prompted many newspaper and magazines stories about the "U.S. productivity crisis." However, there are such severe problems in measuring productivity that economists disagree about whether this crisis is waning, or even whether it ever existed.

At one extreme, economist Harry Magdoff argues that productivity data are unable to "tell us anything fundamental about the nature of

Figure 7.1.

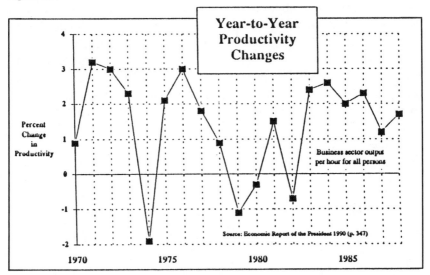

the economy itself." In his view, productivity problems are a myth, generally accepted "by constant repetition and widespread publicity." Other economists accept the measured productivity collapse of the 1970s as a real economic event, but maintain it was a transient setback, probably caused by the energy crises of the 1970s. And, of course, there are many economists who believe there is an ongoing productivity crisis. Why is productivity so difficult to understand? At least three measurement problems confront researchers.

Which Years?   The first problem is identifying the trend in productivity. As shown in Figure 7.1, annual productivity statistics jump from year to year in an apparently erratic manner. Selective choice of years can lead to a misleading picture of productivity, as for example in a widely distributed U.S. Chamber of Commerce program supporting President Reagan's economic policies that used productivity data for 1966, 1973, 1978, and 1979, conveniently selected to show a steady decline in productivity. Other years—1969, 1973, 1976, 1983, for example—would have indicated *increasing* productivity.

These erratic year-to-year productivity changes are caused by fluctuations in the business cycle, that is, alternating periods of growth and stagnation in the economy. When sales begin to falter, employers cut back on output, thereby causing measured productivity to fall until workers are laid off. Conversely, when the economy starts to pick up after a recession, output at first increases faster than new hiring, causing an apparent increase in productivity. Accurate use of productivity data requires correction for the business cycle, for example, looking at productivity changes between peak growth years. On this basis, a definite productivity decline occurred between 1973 and 1979 (two peak years), and appears to have partially reversed itself during the post-1982 economic recovery. But this interpretation is clouded by two less easily resolved measurement problems.

Services   The most vexing challenge is measuring the productivity of services that are not associated with a physical product. In other words, what is productivity of a physician, a school teacher, or a police officer? Is the physician more productive for seeing twice as many patients in an hour, or the teacher more productive with a larger class size, or the police officer more productive for giving more tickets? In the goods-producing sector, productivity is based on the number of items produced. Although this task is complicated by changing quality of goods (see below), at least government statisticians have data, for example, on the number of cars, computers, and shirts that are produced.

As a result of problems in measuring service productivity, U.S. Bureau of Labor Statistics productivity measures do not cover the entire economy. The most comprehensive statistic, "private business" productivity, leaves out government and nonprofit institutions (where output is measured by adding up the cost of labor inputs), which account for more than 20 percent of the national economy. During the 1980s the Bureau of Labor Statistics embarked on an ambitious project to measure output quantities in services, making it possible to estimate productivity in selected services. These data provide important new policy guidance in areas such as government and health care, where it is alleged that costs have increased without comparable improvement in output. Unfortunately these data often are cited without much-needed caveats about their experimental nature. For example, even though productivity in the "business sector" leaves out government and the nonprofit sector, this frequently used statistic nonetheless includes potentially unreliable estimates of service-sector productivity.

Changing Products   The second major problem for productivity statistics is that today's output includes items that once did not exist. Thus, it is difficult to measure productivity for the manufacture of VCRs and microwave ovens. In addition, other products changed so quickly in quality: a typical home computer purchased in 1980 is entirely obsolete and no longer manufactured in 1990. The U.S. Commerce Department attempts to measure these changes in GNP accounts, but substantial gaps remain. For example, according to one study, *all* construction-sector productivity improvements between 1948 and 1986 were overlooked because of problems in measuring the value of buildings. Other researchers charge that despite new procedures introduced during the late 1980s, major errors remained in the measurement of computer productivity, causing as much as a 20 percent overestimation in productivity.

Implications   The problem of year-to-year changes in productivity caused by the business cycle can be resolved with the adjustment suggested above. But the problem of changing products and services is a dilemma that requires far more caution in the use of productivity statistics than is commonly found in media reports or even some research projects. Ongoing cooperation between the Commerce Department and its critics may result in better productivity data, in particular for fast-changing sectors such as the computer industry. However, problems in measuring service-sector productivity are so fundamental that they will not be easily overcome. Researchers should interpret these numbers with extreme caution, realizing that some overall productivity statistics such as "private business productivity" include questionable productivity inferences for the service sector.

The Savings Rate

In an unusual display of unanimity, both Democrats and Republicans on Congress's Joint Economic Committee declared in a 1989 report that the nation's chief economic problem is a low savings rate. As evidence, policy makers point to the Commerce Department's estimate of personal savings as a percentage of disposable income, which fell from an average of 8 percent during the 1970s, to about 3 percent by the late 1980s. But according to many economists, this statistic is misleading because there are both problems in measuring the personal savings rate, as well as theoretical questions about its appropriateness for assessing the health of the national economy.

Measurement Problems   As described above, the underground economy causes errors in GNP accounts. Some experts believe this inaccuracy is asymmetric, causing income to be underreported far more than expenditures. As a result, there may be underestimation of the savings rates, that is, the difference between underestimated income and more accurately measured expenditures. One study for the Commerce Department estimated an error of about 10 percent because of this effect.

A second measurement problem arises because the traditional savings rate does not take into account the value of real estate, stocks, and bonds, which are for many households a form of savings. Paradoxically in recent years, many U.S. households became richer even as they spent a greater proportion of their income because the skyrocketing value of these assets created windfall wealth for many households who then thought they could safely spend more of their income. An alternative savings rate based on the value of assets calculated by the U.S. Federal Reserve Board does not show the same decline in savings measured by the Commerce Department.

Which Savings Rate?   To complicate matters further, many economists believe that the commonly cited *personal* savings statistics are not very important. Although popular newspaper and magazine articles suggest a link between declining personal savings rates and declining U.S. investment, the two trends may not be related. The reason is that most investment comes from *business* savings, a source of funds that increased in many recent years, compensating for the decline in personal savings. There may still be severe problems in total U.S. savings caused by U.S. government deficits (see chapter 11), and international deficits, but in this view emphasis on personal savings is misplaced.

Implications   Controversy about the savings rate is instructive in the dangers of trying to oversimplify economic problems to a single statistic. The idea of ''spendthrift'' U.S. households hurting the U.S. economy carried a moral tone that gained attention in popular accounts. But when analyzed closely, savings are a complex concept, both difficult to measure and tricky to conceptualize in terms of their effect on the economy. Researchers need to take care to assess the accuracy of the numbers they use, as well as the relevance of those statistics to the policy question at hand.

International Statistics

In recent years, the U.S. international economic situation came under increased scrutiny. Headlines asked: Is the U.S. trade deficit too large? Are foreigners buying too much of the United States? Answers to these questions depend critically on the accuracy of statistics collected by the U.S. Commerce Department and the U.S. Federal Reserve.

Month-to-Month Volatility   Month-to-month changes in U.S. trade typically are reported as important news: "October's trade deficit highest ever," followed confusingly by "November trade deficit falls." These sudden shifts in monthly trade figures do not usually signify a trend. Often a single event unrelated to the economy's health will cause trade figures to change, as for example, in 1986 when the Japanese government bought more than $2 billion worth of gold for medals honoring Emperor Hirohito's sixtieth anniversary. Because the gold was shipped through the United States (it was purchased in Europe), exports temporarily appeared to improve.

Most experts recommend that we look at quarterly or annual data instead of monthly data. Even so, the extent of the U.S. deficit was difficult to measure because of measurement problems.

Poor-Quality Data   One indication that worldwide trade data are inaccurate is the difference between all countries' imports and all countries' exports, which should match because every import is also another country's export. But according to the Organization for Economic Cooperation and Development there has been as much as an $80 billion excess in total imports measured worldwide compared to total exports. Much of this error may occur because of the difficulty in measuring services. According to Harry L. Freeman, vice-president of American Express, for the United States alone, as much as $40 billion in administration, legal advice, consulting, and other services provided in other countries was underreported in 1983.

To make matters worse for U.S. data, because of budget cuts in the early 1980s, the number of Customs agents who gather the basic data on imports was reduced at precisely the time when imports surged. In 1985, more than one-half of the trade entries were behind schedule so that shipments were not recorded in the month they actually occurred. In addition, investigators found significant nonreporting by truckers carrying goods to Canada, the United States' largest trading partner, and comical miscoding of country origins, such as "not available" data mistakenly ascribed to Namibia, which is also abbreviated as "NA."

The Real Deficit?   Finally, some researchers argue that the official statistics misrepresent the actual trade situation by not including production in other countries by U.S.-owned firms. This adjustment causes the U.S. deficit with Japan to disappear entirely because the Japanese spend nearly twice as much on IBM, Coca Cola, Xerox, and other U.S. brand goods manufactured in Japan, than U.S. consumers spend on Japanese imports. On this basis, some economists argue that the United States competes well in the international arena, a success masked by the official trade deficit.

Implications   These measurement problems in trade statistics pose different challenges to researchers. The misleading character of month-to-month trade data is widely recognized by economists, if not by newspaper and magazine reporters. Longer-term data are an easy solution. The issue of inaccurate or missing data is less controversial, but one that will have no solution until international trade statistics are improved. The final controversy about the role of foreign production is a complex theoretical question. Because economists disagree about how to deal with the issue, researchers should be wary in using data "corrected" in this manner.

SUMMARY

In this chapter we have seen debates about a wide range of national economic issues. One goal was to unravel the source of apparently contradictory findings that appear both to applaud the success of the U.S. economy during the 1980s, and also to measure apparent continued economic decline. Three major problems contributed to contradictory statistics.

First, the time period of analysis is critical. For productivity, it was necessary to take into account the business cycle that causes swings in the rate of productivity that are unrelated to the long-term historical trend that researchers want to measure. For GNP and trade statistics, the lesson was to use data covering a long enough time period to smooth out short-term fluctuations unrelated to the overall economic issues of interest. Both of these research precautions are relatively easy to follow with well-documented procedures available in the economics literature.

Second, and less easily resolved, is the problem of unavailable information. Many areas of economic activity are not readily measured because there are no prices attached to products, or because the prices used do not represent actual value. Gross national product leaves out entire sectors of production such as housework, because no prices are attached to those services, a bias that strongly affects comparisons between countries. The same problem also affects comparison of countries with different levels of vacation benefits because leisure time is not a commodity with a price. Similarly, investment in the form of education and training is not counted as part of the investment category of GNP accounts because the increased value of human "investments" has no easily measured resale price (see case study question 2). Commerce Department statisticians recognize these measurement problems and have commented extensively on them. Nonetheless, it is the responsibility of researchers to make sure that their use of the statistics is not unduly influenced by what is not included in the underlying data.

Third, the service sector is a problem area for economic statistics, complicating the measurement of productivity and international trade. This sector is growing, and thus will provide an increasing challenge to researchers. In response to the issue, government researchers have developed new statistics, but whether a service-dominated economy can be measured as accurately as one dominated by the production of tangible goods remains to be seen.

The challenge for researchers is to make discriminating judgments when competing statistics are available: when should a statistic be used and what are its shortcomings? For example, as this chapter demonstrates, there are objections to official GNP accounting methods—and economic textbooks list even more. However, there are practically no widely accepted alternative statistics, so that most researchers have little choice but to use official numbers. At a minimum researchers can recognize and cite the importance of the assumptions that lie behind the traditional methods.

Competing measures also exist for the savings rate, the trade deficit, and international investment. In these cases, researchers can use economic theory to make informed choices between different statistics. This link between theory and the use of data should be clearly stated. Failure to do so is a major shortcoming in many research projects. Such lack of theoretical clarity contributes to the confusing state of affairs in which it seems that statistics can be chosen to fit any conclusion, when in fact it is the implicit economic theory that leads researchers to use of particular statistics.

CASE STUDY QUESTIONS

1. During the 1980s, U.S. Commerce Department statistics measured the United States as a net debtor nation for the first time in many decades because investment by foreigners in the United States was greater than United States investment abroad. But these data have been criticized because the U.S. Commerce Department measures investment at its original cost. Why might this accounting procedure (for which there is no ready substitute) cause overestimation of the gap between foreign investment in the United States and U.S. investment abroad?

2. In U.S. national economic statistics, investment includes only physical investments such as machinery or buildings. But according to economist Robert Eisner, almost one-half of U.S. stock of productive capital takes the intangible form of investment in people and ideas. How might the traditional measure including only physical investments lead to inefficient policies regarding investment?

3. During the 1980s, the Bureau of Labor Statistics developed measures of productivity for some government services. For which types of government employment would it be possible to measure productivity with reasonable accuracy? Which government services do not lend themselves to easy measurement of productivity?

4. Critics of the World Bank charge that the use of official GNP statistics causes a bias against investment projects that would help women. Why might this occur?

5. Assume the underground economy is 10 percent of GNP, and GNP is about $5,000 billion, and there are about 100 million U.S. households. Based on these data, approximately how much does each household consume in "underground" products? Does this number seem a reasonable estimate? Explain.

Where the Numbers Come from

Organizations	Data Sources	Key Publications
Board of Governors U.S. Federal Reserve System	Survey of Consumer Finances	*Federal Reserve Bulletin*
Bureau of the Census U.S. Department of Commerce	Survey of Income and Program Participation; U.S. Census of Population; Current Population Survey	*Census of Population; Current Population Reports* (Series P–60, P–70)
Bureau of Labor Statistics U.S. Department of Labor	Establishment Survey	*Employment and Earnings; Current Wage Developments*
Internal Revenue Service U.S. Department of the Treasury	Tax returns	*Statistics of Income*

Summary data in *Statistical Abstract of the U.S.*

(see chapter 11). At three-year intervals during the 1980s, the Fed conducted its own independent survey of several thousand households, asking 100 pages of questions about each family's financial status.

> *Data Sample:* The 1986 Survey of Consumer Finances found that 19.3 percent of households owned stocks, with a median value of $6,000, and an average value of more than $80,000.

Survey of Income and Program Participation   The second major U.S. wealth survey is conducted by the Census Bureau. These data were collected on a regular basis only between 1850 and 1890, and then not again until 1984 in the Survey of Income and Program Participation (SIPP).

Wealth, Income
and Poverl

Economists differentiate between wealth, a stock of value such a house or stock, and income, a flow of value over time, such as a sal or interest payment. Data on wealth and income typically come fr different sources, each with its own set of problems. There is relativ little information on the distribution of wealth in the United Stat One reason for the scarcity is difficulty of measurement. Beca many items of wealth have not been sold recently, they do not hav readily identifiable price. A second reason for the lack of data wealth is its ownership by a relatively small group who are not eage share information about how much wealth they own. As the contro sies below illustrate, this second factor severely restricts how much know about wealth. Unlike wealth, incomes leave a "paper trail" readily measured dollar amounts. As a result, income is well do mented in a variety of government and private-sector sources. But this chapter demonstrates, there is still serious disagreement about f damental findings, including the trend in well-being for the typ family, and the extent of poverty in the United States.

DATA SOURCES

Wealth

Federal Reserve Survey   The most comprehensive survey on we holdings is conducted by the U.S. Federal Reserve, a quasi dependent government body that acts as the country's central t

Data Sample: In the 1984 survey, equity in homes comprised 59.7 percent of the wealth of households with incomes less than $10,000, but only 30.1 percent of the wealth of households with incomes over $48,000.

Indirect Estimates from Tax Records   Historical data on wealth distribution are calculated by two major methods. The "estate-multiplier" method pioneered by Robert J. Lampman of the National Bureau for Economic Research uses Internal Revenue Service records for the 1 percent of estates subject to taxes (only holdings greater than $600,000 in 1987). A related method called "income capitalization" works backwards from tax reports of rent, dividends, and interest to estimate wealth from which these incomes are derived.

Data Sample: Lampman measured a decline in the share of wealth held by the top 1 percent from 36 percent in 1929 to 26 percent in 1956.

Direct Counts   The extraordinarily rich usually are well-known individuals about whom information can be obtained from public sources. Based on stock-ownership records, media coverage, and independent investigation, *Forbes* and *Fortune* magazines each estimates wealth holdings for a select number of these individuals.

Income

U.S. Census   Every decennial Census of Population since 1940 has included questions about income, providing researchers with a tremendously detailed data source, but one that is available only at ten-year intervals.

Data Sample: In the 1980 U.S. Census, McAllen-Edinburg-Mission, Texas, had 35.2 percent of the population below the poverty line, the highest rate for all U.S. metropolitan areas.

Current Population Survey   By far the most frequently cited source of income data is the Census Bureau's Current Population Survey (CPS). Covering over 60,000 households, the CPS is the largest survey taken in between census years. (See chapter 9 on the origins of the CPS.)

Data Sample: According to the Current Population Survey, Manchester-Nashua, New Hampshire, had the fastest increasing per capita income between 1979 and 1983 of all U.S. metropolitan areas.

Bureau Labor Statistics' Establishment Survey   Data collected in the BLS Establishment Survey are often quite accurate because the survey is based on employer records, rather than on respondent recall. But the Establishment Survey measures earnings for individual jobs, not the total income for a worker, who may have more than one employer, or for a family with several separate sources of income.

Data Sample: In the March 1985 Establishment Survey, the lowest-paying manufacturing industry was "Children's dresses and blouses," with average weekly earnings of $170.16 for nonsupervisory production workers.

Panel Study of Income Dynamics   For comparisons over time, or longitudinal studies, researchers frequently turn to a private survey, the University of Michigan's Panel Study of Income Dynamics (PSID). Begun with 5,000 households in 1968, PSID followed 7,000 households in 1986, including many of the original sample, as well as those split off when children married or couples separated.

CONTROVERSIES

Are the Rich Getting Richer?

Are the rich getting richer? The answer is "we don't know." Attempts during the 1980s to measure wealth distribution generated considerable controversy, but ended in continued uncertainty whether wealth ownership is becoming more or less concentrated. Nonetheless, this research failure illustrates the problem of surveying wealth, or any other variable so unequally distributed that even large surveys are unlikely to include those who own a significant part of the total wealth.

In 1983 the U.S. Federal Reserve changed its usual format for measuring wealth by adding 438 individuals already known to be wealthy. In theory, this commonly used method of "enriching" the data sample should have increased our knowledge about wealth holdings. Indeed, the survey indicated that the share of wealth going to the top 0.5

percent increased to 35 percent in 1983 from 25 percent in 1962. But these startling results were not destined for much public notice. As usual, the Federal Reserve survey was published in the *Federal Reserve Bulletin*, from which the numbers made their way into academic studies and textbooks.

Then, in 1986, the Joint Economic Committee of Congress released its own interpretation of the Federal Reserve's study using catchy labels—"super rich," "very rich," "rich," and "everyone else"—to underscore the vast holdings of the wealthy that apparently increased since 1962. After a barrage of media reports on these results, the Reagan administration asked the Federal Reserve to reexamine the survey. Suddenly an error appeared: one of the 438 wealthy individuals was not as rich as he or she reported. Removing this individual caused the estimate for the share owned by the super rich to fall by almost 10 percent, wiping out the apparent increase since 1962.

The accuracy of the one data point is difficult to determine. A 1986 follow-up survey showing this person's wealth to be only $2.3 million led the Fed to conclude that the reported 1983 wealth of $200 million was a coding error. Critics responded that the individual, known to own Texas oil and gas wells, indeed may have suffered a financial setback reported between 1983 and 1986. Whatever the actual circumstances of this one Texas magnate, the dispute shows how difficult it is to measure wealth. A basic research principle is to include a survey sample that is large enough that errors for a single individual do not affect overall findings. Even the relatively large Federal Reserve survey—less than 4,000 households—was still too small to accurately measure changes in wealth holdings because so few individuals owned so much.

What Is Wealth?

For the less-than-extremely wealthy, Federal Reserve Board data are relatively accurate. Overall they measure total average net worth in 1986 at over $145,000 per household, while the median net worth was nearly $44,000 (see Box 8.1 on the difference between average and median). For black and Hispanic households, median net worth was only $11,000 in 1986, about one-fifth of median net worth for white households.

Most household wealth is in housing, an average value of $80,000 in 1986 for those who owned a home. For some research purposes, it is best to exclude ownership of homes and other consumer durable goods

---

Box 8.1. **Mean, Median, and Mode**

The *median* is the data point for which one-half the observations are above and one-half below; the *mean* is the average, or in this case, total income divided by number in the sample; the *mode* is the data point with the most observations, a statistic rarely used in income analysis. Median income is the most common starting point for research on the "typical" household. A relatively small number of families with very high incomes skews the mean at about 15 percent higher than the median. Thus, mean annual family income in the United States was about $24,000 in 1980, while the median income was $21,000. The major drawback to using the median is that it is unchanged by redistribution of income above and below it. For example, when the poor become poorer and the rich become richer, it is possible for the median to stay the same.

---

in order to focus on ownership of wealth that is a source of economic power such as stocks and bonds. This "financial wealth" is even more unequally distributed than total wealth; the top 10 percent of households owned 86 percent of financial wealth in 1983. Some researchers argue that we should move in the other direction, expanding the definition of wealth to include the value of pensions and social security. Although most people do not consider these benefits to be wealth, they are similar to bonds and other arrangements that promise a source of future income. Former chief economic adviser in the Reagan administration, Martin Feldstein, advocated such an approach, by which measured inequality in U.S. wealth holdings would be reduced by nearly 30 percent.

Researchers need to choose carefully between these different measures of wealth. For analysis of the distribution of resources, total wealth measures are appropriate, perhaps also including the value of retirement funds. But if the research goal is to understand how wealth affects power, then it might be proper to use a narrower definition that excludes housing and retirement benefits.

Who Is the Richest of Them All?

In 1987, the wealthiest individuals in the *Fortune* and *Forbes* surveys were as follows. Both *Forbes* and *Fortune* openly discuss problems in

Fortune (worldwide)	_Forbes_ (U.S. only)
Wealth (in billions)	
1. Sultan Hassanal Bolkiah $25.0	1. Sam Walton $8.5
2. King Fahd $20.0	2. John Werner Kluge $3
3. Samuel and Donald Newhouse $7.5	3. Henry Ross Perot $2.9

finding out about wealth; every year an individual will catapult to near the top when it is discovered that he or she is in fact quite wealthy. A previously uncounted Mars Candy Company benefactor, billionaire heiress, Jacqueline Mars Vogel, was belatedly "discovered" and added to the _Forbes_ list in 1987. Lester Crown, owner of General Dynamics stock inherited from his father, as well as real estate and sports teams, weighed in at $5.7 billion in the 1987 _Fortune_ list, but only $2.1 billion according to _Forbes_.

One source of such discrepancies is the lack of information on privately held wealth. The Mars Company, for example, is one of the small number of large firms still owned entirely by a few individuals. Unlike publicly held corporations, there is no stock price to estimate the value of the company (see chapter 10). Similarly, _Forbes_ and _Fortune_ must estimate the value of property that has not been bought or sold in recent years. Finally, family trusts complicate wealth measurement by dispersing fortunes among various descendants. As a result, _Forbes_ publishes a separate wealth list for total family holdings, led by the DuPonts, Gettys, and Rockefellers.

Are We Better Off?

Is the typical American better off than twenty years ago? This simple question has provoked a broad spectrum of answers depending on the data source used. Between 1970 and 1987, Americans were somewhere between 10 percent _worse_ off measured by average weekly earnings and more than 30 percent _better_ off measured by income per capita. At stake in the interpretation of these data is the direction of U.S. economic policy. During the 1980s, supporters of the economic policies of presidents Reagan and Bush pointed to the optimistic income data, while critics emphasized data that showed an income decline.

Figure 8.1.

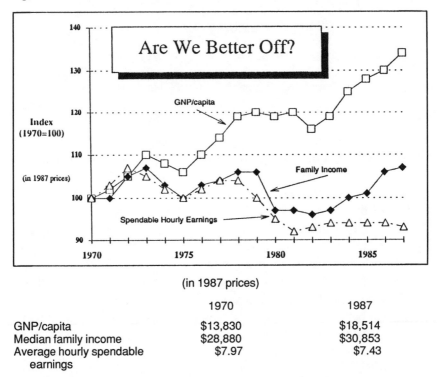

Are We Better Off?

(in 1987 prices)

	1970	1987
GNP/capita	$13,830	$18,514
Median family income	$28,880	$30,853
Average hourly spendable earnings	$7.97	$7.43

Sources: Statistical Abstract of the United States, 1989 (Washington, D.C.: U.S. Government Printing Office, 1989), pp. 424, 444; Thomas E. Weisskopf, ''Use of hourly earnings proposed to revive spendable earnings series,'' *Monthly Labor Review*, Nov. 1984, p. 40 (updated courtesy Thomas E. Weisskopf and David M. Gordon, Graduate Faculty, New School for Social Research).

Per Capita Income   The rosiest view of economic progress during the 1980s, indicating 20 percent growth, is based on per capita personal income, a statistic from the U.S. Commerce Department national income accounts (see chapter 7). Per capita income is simply the total of all wages, interest, rents, and other incomes divided by the number of people in the country. Although this number is often cited as evidence of success in the Reagan-Bush economic program, critics charge that the statistic is misleading because the number of wage earners has increased relative to the number of dependents. Or to make the same point with a story: Assume a household of four people in 1980 with one person working outside the home earning $20,000 had a per capita income of $5,000. If in 1990, the original worker's income falls to $18,000, but a second family member now works outside the home, and earns $10,000, then per capita income increases to $7,000 ([$18,000 + $10,000] ÷ 4). In other words, total income increased, but only because more people were working, each of whom earned less.

Earnings   What is the trend in earnings of the typical worker? This question changes the original question from one of *income* from all sources including rents, interests, and dividends, to one of *earnings*, including only wages and salaries. (Sometimes earnings is defined also to include self-employment income and farm income.) For many years the Bureau of Labor Statistics Establishment Survey measured "spendable weekly earnings for the typical family of four with one full time worker and three dependents." According to this measure, this statistically "average" family was better off in 1959 than in 1981! In 1982, the Reagan administration suspended publication of the series on the grounds that it was inflammatory and inaccurate.

Even critics of the administration agreed that this measure used outdated assumptions about tax rates and the composition of the workforce. But, even though correcting for these deficiencies was a relatively simple matter, no official replacement data were introduced. Consequently, University of Michigan economist Thomas E. Weisskopf attempted to revive the series on his own, using spendable *hourly* earnings data in order to avoid the problems with the discredited *weekly* earnings data. According to Weisskopf, this new statistical series still shows steady deterioration of earnings after 1972, falling by more than 13 percent by 1987. Thus, it appears that pay levels for U.S. workers indeed stagnated during the 1970s and 1980s (see Figure 8.1).

Family Income   One way to combine the effect of additional workers with the effect of lower earnings is to look at the trend in income for household units. In fact, the most widely cited statistic on income is featured in the annual Current Population Survey publication, "Money and Income of Households, Families and Persons." According to this source, income was nearly constant during most of the 1970s and 1980s at about $29,000 in 1987 buying power, and improved to only

---

Box 8.2. **The Economic Consequences of Divorce**

According to Lenore Weitzman's 1985 book, *The Divorce Revolution*, women suffer a 73 percent loss in economic status after divorce. Criticism published subsequently in the journal *Demography* suggested that this widely cited statistic is quite inaccurate. Weitzman's sample consisted of only 228 men and women who became divorced in Los Angeles County in 1977. Data from the far larger Panel Study of Income Dynamics measured an average of about 30 percent loss in economic status for women in the first year after divorce. The critics conclude that the economic well-being of men and women indeed diverges substantially in the years after divorce, but not nearly to the extent publicized by Weitzman's findings.

$30,853 in 1987. This statistic is often quoted, but usually without reference to serious shortcomings in the data.

One problem is that the U.S. Census carefully defines a "family" as two or more related individuals living together, thus leaving out more than 30 million individuals in 1990 who lived in nonfamily households, either as single-person households or with unrelated individuals. Median income for families is more than double the median income for nonfamily individuals, so looking only at families overstates the typical income of U.S. households. On the other hand, in recent years nonfamily household incomes increased faster than the average, so research only on families underestimates improvement in overall well-being.

 A second problem with family income data is that they do not take into account the decline in family size from 3.58 in 1970 to 3.28 in 1980. According to one measure of family well-being, these smaller families are 20 percent better off because there are fewer children to support. However, other researchers object that these families might have fewer children precisely because of stagnating incomes. In this view, families are worse off because they could not afford as many children as they might have liked.

Because of these problems, researchers need to be careful in using the family income data. Overall, the limited improvement in the median family income level was a worrisome trend during the 1970s and 1980s. But used by itself it does not tell the whole story about changing living standards.

Good Jobs, Bad Jobs

Average well-being, whether measured by per capita income, earnings, or family income, is based on a single statistic that may hide important changes in the *distribution* of income. For example, it is possible for average income to remain unchanged at the same time that it is possible for the rich to become richer and the poor to become poorer. In fact, according to some researchers precisely this trend was underway during the 1980s, an assertion that provoked an often bitter debate about the actual distribution of pay for newly created jobs in the U.S. economy.

This controversy is a lesson for researchers about the potential pitfalls in using income data. Popular magazine articles titled "A Surge in Inequality," "The Shrinking Middle Class," "Low-Pay Jobs: The Big Lie," and "Chicken Little Income Statistics" confused readers with seemingly convincing statistics for opposite conclusions. Less frequently reported were the reasons for these differences. When the political controversy ended, it turned out that we had learned quite a bit about trends in U.S. income distribution.

It is well documented that pay levels decline during economic bad times, sending individuals down from middle to lower income levels. The debate about the disappearing middle class occurred just after the 1981–82 recession, so results depended critically on how those years were treated. For example, economists Barry Bluestone and Bennett Harrison received nationwide attention for their study showing that nearly one-half of net new jobs created between 1979 and 1985 paid less than $7,400 (in 1986 buying power). But researchers at the Bureau of Labor Statistics attributed the trend to changing economic conditions, in particular the 1981–82 economic downturn.

A second rejoinder to Bluestone and Harrison came from Brookings Institution economist Robert Lawrence, who attributed most of the growth in low-wage jobs to the sudden appearance of baby-boom youth in the labor market. As these workers gain in age and experience, Lawrence believed income distribution would move closer to its previous norm. Finally, other researchers attributed Bluestone and Harrison's results to incorrect use of inflation adjustments. The relationship between inflation measures and the measurement of income distribution is discussed in chapter 11. To summarize, by using a different inflation index, American Enterprise Institute researchers Marvin Kosters and Murray Ross measured a *decline* in low-wage jobs for the same time period that Bluestone and Harrison measured their much-publicized increase in low-wage jobs.

Each of these researchers made quite different policy recommendations. Bluestone and Harrison advocated government-sponsored industrial policy to increase the number of high-paying jobs. Lawrence argued against industrial policy, calling instead for retraining and relocation assistance for low-paid, young workers. Kosters and Ross opposed all such government intervention in favor of continued reliance on private markets. The jury is still out on which policies will best help the U.S. economy. Nonetheless, it is possible to assess what we have learned about income distribution in this debate. First, there is widespread agreement that a shift has occurred toward low-pay jobs for some groups. Even Kosters and Ross, who gave the most optimistic appraisal of the U.S. economy, measured an increase in the proportion of low-paid jobs for full-time, year-round workers. In addition, the number of part-timers (who obviously earn less) has increased, although there is debate about how to measure the effect of the increase in part-time work on overall pay levels. Overall, there has been an increase in the proportion of low-income individuals, but the impact on households or families is a more complex picture because, as noted above, households may have higher earnings at the same time that each individual earns less.

Statistics for Every Theory?   At this point it may be tempting to question the usefulness of income statistics that tell such conflicting stories. If policy advisers from every political persuasion can find ample evidence to support any position, what good are income statistics? The answer is that each income statistic measures a slightly different concept; they must be used together, with careful distinction about what is being measured. For example, per capita income provides an indication of well-being, but it tells us nothing about the distribution of that well-being, which must be measured by other statistics. The confusing statistics on earnings and family income showed that major changes were occurring in the labor force and the family in addition to an underlying slowdown in the growth of income. Finally, the good jobs–bad jobs debate illustrated what can go wrong when researchers and the popular media reporting the findings do not pay careful attention to the limitations inherent in the data. Research by

Bluestone and Harrison faced considerable criticism when it was shown that alternative assumptions caused a reversal in their findings. The lesson for researchers is that it is necessary to anticipate objections by proving the robustness of results under different assumptions. Indeed, subsequent research confirmed Bluestone and Harrison's conclusion that low-pay jobs increased, but in a politically acrimonious climate opposed to their interventionist policy recommendations, these later findings received little attention.

What Is Poverty?

Research on poverty typically confronts a perplexing question: how to define poverty? The easy solution is to rely on the official U.S. Census Bureau poverty line, the most commonly used in social science research. But, as demonstrated by its origins, the Census Bureau poverty line is quite arbitrary, and therefore inadequate for some purposes.

The Official Poverty Line During the early 1960s, Molly Orshansky, a Social Security Administration staff economist, was asked to develop a definition of poverty for the War on Poverty. By her own admission, this "Orshansky" poverty line was a compromise between scientific justification and political expediency. She began with a U.S. Agriculture Department estimate for a nutritionally sound diet, and then estimated the total poverty budget based on the proportion of food expenditures in a typical total family budget. Orshansky was unhappy with these assumptions, in particular the food budget, which was intended as a stop-gap grocery list but required a sophistication of purchasing and food preparation that was not likely to be practiced by poor families. But Orshansky was under pressure from the administration to calculate a poverty line at about $3,000 for a family of four, low enough so that the War on Poverty could reasonably be expected to help all those designated as poor. She had more leeway in defining poverty for other-size families, so she set the poverty line on slightly more favorable terms for smaller-size households and families with more than four people.

Not surprisingly, these highly arbitrary poverty lines have been criticized on many grounds. But researchers disagree whether this measure under- or overestimates the actual rate of poverty.

The Poverty Line Is Too Low   The official U.S. poverty line is an absolute standard, adjusted only for inflation. (In 1990 there was renewed debate about how to adjust for inflation, including a Census Bureau proposal to use a new inflation adjustment that would substantially reduce the official poverty line; see chapter 11.) Over the years since 1965 the standard of living in the United States has increased, so that on a *relative* basis, the poverty line has fallen. In 1965, it was just under one-half the U.S. median income; by 1986 the official poverty line was less than one-third of the median income. If the poverty line measured poverty at a constant *relative* rate, then measured poverty would have increased between 1965 and 1983, instead of falling, as it did in the official absolute standard.

The Poverty Line Is Too High   Others have criticized the Orshansky poverty line for overestimating the poverty line. For example, economist Rose Friedman points out that poor families spend a higher proportion of their income on food than the ratio used by Orshansky. Friedman recalculates Orshansky's poverty level with new ratios, estimating U.S. poverty at one-half its official level.

A second correction that reduces the apparent level of poverty is to include the value of noncash government programs such as food stamps, school meals, housing subsidies, and medical care. One such effort measured government programs at their market value, that is, what it would cost the poor to buy services comparable to those provided by the government. By this estimate, the poverty rate falls by about one-third, which prompted President Reagan's chief economic adviser Martin Anderson to conclude that the War on Poverty had been "won." But many economists question the relevance of market values for adjusting the poverty rate. In particular, medical care is so expensive in the private sector that the market value of Medicare and Medicaid is sufficient by itself to lift—in theory—almost all the elderly poor out of poverty.

Implications   The official "Orshansky" poverty line has withstood the test of time. It makes sense for many research projects because conclusions can be compared readily with other studies that also use this poverty line. Nonetheless, researchers should be aware of biases in the official number. Most notably, the absolute standard means that poverty today is measured by the same living standards used in 1965 (again, corrected only for inflation). The arbitrary assumptions made by Orshansky may be less of a problem. *Any* poverty line will be arbitrary, and the problems with the official one in part cancel out one another: Friedman's complaint about the food budget ratio is offset by the low food budget originally used, and the failure to include noncash benefits for the poor is offset by tax breaks and other government assistance available to the nonpoor.

One alternative research strategy is to adopt more than one poverty measure, including both absolute and relative standards. By using several poverty lines, it is possible to demonstrate the constancy, or robustness, of results under alternative assumptions. For example, the issue of how to count noncash benefits can be resolved by looking at alternative poverty measures published by the U.S. Census Bureau. Replacing the questionable market valuation for noncash benefits with more realistic assumptions reduces by about one-half the number of the poor who are raised above the poverty line by their noncash benefits.

Do the Poor Stay Poor?

The official poverty rate is based on a snapshot view. If our research interest is to find out if the same households are poor in different years, then we need longitudinal studies, that is, surveys that reinterview respondents over a long period of time. Surprising data from the University of Michigan's Panel Study of Income Dynamics (PSID) and the Census Bureau's Survey of Income and Program Participation (SIPP) show remarkable movement in and out of poverty. The PSID found that only 2.6 percent of the population was poor in eight out of ten years between 1969 and 1978, while over 24 percent were poor for at least one year. Similarly, in SIPP, only 6 percent of the population was poor in *every* month of 1984, but 26 percent were poor for at least one month.

For some conservative policy advisers, these data prove that poverty is less serious than CPS data indicate. In this view, most poor people require little government assistance because their poverty is temporary. Moreover, the small number who stay poor have become dependent on welfare programs and would gain by being forced to find regular employment. On the other hand, liberal social scientists often emphasize the surprisingly large proportion of the population experiencing temporary poverty. In this view, the welfare system is a much-needed security cushion for many families who are precariously close to the poverty line. Along similar lines, sociologist Mary Jo Bane used longitudinal data to show that most poverty occurred because of income or job changes, not because of family composition changes such as divorce or abandonment. Bane concludes: ''the problem of poverty should be addressed by devoting attention to employment, wages and the development of skills necessary for productive participation in the labor force rather than hand-wringing about the decline of the family.'' This policy recommendation has not been tested, but it shows how one can use dynamic data available in the PSID or SIPP to go beyond the debate about the ''actual'' low or high rate of poverty.

SUMMARY

Without improved data on wealth, we will not understand its distribution in the United States. At present, however, the barriers to better data appear insurmountable. The uneven distribution of wealth means that even extremely large surveys will tell us nothing about the very wealthy; it is unlikely that any of the *Forbes* 400 will be interviewed in the extremely large-sample Current Population Survey, and even more improbable that they will be included in the Federal Reserve survey. For example, the enriched sample of 438 known-to-be-wealthy households in the 1983 Federal Reserve survey included none of the wealthiest Americans identified by business magazines.

Additional data on income also would be helpful, for example, replacing the spendable weekly earnings series and increasing funding to the Survey of Income and Program Participation. But in general, simply increasing the quantity of data will not be sufficient. As economist Isabel Sawhill concludes, ''We are swamped with facts about people's incomes and about the number and composition of people who inhabit the lower tail, but we don't know very much about the process that generates these results.'' In other words, we need more data about income dynamics, that is, when and how income changes over time, and we need data about why incomes differ for different jobs.

Controversies about the distribution of income and the rate of poverty both demonstrate the need to test different assumptions in research projects. This kind of sensitivity analysis can preempt criticism about what may appear to be arbitrary choices such as years chosen for study, inflation indexes, or poverty lines. Such care can help researchers reach an audience beyond the already convinced.

Finally, despite the apparent existence of contradictory statistics, researchers have been able to reach important conclusions about income distribution and poverty. In other words, although it is possible to "lie with statistics," bending the numbers to agree with one's prejudice, it is also possible to use income statistics correctly if one understands the limitations of the underlying data.

CASE STUDY QUESTIONS

1. Even though the Census Bureau spends considerable effort training its survey takers to gather accurate data, respondents may nonetheless misrepresent their income. One study comparing Current Population Survey (CPS) data with tax returns showed that actual self-employment income was 24 percent higher than reported in the survey, actual government transfer programs other than social security were 42 percent higher, and acutal property income such as interest, rent, and dividends was 135 percent higher. How might these possible errors affect research on wealth and income distribution?

2. Current Population Survey data on income exclude capital gains, that is, income derived from the profitable sale of homes, stocks and bonds, or other investments. What effect does this exclusion have on studies of the distribution of income?

3. A 1987 *Ebony* magazine article celebrated a more than 50 percent increase between 1980 and 1986 in the number of black families with incomes between $25,000 and $50,000. By contrast, there was only an 18 percent increase in white families within this income bracket. How might these statistics exaggerate the improvement of income for blacks relative to income for whites?

4. The "feminization of poverty" has received much attention based on statistics showing that over one-half of all poor families were headed by women during the 1980s, up from only 25 percent in 1959. But research on the dynamics of poverty by Mary Jo Bane shows that for blacks, most poor female-headed households were formed from households that were *already* poor. Based on this data,

why do some policy advisers recommend employment programs instead of increased child support enforcement as the best way to reduce poverty rates?

5. Many studies of income focus exclusively on family incomes. What biases are introduced by leaving out nonfamily households when we study the well-being of the "typical" household?

6. The gap between men's and women's pay has received much attention in recent years. Usually the gap was measured by the ratio of women's pay to men's pay, which was approximately 69 percent in 1987. But there are several potential problems with this measure.

a) Most researchers use *weekly* earnings measured in the Current Population Survey. However, *annual* earnings that include second jobs measure a slightly larger pay gap. Why?

b) Most researchers compare pay for only full-time, year-round workers. Why would the pay gap appear larger if all workers were studied? What are the reasons for studying only full-time, year-round workers? What would be the reasons for studying all workers?

c) The measured pay gap between men and women closed by 7 percentage points between 1979 and 1987. But during this period men's median pay fell by more than 7 percent. How does this additional statistic affect assessment of women's progress in achieving equality?

Chapter 9

Labor Statistics

This chapter examines labor statistics, a broad range of data on unemployment, the number of jobs, occupations, union membership, strikes, and workplace safety. Because these statistics directly affect so many lives, they are mainstays of public policy. American macroeconomic policies, government training and education programs, equal rights efforts, and regulation of labor relations and the workplace all depend on labor statistics. In each case, however, there are significant measurement problems that complicate policy choices.

DATA SOURCES

U.S. Bureau of Labor Statistics

A researcher's first stop often will be the U.S. Department of Labor's Bureau of Labor Statistics (BLS), which publishes a wide range of information about the U.S. workforce. The most well known statistics on unemployment are computed by BLS based on survey data from the U.S. Census Bureau. In other cases, BLS simply publishes statistics collected by other U.S. government agencies. These include job injuries counted by the Occupational Safety and Health Administration (OSHA) and union membership estimated by the U.S. Census Bureau. Finally, BLS collects its own statistics, most important of which is the Establishment Survey, a monthly survey covering 200,000 employers for data on the number of jobs and average pay levels.

Where the Numbers Come from

Organizations	Data Sources	Key Publications
Bureau of Labor Statistics U.S. Department of Labor	Current Population Survey; Establishment Survey; Occupational Safety and Health statistics; international comparisons	*Employment and Earnings; Monthly Labor Review; Handbook of Labor Statistics; Occupational Injuries and Illnesses; Current Wage Developments*
U.S. Bureau of the Census U.S. Department of Commerce	U.S. Census of Population; Economic Censuses	*U.S. Census of Population; Census of Manufactures* (and other economic sectors)

For summary data see *Statistical Abstract of the U.S.*

Data Sample: For April 1985, the Bureau of Labor Statistics estimated the unemployment rate for married men at 4.5 percent, for widowed, divorced, or separated men at 10.0 percent, and for single, never-married men at 12.9 percent.

U.S. Census Bureau

While the Bureau of Labor Statistics publishes the most current labor data, the data published by the U.S. Census Bureau are the most comprehensive, although they are untimely (see chapter 2). The long form of the census completed by about 20 percent of the population provides labor force data with great accuracy for relatively small geographic areas.

Data Sample: In the 1980 Census of Population, male hotel and lodging executives, administrators, and managers outnumbered females by 96,637 to 66,178, while hotel and lodging room cleaners were predominately female by a 193,482 to 62,053 margin.

At five-year intervals the Census Bureau surveys businesses in the Economic Censuses. These surveys are also quite detailed, providing labor force data by economic sector.

> *Data Sample:* In the 1982 Census of Government, Harlan County, Kentucky, employed 967 workers: 640 in education; 48 in the police force; and 25 in firefighting.

CONTROVERSIES

Unemployment

On the first or second Friday of every month, the U.S. Bureau of Labor Statistics announces the unemployment rate for the previous month. It is a touchstone for U.S. economic policy; changes of a fraction of 1 percent are headline news, enough to bolster or shake confidence in a national administration. But practically unnoticed by the media is uncertainty about the interpretation and accuracy of the measured unemployment rate.

How It Came to Be   The Bureau of Labor Statistics came into prominence because of an embarrassing gap in U.S. social statistics. At the height of the 1930s' Great Depression, no one knew how many people were out of work. Limited funding prevented the BLS from conducting the kind of nationwide survey necessary to measure unemployment accurately. Instead, the BLS relied on partial surveys of the *employed* by individual states where strong labor lobbies had pressured for comprehensive workplace surveys. These data were misleading as a measure of unemployment; for example, in January 1930 President Hoover declared "the tide of employment has changed" based on an apparent upswing in the job count, although within one year more than 3 million people lost their jobs.

After a 1937 postcard survey yielded worthless returns by leaving out everyone without a permanent residence, the Roosevelt administration finally agreed to a large-scale house-to-house survey. Ironically, the task was assigned to the Works Progress Administration, itself a government effort to provide jobs. The resulting 15 percent unemployment rate estimate proved that the country still suffered from economic depression. Once it had been demonstrated that a direct sampling of individuals could measure unemployment, the U.S. Census Bureau

---

Box 9.1. **Fewer Statistics; Less Money**

In 1988, the CPS ended a special sample that permitted unemployment rates to be calculated for New York City and Los Angeles. As a result, those two cities were forced to rely on statewide unemployment estimates, a procedure that local officials feared would reduce federal revenues formerly allotted on the basis of city unemployment rates, which usually were higher than unemployment rates for the state as a whole.

---

took over, initiating the monthly Current Population Survey in 1947. Today it is the largest regularly conducted poll in the world, covering about 60,000 households, and is used to estimate many important social science statistics (see chapters 2, 4, and 5), but its key focus remains the unemployment rate. In the CPS, unemployment has a specific, technical definition: those respondents who are not working (but are not on sick leave) and who actively searched for work during the last four weeks. The unemployment rate is the number of unemployed divided by the labor force, consisting of the employed plus the unemployed. Researchers disagree whether this method causes under- or overestimation of the actual unemployment rate.

Undercount   There are two well-documented shortcomings in the official definition of unemployment causing it to underestimate the actual number of people in need of work. First, the official statistic leaves out part-timers who would like full-time work; anyone who works, even as little as one hour per week, is counted as employed. Second, discouraged workers who are not actively seeking a job are left out of the labor force entirely, that is they are neither employed nor unemployed. Only those who made specific effort to find work, such as writing letters, canvassing, or reporting to an agency, are counted as unemployed.

The BLS recognizes these potential limitations to the official unemployment rate by publishing different unemployment rates labeled U–1 through U–7. But the news media typically report only the official one called U–5.*

---

*There is also a U–5a (including the armed forces as employed workers) and U–5b (excluding the armed forces from the labor force). Because both U–5a and U–5b are commonly used, the "official" unemployment rate varies in media reporting, but typically by only 0.1 percent.

The other rates provide researchers with alternative—although seldom-used—statistics. For example, U–7 is a comprehensive measure of unemployment, including part-timers seeking full-time work (counted as one-half worker each) and discouraged workers. Typically U–7 is 50 percent higher than the official unemployment rate. Some researchers suggest that the actual unemployment rate is even higher than U–7 because the BLS count of discouraged workers leaves out those who identify themselves as students or homemakers. A 1979 Brookings Institution study found that 50 percent of this group wanted a job, indicating an actual unemployment rate more than double the reported rate. In other words, in 1990 unemployment was actually more than 10 percent, rather than the official rate of about 5 percent.

Overcount   Two measurement problems can cause overestimation of the official unemployment rate. First, some individuals likely misrepresent their work status to CPS surveyors in order to cover up illegal jobs. No one knows the precise size of the unreported workforce (see chapter 7), but underground economy expert Peter Gutmann argues that it causes official unemployment rates to be 30 percent too high.

A second problem arises because the single official unemployment statistic does not take into account *who* is unemployed. When there is an increasing proportion of women and youth in the workforce, the unemployment rate may rise because these inexperienced workers possess fewer skills and are more likely to change jobs frequently. One interpretation of this trend is the existence of a rising "natural rate" of unemployment compatible with nonaccelerating inflation. In this view, attempts by the government to achieve lower unemployment than the natural rate, about 6 percent during the 1980s, would have been inflationary. Other economists dispute these findings on the grounds that the term "natural" rate gives the false impression of immutability, when in fact the natural unemployment rate can be lowered with better investment and training programs.

Alternate Measures   In *Out of Work: The First Century of Unemployment in Massachusetts,* historian Alexander Keyssar explores the importance of an alternative measure of unemployment, the proportion out of work at some point during a year. Between 1830 and 1930 this statistic frequently reached as high as 40 percent, indicative of a far greater impact of unemployment than the traditional unemployment rate would suggest. In other words, if we want to measure how many individuals are affected by unemployment, either because they are currently unemployed, or have faced unemployment recently, then the statistic used by Keyssar is more accurate.

A more optimistic appraisal of the labor market occurs when researchers use statistics on the number of jobs rather than unemployment. For example, the BLS Establishment Survey provides a frequently updated count of jobs. Because these data are collected directly from employers, there are no problems caused by survey respondents who do not want to admit unemployment. The disadvantage of the Establishment Survey is that it counts all jobs, thereby overstating the employment picture when more individuals have two jobs. During the 1980s Establishment Survey data were used in political debate about the health of the U.S. economy. In the 1984 presidential campaign, President Reagan pointed to the Establishment Survey count of 5 million new jobs created during the previous two years, despite record-high unemployment. Similarly, in 1988, presidential candidate Bush boasted of 17 million jobs created between 1982 and 1987 while he was vice-president. This was a far more favorable statistic than the unemployment rate, which averaged just under 8 percent during this period.

Implications   Debates about labor market statistics teach several lessons about the use of data. First, the existence of data depends on social priorities. Students of the labor market are fortunate that because of its origins, the largest monthly U.S. survey, the CPS, has more questions on unemployment and employment than on any other single subject. The challenge for social scientists is to select from these numerous labor statistics choices that depend on the research purpose. For example, in studying the social consequences of unemployment, or social distress, the official U–5 unemployment rate is inadequate. Researchers may need to use less-often-consulted statistics such as U–7, or to make further adjustments to take into account measurement problems in official statistics.

If the research goal is to measure the overall state of the macroeconomy, then the official unemployment rate has the advantage of tradition. But because of changing labor force characteristics, the official unemployment rate may not be a constant measure of how well the macroeconomy is using labor resources. The debate about whether or not to call this effect the "natural" rate of unemployment illustrates the significance of language in social science research. More substantively, additional data provided in the CPS on *why* individuals left their jobs and *how long* they were unemployed can give us a better understanding of changes in labor markets. In a similar fashion, differences between the official unemployment rate, the frequency of unemployment studied by Keyssar, and job data emphasized by presidents Reagan and Bush demonstrate the need for researchers to keep an eye on more than one statistic. During many recent years, the increased size of the labor force caused both increasing unemployment *and* more employment.

Better Jobs?

Researchers on occupational change owe much to U.S. Census Bureau statistician Alba Edwards who between 1910 and 1940 undertook the massive task of classifying jobs into a usable number of occupations. The major categories developed by Edwards are the basis for much research on occupations, including controversial conclusions about the trend in job quality and intergenerational mobility.

Self-fulfilling Scale   Historian Marjorie Conk charges that some of Edwards's assumptions about job status were based on sexist and racist biases. For example, the nurses and midwives occupation was graded "semi-skilled" because it included mostly women workers. Similarly, other occupations were labeled low-skill because they were dominated by black or foreign-born workers. The system appeared satisfactory to Edwards because it reflected existing notions of "high" and "low" status. Other researchers point out that Edwards overestimated the increase in the skill level of U.S. jobs because of mistaken assumptions in the semi-skilled category, which was first introduced in 1910 as a category for work with machinery. On this basis, a large number of workers were promoted out of so-called unskilled occupations based on work with machinery—even if the tasks involved were less complex than the "unskilled" occupations. Later, repetitive task assembly-line jobs also were classified as semi-skilled, likely overstating the increase in the average occupational skill level.

White Collars   One of the major uses of the Census Bureau occupational classification is for the study of intergenerational mobility.

Based on a special set of questions in the 1962 and 1973 Current Population Survey, a 1967 study by sociologists Peter M. Blau and Otis Dudley Duncan, and updated by David L. Featherman and Robert M. Hauser in 1978, found significant upward mobility when sons of low-status fathers moved into higher-status white-collar jobs. (Data on mothers were not collected. Later studies found the effect of mothers' educational attainment outweighed the effect of fathers' status.)

Critics of the Blau and Duncan approach charge that categories based on the original Edwards classification may be misleading about status levels. In particular, jobs grouped as "white collar" do not necessarily involve more skill than the manual occupations they replace. For example, clerical occupations are white collar even though they include low-status filing and typing jobs with what is today the second-lowest pay of all major census classifications. The white-collar designation is a holdover from the nineteenth century, when clerical workers were a tiny enclave of privileged male workers. On the other hand, the "non-household service worker," a 1950s category introduced to separate service workers employed by corporations and government from personal maids and butlers, still retains the "lower manual" designation, even though these occupations include relatively high-skill jobs such as nursing, firefighting, and police work. Finally, the Census Bureau measured an increase in the number of managers, but made no distinction between the head of a major corporation and the person responsible for a fast-food franchise. Thus, although there are more managers, not all possess the status once accorded to this job title.

New Classification   Many anachronisms in the old classification scheme were rectified in the 1980 census when individual job titles were reallocated within the classification hierarchy. These corrections were welcomed by researchers, for example, shifting 240,000 practical nurses from the catch-all service category to the more specific—and higher-status—technician occupation. But as a result of the new classification, historical comparison with previous censuses is nearly impossible (although part of the 1970 census was recoded, making it compatible with 1980 data). Moreover problems remain, such as "managers, not elsewhere classified," the largest detailed classification including over 5 million individuals in 1980. But this catchall classification covered such diverse work settings that it was not useful for many research purposes.

Implications The pre-1980 Census Bureau occupational classification demonstrates the problem of fitting data into a few usable categories. In the case of Edwards's scheme, there were obvious initial biases, as well as subsequent changes in many occupational characteristics. Even though "semi-skilled" and "white and blue collar" were commonly used groups, they may not have measured what researchers intended. Extensive reclassification in the 1980 census presents another challenge to researchers because of incomparability between recent and past data.

Unions

The U.S. Bureau of Labor Statistics is the main source of national data on labor unions. Recent problems in measuring union membership and strike activity illustrate how researchers must pay careful attention to changes in data-collection methods.

Membership Prior to 1973, the only data came directly from union reports of their own membership. After 1973, the Current Population Survey added a question on union membership, which, beginning in 1981, replaced the direct count in government publications. Some social scientists charge that antiunion sentiment in the Reagan administration prompted the abandonment of the direct count. However, even the critics admit that there were problems with the older data source, in particular an upward bias caused by exaggerated union membership reports from unions wanting to present a strong image to employers, as well as a downward bias when local unions failed to report all members to the national union in an effort to avoid dues payment. No one knows the extent of either bias.

By avoiding self-serving membership reports, CPS data may be more accurate. Moreover, CPS unionization data can be correlated with other CPS questions on industry of employment, occupation, race, sex, and other variables. But such survey data are only as good as the informants' knowledge. There is evidence that respondents may not know whether they or other household members actually belong to a union. The primary problem is that many unions, most notably teacher and nursing "associations," do not use the title "union." The original 1973 CPS question about union membership was changed in 1976 to include "associations." But it was found that respondents answered "yes" if they simply belonged to a workplace club or "association." So the question was changed once again in 1979, to read "union or employee association similar to a union."

Researchers need to be aware of changes in the way in which union membership has been measured. Although all statistics show a dramatic decline in U.S. union membership during the 1970s and 1980s, the extent of this decline and the years in which it occurred depend on which data source is used.

Strikes The CPS sample is too small to estimate accurately the number of workers on strike. Consequently, the BLS relies on newspaper, magazine, and government reports to assemble data on the number of strikes, number of workers involved, and days idle. These data are comprehensive for strikes involving more than 1,000 workers. However, budget cutbacks in 1981 caused termination of data on smaller strikes (involving at least six workers for one eight-hour shift). According to BLS officials, these data were deleted in order to preserve the quality of such statistics as the Consumer Price Index, which is more important for policy decisions.

Researchers may agree that it was important to maintain the integrity of the Consumer Price Index, but the reduced quality of strike data is a major handicap for labor relations research. It is true that larger strikes account for most strike-days lost, but these large strikes were less than 10 percent of the total number of strikes in 1981. Thus, a full picture of labor relations requires information that is no longer collected.

Is the Workplace Safe?

Concern about occupational safety and health is a longstanding BLS tradition. In 1909, a BLS study documented phosphorus poisoning in the match industry, causing Congress to impose a tax on the dangerous product. In 1910, the BLS began publishing accident statistics based on reports from individual states and insurance companies. Congress refused authorization for a separate division on safety, so in subsequent decades safety data covered only 25 percent of the workforce. Under the 1970 Occupational Safety and Health Administration (OSHA) legislation, BLS coverage was expanded. But as of the late 1980s, it still excluded most small farms, the self-employed, government agencies, and employers with fewer than eleven employees (except in some high-risk industries). Critics charge that OSHA data should be comprehensive because, unlike other government surveys, the information is used both for enforcement as well as for research purposes. In fact, the most common penalty meted out by OSHA is for not reporting accidents.

Overall, OSHA presents researchers with a new and not well understood data set. Recent debate about the effectiveness of OSHA illustrates the limitations of available data. A significant decline in deaths, injuries, and illnesses is evident in the decade after OSHA was created (1971–81). By the mid-1980s, improvement begins to level off, but the data are not accurate enough to interpret this new trend with confidence. For example, the fatality rate per 100,000 workers, rose from 5.6 in 1983 to 6.4 in 1984, but then fell back to 6.2 in 1985. Perhaps the rapid improvement during the 1970s was a result of long overdue enforcement, so further reduction in death and injuries may be slower in coming. However, critics of OSHA policy charged that additional injuries resulted from a nearly 25 percent cutback in the number of inspections.

International Labor Statistics

Intercountry comparison of labor statistics are tricky because similar-sounding statistics—the labor force, unemployment, and employment—may differ in meaning. Researchers would be at a loss if it were not for the help available from statistical agencies. Regularly published BLS bulletins provide comparable data on the labor force, employment and unemployment in large industrial countries. Additional comparison data are assembled by the International Labor Organization, based in Geneva, Switzerland, and the Organization for Economic Cooperation and Development, based in Paris.

Unemployment   Two sets of problems confound direct comparison of unemployment rates in different countries. The labor force is defined variously to exclude those people under sixteen years old (in the United States), those under fifteen years old (in many other countries), full-time students looking for work (Sweden), and those waiting for a job to begin (Japan). Also, definition of those available for work varies from those who actively searched for a job during a four-week period in the United States, to a sixty-day period in Sweden, to an unspecified amount of time in Germany and Japan.

A second problem is variation in the level of distress caused by unemployment in different countries. Relatively comprehensive social welfare systems in Western Europe cause unemployment rates to mean quite different economic circumstances than they would in the United States. In the Netherlands, for example, it is estimated that reported unemployment would rise by 3 percent if it were not for relatively generous benefits that enable otherwise unemployed workers to retire and thus leave the labor force. Similarly, in Sweden, unemployment appears to be extremely low, below 3 percent until 1981, in part because job losers are given subsidized public employment.

The low Dutch and Swedish unemployment rates accurately portray the relatively low level of social distress in those two countries; a smaller proportion of the population suffers the economic and social problems of unemployment. But for a researcher studying economic growth, the unemployment rates may be misleading. Whereas in other countries, low unemployment usually implies fast economic growth, the Dutch and Swedish economies have been relatively stagnant.

Employment   Which country creates the most jobs? During the 1980s, supporters of the Reagan and Bush administrations pointed proudly to Establishment Survey statistics measuring more new jobs in the United States than similar surveys counted in all of Western Europe and Japan *combined*. But data incompatibility clouds interpretation of these intercountry comparisons. The European workforce is older than the U.S. workforce so that a smaller proportion of the population is in the traditional working-age group for whom jobs must be created. (The reverse, however, is true in Japan.) In both Europe and Japan, many fewer teenagers work, again reducing the need for new jobs, although in West Germany, it appears that many teenagers have left the labor force precisely because work was unavailable. (Japanese teenagers have never worked in large numbers.)

In summary, international comparisons require careful attention to how data are collected. Again, this problem is recognized by the U.S. Bureau of Labor Statistics as well as by the international statistical organizations that provide standardized statistics for most major countries.

SUMMARY

Seemingly small changes in labor statistics can have dramatic human consequences. Consider the U.S. unemployment rate, where every 1 percent change translates into at least one million more jobs. An increase of 1.0 per 100,000 in U.S. job-related fatalities means more than 1,000 additional deaths. But as this chapter demonstrates, there are many problems in measuring labor statistics, ranging from definitional issues for the unemployment rate, to changing survey techniques for union membership. The challenge for researchers is to understand the limitations of these numbers, without losing sight of their effects on human lives. For example, the official U.S. unemployment rate is an extremely limited and easily criticized single statistic. But it is possible to obtain a fascinating, and relatively complete, picture of the U.S. labor markets—*if* researchers look at all the statistics available, including alternative unemployment statistics, employment counts, and the causes and duration of unemployment. Similarly, there are flaws in the most commonly cited statistics about job quality, union membership, strikes, and workplace safety. International data compound each of these issues, requiring yet more skepticism about comparisons of simple statistics. But properly interpreted, the vast quantity of data collected has the potential to illuminate our understanding of labor issues.

CASE STUDY QUESTIONS

1. The official unemployment rates for teenagers are quite high, over 15 percent in many recent years. But this statistic does not mean 15 percent of all teenagers are out of work. What does it in fact measure?

2. Sometimes the Current Population Survey and the Establishment Survey measure different direction of changes in the number of jobs. In August 1988, for example, households reported job loss in the Current Population Survey, while businesses reported substantial employment gains in the Establishment Survey. Economists believe that the following factors are responsible: multiple job holders, newly created businesses, and undocumented aliens. How does each factor cause a difference in the number of jobs counted in the CPS and the Establishment Survey?

3. The average duration of unemployment depends on the state of the economy. During the economic recession of the early 1980s, unemployment lasting more than six months comprised about one-quarter of all unemployment, but only one-eighth of unemployment during subsequent years of economic recovery. How might this change affect public policy based on the official unemployment rate?

4. Some researchers complain that traditional census categories understate the degree of job segregation between men and women as well as the low status of jobs held by women. How might a large category such as "sales workers" cause this bias?

5. In Japan between 1955 and 1975 there was a twofold increase in the number of women attending college. Also, many women moved from farms, where they had combined farm work with child care, to cities where they had no paid employment. How might these factors explain declining labor force participation for Japanese women, the opposite of the trend in most other countries? (Hint: Few Japanese college students have outside jobs.)

Chapter 10

Business Statistics

Information about business is itself a very profitable business, serving a large market of information-hungry investors. Thus for research purposes, primary data directly from businesses are plentiful, as are secondary sources interpreting these data. The Data Sources section below reviews this vast field. The Controversies section focuses on one fundamental aspect of business statistics: the many ways to measure business size, including sales, assets, stock market price, and profits. These statistics are important as indicators of the success of individual firms, and for public policy, especially the enforcement of antitrust law.

DATA SOURCES

The availability of data depends critically on the type of business being studied. The approximately 17 million U.S. businesses divide into two basic forms of legal organization. Corporations are least in number, about one-sixth of all businesses, but predominate in economic importance, accounting for four-fifths of sales and profits. Corporate data are voluminous, and usually publicly available. On the other hand, more than 14 million sole proprietorships and partnerships account for only about one-tenth of business revenues. Data on these mostly smaller businesses are much less accessible.

Public Corporations

SEC Disclosure   The financial distress of the Great Depression, coupled with complaints about corporate misrepresentation, led to the cre-

Where the Numbers Come from

Organizations	Data Sources	Key Publications
U.S. Securities and Exchange Commission	Corporate reports	*SEC Monthly Statistical Review; Official Summary of Security Transactions and Holdings*
U.S. Small Business Administration	Small Business Data Base	*State of Small Business; Handbook of Small Business Data*
Federal Trade Commission	Corporate reports to FTC	*Quarterly Financial Reports; Statistical Report on Mergers and Acquisitions; Annual Line of Business Report*
Dun and Bradstreet	Credit reports	*The Failure Record*

ation of the Securities and Exchange Commission (SEC) in 1933. In addition to monitoring the stock exchange and other capital markets, the SEC sets strict guidelines for corporate disclosure, that is, what corporations must tell the public about the type of goods or services produced, the names of corporate officers, the names of major stock-holders, and most importantly, a summary of corporate finances. Lists of companies reporting to the SEC and the data itself are available directly from the SEC offices, or through private firms that employ researchers who will locate and photocopy SEC files for a fee. A few large corporations are privately held, that is, they do not sell stock to the public. Data on these private firms are considered separately below.

Annual Reports   The SEC's financial disclosure requirements for stockholders are fulfilled by the annual report, a publication expanded by most corporations to a multipage glossy magazine that advertises the company's investment potential. The annual report is an easily accessible source of data, available in many public libraries or from the corporation itself. However, experts warn users not to rely entirely on annual reports. Additional, possibly more revealing, information is publicly available in SEC reports. Moreover, the text that fills most space in annual reports can be misleading; corporations are under no obligation to discuss unsavory prospects in this written material.

> *Data Sample:* In the 1988 General Motors Annual Report the president and chairman told shareholders: "We are very pleased with GM's performance in 1988. . . . With its accelerating momentum, GM is well positioned to achieve its ultimate objective of strong profitability. . . ." Nowhere do they mention GM's share of the U.S. auto market, which declined to 34.7 percent in 1987 from 38.5 percent the previous year.

Handbooks   For research on a number of corporations, it is most convenient to consult handbooks containing data collected by private companies such as Moody's, Standard and Poors, Value Line, and Dun and Bradstreet. Each of these handy reference books is updated frequently to include all key data from SEC reports, as well as recent stock prices, debt, capitalization, and usually to add an impartial assessment of each corporation's current financial status. Supplementary handbooks help researchers find corporate addresses, subsidiary ownership, corporate leadership, and product lines.

Business Magazines   Based on the popularity of the *Fortune 500* largest industrial corporations, first introduced in 1955, we now have the *Business Week 1,000*, several *Forbes 400* rankings, and an expanded *Fortune 500* to include nonindustrial corporations as well. These business magazines also publish special issues with comprehensive listings of corporate management, corporate compensation, and data on unusually successful small businesses. Because of deadline pressures, errors appear regularly in these issues. Researchers should look out for anomalous-looking data and should consult subsequent issues for corrections. Nonetheless, these compilations are quite handy for home and office use because they are far less expensive than corporate handbooks.

Privately Held Corporations

Some major U.S. corporations are nearly exempt from public scrutiny because they do not have publicly traded stock. Most are companies owned by only a few shareholders, for example, the Mars Candy Company, which is owned by members of the Mars family. *Forbes* magazine uses outside sources, and in some cases voluntary disclosure, to estimate the size of the 400 largest privately held firms, topped in recent years by Cargill Inc, a Minneapolis grain-trading company with more than $38 billion sales in 1988. Overall, these 400 private corporations averaged slightly over $1 billion in sales, compared to more than $5 billion for the 400 largest corporations with stockholders.

For data on privately held companies that are not large enough to be described in the *Forbes 400,* researchers face a substantial challenge. A helpful resource is *A Guide to Information on Closely Held Corporations*, developed by labor relations experts with experience in researching corporations. The *Guide* recommends first checking business magazine and newspaper indexes to see if a reporter has already conducted the research you wish to do. Next look in directories such as Dun and Bradstreet and Thomas Register, which include privately held firms. Finally, additional information can be gained from records of corporate formations filed with state offices, and real estate, litigation, and court judgments in local jurisdictions.

> *Data Sample:* In Dun's Marketing *Million Dollar Directory* we learn that Kut Rate Fashions, Inc., of Columbia, South Carolina, has 85 employees and annual sales of $11 million.

Small Businesses

The great majority of U.S. businesses are small. Defined as employing less than 100 workers, small businesses comprise over 98 percent of all businesses, although these small firms take in less than 40 percent of all business sales. For data on individual small businesses, a researcher may need to do some data digging. Local libraries are a good place to start; librarians often are familiar with sources on local businesses, and reference works on local economies are frequently in their collections. Private data firms, most notably Dun and Bradstreet, collect data on small firms, but access to the data is expensive.

Aggregate Statistics

Many research projects require aggregate statistics, that is, combined data for groups of businesses, perhaps in a single location or in a single line of business. For these numbers, U.S. government statistics are almost certainly a researcher's starting point. The U.S. Commerce Department's economic surveys (see chapter 7) provide a core set of data, detailed by geographic area and product lines. The U.S. Labor Department's Establishment Survey uses similar organization by locale and product, but is limited to data on the workforce.

For aggregate data on small businesses, a recently developed source is now available from the Small Business Administration, an independent federal agency. The "Small Business Data Source" is unusual in that it follows the record of individual businesses, rather than the typical single-point-in-time "snapshot" view of most aggregate statistics. As a result, the Data Source will answer important questions about which small businesses grow—and which fail. In addition, the Data Source fills a data gap on business startups not always recorded immediately in U.S. Census reports.

> *Data Sample:* The Small Business Data Source analyzes changes in the number of jobs for 1976 to 1984 as follows:
> New business startups: 26 million new jobs
> Existing business expansion: 8 million new jobs
> Businesses going defunct: 16 million jobs lost
> Layoffs: 3 million jobs lost
>
> Net change: 14 million new jobs.

CONTROVERSIES

Who Is the Biggest of Them All?

The size of a business can be measured in many ways: by the value of a firm's sales; by the value of a firm's assets; by the value of a firm's profits; or by the number of a firm's employees. As shown in Table 10.1, these measures of size cause different rankings of U.S. companies; General Motors, IBM, and Citicorp can all legitimately claim the number one spot. There are advantages and disadvantages

Table 10.1

Big by Any Measure: Corporate Size, 1989 (in billions)

	Sales	Assets	Stock Market Value	Profits
1.	General Motors $127	Citicorp $231	IBM $62	General Motors $4.2
2.	Ford $96	General Motors $173	Exxon $59	General Electric $3.9
3.	Exxon $88	Ford $161	General Electric $58	Ford $3.8
4.	IBM $127	American Express $231	AT&T $62	IBM $4.2
5.	Mobil $57	General Electric $128	Phillip Morris $36	Exxon $3.0

Source: The Business Week 1,000, April 13, 1990, pp. 158–60.

to each measure of size, so researchers must consider carefully which to use.

Sales   The oldest and most famous ranking of U.S. corporations, the *Fortune 500*, is based on annual sales. When the list was first published in 1955, economist M.A. Adelman wrote to the magazine to complain that sales data are "almost meaningless" because they include production by the company's suppliers that is passed on in the company's sales. As an example, Adelman pointed to the Dupont Corporation with $1.7 billion sales, which appeared smaller than meat processor Swift and Co. with $2.5 billion sales. But almost all of Dupont's sales were based on its own production, whereas 90 percent of Swift's sales came from supplier costs passed on to customers. *Fortune* admitted the data were imperfect, but defended them as the best available.

Because of the problem with incomparability between different industries, the *Fortune 500* initially was limited to only industrial corporations. In later years, *Fortune* added a separate list of the largest service corporations. But the distinction between these two lists is

Box 10.1. **Which Is Larger: GM or Switzerland?**

A frequently cited criticism of the power of large corporations is their size, measured by annual sales, in comparison to the GNP of relatively large countries. In this manner, General Motors, the largest U.S. corporation in sales, ranks ahead of Switzerland, Indonesia, and South Korea.

GNP or Annual Sales—1985 (billions)

1. U.S.		$3,947
.		.
.		.
20. GENERAL MOTORS	$	96
21. Switzerland	$	93
22. EXXON	$	87
23. Indonesia	$	86
24. South Korea	$	86

Technically this list is an invalid comparison of statistical apples and oranges. Gross national product measures a country's total production, whereas corporate sales include that corporation's production *plus* production by other firms used as raw materials, machinery, and other inputs. A correct comparison would measure corporate production by what economists call "value added," the concept used in GNP accounts to avoid the double-counting that arises in corporate data. On this basis, GM is nevertheless still quite large, outranking the Philippines, Greece, and Pakistan, although not Switzerland, Indonesia, and South Korea, as comparison of sales with GNP misleadingly implies.

increasingly difficult because more firms are diversifying to include both industrial and service-type production. This causes crossover and ambiguity in the rankings: for example, during the 1980s International Telephone and Telegraph, Union Pacific, Charter, and Gulf & Western left the top 100 of *Fortune*'s industrial list when they were reclassified as service corporations.

Assets   In theory, a second measure of size, the value of assets, should give a good comparative size statistic valid between different sectors of the economy. The problem with assets, as every accounting student quickly learns, is that unlike the items measured in sales data, few assets are actually bought or sold during a given year. As a result, accountants must estimate asset value based on changes in value since they were first purchased. The procedure is called depreciation, a complex formula oriented toward taxation, not actual demise of the asset. Smart investors know to investigate closely before trusting the measured assets as the actual value of a company. Despite this drawback, asset value is commonly used in research on diverse sectors of the economy where sales data would be misleading. For example, the debate about the concentration of corporate power discussed below is based on estimates of assets owned by the largest corporations.

Market Value A third measure of size, used in the *Business Week 1,000*, is based on the combined value of all stock owned in the corporation. This number reflects both the value of funds invested in the corporation when stock was first issued, as well as subsequent changes in the corporation's value based on the rise and fall of the stock price. In theory, the combined knowledge of all stock investors may provide a better measure of corporate values than any single number in the corporate accounts. The drawbacks to stock values as a measure of size are twofold. First, changing stock prices mean that the "value" of the firm changes literally from moment to moment as the stock price varies. Typically researchers must choose an arbitrary day for measuring stock prices; even a short time earlier or later, stock prices may be significantly different.

Second, aside from day-to-day fluctuations, there are uncertainties about the meaning of long-run stock prices, in particular whether this is actually a measure of underlying corporate values. There is ongoing debate among economists and business analysts about the efficiency of the stock market, both as an indicator of differences between corporations in terms of their productive capacity, and the ability of the stock measure to measure the economy's overall strength.

In summary, stock prices are a convenient statistic in the sense that they are widely reported and therefore are readily available in print or electronic format. The problem is that no one knows for certain what these voluminous data are telling us.

Employment Finally, the number of employees is an indicator of size. For organizing data on varied types of firms, employment is a

convenient size criterion for several reasons. First, counting employees is less ambiguous than using accounting principles to estimate sales or assets. Second, employment data are applicable to all firms, whether incorporated or not. And third, employment size is a statistic likely to be known by employees, and thus can be measured in household surveys as well as business surveys.

Two precautions in using employment data are required. First, employment gives only a general indication of size, differentiating between "large" and "small" businesses, but it cannot be used for comparing two companies of similar scale. For example, labor-intensive companies such as Fruit of the Loom apparel company had over 23,000 employees in 1988, but was comparable in size as measured by other criteria to machine-intensive Clorox with only 4,800 employees. Second, researchers must distinguish between business establishments (locations where the business operates) and enterprises (legally constituted business that may have many establishments). The distinction is important especially in household surveys where respondents may not know about enterprise employment beyond their workplace establishment.

Implications   One obvious solution to the problem of too many ways to measure size is to use more than one statistic; indeed, studies by investors typically use all the information provided by sales, assets, market value, and employment. When it is necessary, however, to choose one of the rankings, researchers should ascertain which indicator is most appropriate. For example, investigation of market control within an industry typically looks at sales data, whereas research on the source of profitability—are big firms more successful?—uses asset data, and, as a third option, studies of corporate takeovers are based on market value. A well-justified research project will explain why one size measure was chosen instead of the others.

Are the Big Too Big?

Probably the most important public policy use for data on business size is antitrust law. At issue is government intervention to limit the power of one business entity if it is too big, or to restrict the power of several corporations, if together they wield too much economic power. Not surprisingly, the criteria for "too big" and "too much economic

---

Box 10.2. **Top of the World**

Japanese businesses dominated worldwide rankings during the 1980s.

Sales	Market Value (1988)	Profits
1. C Itoh	1. Nippon Telegraph and Telephone	1. IBM
2. Mitsui	2. Sumitomo Bank	2. Exxon
3. Marubeni	3. IBM	3. Royal Dutch/Shell
4. Sumitomo	4. Dai-Ichi Kangyo Bank	4. Ford
5. General Motors	5. Fuji Bank	5. General Motors

Overall, among the top 1,000 firms, Japanese companies account for 48 percent of the market value, while U.S. firms comprise 30 percent. These rankings, however, overstated the total Japanese influence for two reasons. First, the Japanese economy has fewer, and therefore larger, corporations, so that they comprise a greater percentage of the top rankings than they do of the total world economy. Second, Japanese stock market prices are higher relative to corporate earnings; in terms of *profits* earned in 1988, U.S. corporations held four of the top five spots.

---

power'' are a sticking point, and the source of much statistical controversy.

In some cases there was consensus that corporations became too big, as in the nearly total monopoly gained by the American Tobacco Company and the Standard Oil Company. In 1911, both these firms were forced to split into smaller, competing entities. Most antitrust cases, however, involve a middle ground in which no single firm dominates an industry, and instead there are a few large firms that share the market. Antitrust laws are vague about what to do in such situations. The Sherman Antitrust Act forbids the "attempt to monopolize," while the Clayton Antitrust Act forbids business behavior that will "substantially lessen competition." Consequently, the U.S. courts and federal regulators have attempted to develop more specific guidelines for antitrust policy based on measures of market shares of sales.

In recent years federal regulators began using a measure of market

Table 10.2

Concentration Ratios (share of value of shipments, 1982)

Industry	Percent Accounted for by 4 Largest Firms	HHI
Pickles, sauces, and salad dressing	56	1,697
Typesetting	7	23
Tires and inner tubes	66	1,591
Motor vehicles and car bodies	92	Withheld to avoid disclosing data for individual company
Dolls	36	688
Macaroni and spaghetti	42	646

Source: Bureau of the Census, U.S. Department of Commerce, *1982 Census of Manufacturing: Concentration Ratios in Manufacturing* (Washington, D.C., U.S. Government Printing Office, April 1986), MC82-S-7.

shares called the Herfindahl-Hirschman Index (see Box 10.3). Essentially this index has the same impact as the former criteria based simply on market share of sales controlled by the top four or eight firms, a statistic published in the Commerce Department's economic censuses (see Table 10.2 for examples). However, these seemingly straightforward guidelines have been complicated in actual practice for two reasons.

What Is a Market? One fundamental problem in enforcing antitrust rules is determining the relevant market that the firms under investigation are alleged to control. Over the years since the 1890 Sherman Antitrust Act, the U.S. Supreme Count has moved back and forth in defining the level of market control that could be presumed to be in violation of the law. At one extreme, a 1966 decision blocked the merger of Pabst and Blatz beer brewers because they accounted for 24 percent of Wisconsin beer sales, although they comprised only 4.5 percent of the national market over which beer is readily distributed. More recently, the court has been more permissive, as for example in the 1986 acquisition of Republic Airlines by Northwest Airlines, de-

---

Box 10.3. **The Herfindahl-Hirschman Index**

As a key guideline for antitrust enforcement, the U.S. Department of Justice measures market shares by the Herfindahl-Hirschman Index. It includes all firms in the industry, with each firm's percentage market share squared and added together. Thus, an index of 10,000 measures a perfect monopoly (100 percent squared), while 0 measures perfect competition. Guidelines introduced by the U.S. Justice Department indicated that mergers "likely" would be challenged if the index were above 1,800, corresponding to approximately four firms controlling 70 percent of the market, or if the merger would raise the index by an additional 100 points, corresponding to the merger of two firms each with 10 percent of the market. Lower thresholds would bring less scrutiny, down to markets with an index below 1,000, corresponding to four firms controlling about 50 percent of the market, below which merger challenge was "unlikely."

---

spite a 90 percent market share in Minneapolis. In this case, the acquisition was approved on the grounds that many passengers who were connecting through Minneapolis could fly via other airports such as Chicago where Northwest and Republic had a much smaller market share. A similarly expanded market definition was used in 1988 to approve the merger between Owens-Illinois and Brockway, the second and third largest U.S. glass bottle manufacturers. The merger gave the new firm more than 37 percent of the glass bottle market, clearly violating Justice Department guidelines by raising the Herfindahl-Hirschman Index by more than 600 points. Nonetheless, the acquisition was approved on the grounds that the actual market for bottles included plastic, metal, and paper containers, for which the two firms had a much smaller market share.

2. What Is Competitive? Even when the relevant market is identified, antitrust enforcement must still determine *how much* market share will be accepted. Once again, U.S. Supreme Court rulings on the issue have vacillated, shifting from permissiveness during the 1920s when J.P. Morgan's U.S. Steel, with a 60 percent market share, was permitted to survive, to increased enforcement beginning in the late 1930s. Antitrust enforcement peaked during the 1960s, when, for example, the government blocked the merger of Brown and Kinney Shoes, and between Vons Grocery and Shopping Bag supermarkets, even though the combined market shares in each case were less than 10 percent. By the 1980s, the pendulum swung back in the other direction, epitomized by the 1982 dismissal of a thirteen-year suit against IBM's domination of the computer industry. During the first term of the Reagan administration, the number of challenges brought by the Justice Department and the Federal Trade Commission fell to nearly one-half the average of the previous two decades.

The economic issues about what level of market control constitutes undo influence are complex and beyond the scope of this book. In brief, one highly influential school of thought, identified with the University of Chicago, believes competition will be intense even in a highly concentrated market. In this view, the policy priority should be eliminating government price controls in the airline, trucking, banking, and other industries, rather than enforcing allegedly archaic antitrust laws. On the other hand, a great many economists advocate a return to past antitrust enforcement. Economist William Shepherd, for example, former adviser to the Justice Department's Antitrust Division, maintains that today's markets are increasingly competitive *because* of antitrust activity.

Despite over 100 years of antitrust enforcement, there is no consensus about what constitutes the appropriate market for which to measure market shares, nor is there agreement about what level of market shares should be acceptable in any market. The future of market share of sales as a criterion for antitrust action is in doubt. Although the official guidelines still refer to market share of sales, in actual practice during the 1980s, antitrust was not enforced by federal regulators, even when concentration indexes were well above the threshold designated as potentially anticompetitive.

The Urge to Merge—Are the Big Getting Bigger?

During the 1980s an unprecedented number of mergers and acquisitions occurred, capped by the 1988 $24.5 billion purchase by Kohlberg-Kravis-Roberts of R.J. Reynolds-Nabisco, two firms combined in an earlier merger. Even taking into account inflation, the value of mergers during the 1980s averaged more than three times the level of the previous two decades. Because of this trend, some policy advisers called for more antitrust regulation. If the mergers or acquisitions occurred within an industry, then the concentration ratios were relevant, as in the case of Northwest and Republic Airlines described above. However, for mergers or acquisitions across diverse industries, the absolute size of the resulting corporations is more relevant than market share. In such cases, asset value became the relevant indicator.

Interpretation of asset values has generated an ongoing controversy since a 1932 study by Adolf Berle and Gardiner Means, *The Modern Corporation and Private Property*, measured increased concentration of ownership. However, data collected by the U.S. Federal Trade Commission based on corporate financial accounts showed a slight decline in concentration among the top 200 nonfinancial corporations between 1970 and the mid-1980s. These data were used by President Reagan's Council of Economic Advisers to argue that mergers had not harmed the competitive climate. On the other hand, economists in favor of government intervention against corporate mergers pointed to data on *manufacturing* corporations (as opposed to all nonfinancial corporations) that showed *increased* concentration of asset ownership among the top 200 firms, rising to nearly 60 percent by the end of the 1980s.

Who is correct? The data on all "nonfinancial" corporations used by the Reagan administration are more inclusive, thus better representative of the entire economy. However the manufacturing data used by the critics may be more consistent over time because these manufacturing industries have not changed as much as those industries included in the nonfinancial category. (In addition, results depend whether domestic activity alone is considered, for which concentration of ownership by the largest 200 corporations appears unchanged, or whether overseas activity is included, for which concentration of ownership has increased.) Overall, we know there is considerable concentration of ownership, but the long-term trend is a complicated picture, highly dependent upon which data are used.

Line-of-Business Reporting

How much detail should businesses be required to report to government statistical authorities? During the 1970s a program to increase business disclosure to the U.S. Federal Trade Commission caused so much controversy that the new statistics were no longer calculated, and similar proposals by other agencies were curtailed. As a result, information was not collected that would have been useful for government regulators, financial investors, and academic researchers.

At issue was "line-of-business reporting," the disclosure of financial statistics for different product areas under control of a single company. Under existing rules, companies are required to disclose only limited information about multifaceted operations; most financial data could be reported in consolidated form, that is, a single number encompassing the entire business firm. A leading proponent of line-of-business reporting pointed to the example of the General Electric Corporation, which reported much of its financial data to the SEC under the category "consumer products," not further divided into refrigerators, light bulbs, televisions, hair dryers, or other items made by the corporation. Similarly consolidated statements are the most detailed public information available for other large U.S. corporations, most of which also have diversified production.

The proposal for line-of-business reporting was initiated by the U.S. Federal Trade Commission as part of its antitrust enforcement to assess corporate control in individual markets. Proponents argued that disclosure also was needed by the many other agencies as well, including even the Postal Rate Commission, which wanted to assess magazine publisher claims that increased second-class mailing rates jeopardized profits. Because large corporations combined data for magazine and other publishing efforts—and refused to provide the Postal Commission with line-of-business data—profit levels for individual lines of business could not be analyzed. In addition, private investors argued for increased disclosure because current practices enabled diversified corporations to hide losses by unsuccessful parts of their companies.

Opponents of increased disclosure succeeded in preventing extensive overhaul of line-of-business reporting. Arguments against the plan were threefold. First, critics maintained that disclosure would not provide accurate information because of inconsistencies in the Standard Industrial Classification (see Box 10.4) proposed for line-of-business reporting. Second, critics argued that corporate accountants could not accurately measure how overhead costs are distributed among different parts of a business. Third, and most important for the defeat of the proposal, corporations opposed disclosure on the grounds that it would breach financial confidentiality, providing data to possible business competitors.

Box 10.4. **Standard Industrial Classification**

Consistent classification of U.S. industry is so important that responsibility is entrusted to the president's Office of Management and Budget's Statistical Policy Office. They oversee the Standard Industrial Classification (SIC), a numerical coding used throughout the government and in most private-sector research as well. In the SIC, four digits refer to specific industries; for example, 2098 is macaroni and spaghetti makers. The first two digits are larger aggregates; in this case, 20 is for food and kindred products manufacturers. The U.S. Census Bureau adds three more digits to create product-line codes. For example, 2844515 is "suntan and sunscreen lotions and oils" in the "toilet preparation" industry, SIC code 2844.

The major problem with the SIC is that its codes are outdated. For example, until recently, microwave components were included in a catch-all category, 3679, "Electrical Components Not Elsewhere Classified," along with phonograph needles and radio headphones. Service-sector classification is especially obsolete with major industries often categorized in a single four-digit code. Thus, *all* eating places fall under code 5812, while the older food manufacturing industry is divided into many four-digit codes, for example, with a separate code for macaroni and spaghetti products. Researchers and marketing groups (who use SIC codes to target advertising) claim that they are handicapped by these out-of-date categories. But budget restraints have prevented the much-needed overhaul of SIC codes, reducing the Statistical Policy Office to a staff of fewer than ten professional employees in 1987 who had time to recommend only minor changes in the classification system.

More than 100 companies filed lawsuits against the Federal Trade Commission line-of-business reporting program. Similar proposals were considered by the Financial Accounting Standards Board, the private-sector watchdog for business reporting, but only minor modifications were adopted, so that both the Financial Accounting Standards Board and the SEC allowed businesses to report financial data in extremely broad categories, only if the line-of-business constituted at least 10 percent of total sales, and for no more than ten categories. During the 1980s, the Reagan administration halted the Federal Trade Commission line-of-business reporting program at a time when only data through 1977 had been collected.

Box 10.5. **Who Owns the Corporation?**

The dispute about line-of-business reporting is typical of the manner in which U.S. business has resisted mandatory disclosure rules. A proposal during the 1970s to increase reporting of stock ownership met a similar fate, despite complaints by government regulators, investors, and researchers that it was difficult to find out who controlled corporations. Federal regulators required disclosure of major stockholders to varying degrees. For example, corporations must disclose the name of stockholders with greater than 5 percent ownership. But frequently these stockholders were reported as stock nominees such as "Cede and Co." The purpose of these nominees was to facilitate computerized transactions, and the nominees have no power to buy, sell, or exercise any stock's voting rights. However, listing by stock nominees left federal officials unable to ascertain actual ownership, a severe handicap for the regulation of communications, energy supplies, and banking.

The debate about line-of-business reporting is illustrative of a tug-of-war that frequently takes place between government regulators and the business world. In this case, as in other disputes (see Box 10.5), the experience of the past two decades has been soundly against increased disclosure. Ongoing political debate will determine whether additional information will be collected in the future.

How Much Profit?

Even without line-of-business data, considerable information is available about corporate finances. One frequently studied subject is profits, a term that has different meanings to different users. Two recent controversies about profits illustrate potential pitfalls that can occur when a term is not defined precisely.

Are Profits Too High?   American corporations have paid for newspaper and magazine space to respond to what they perceive as widespread misperception on the part of the public about the level of corporate profits. Opinion polls show that the public estimates typical profit rates at nearly 30 percent, whereas according to the Chevron Oil Corporation in one advertisement, profits averaged only 5 percent.

The number reported by Chevron is profit as percentage of sales, based on a statistic in corporate reports called "net income as a percentage of sales." Indeed, for many corporations this figure is no more than 5 percent. However, this statistic has limited applicability for comparative purposes because sales cannot be compared between different sectors of the economy. (See above on sales as a measure of corporate size.) For example, the profit rate on sales can be misleadingly low if the business has a fast turnover that enables high profits to be earned despite a low profit rate. As an alternative, business analysts calculate profits as a percentage of how much has been invested in the firm, a profit rate that averages over 10 percent. For example, in 1988, Chevron's profit as percentage of stockholder equity was 12.3 percent. It is this second definition of profits that the public probably had in mind in the opinion polls, because it is similar to the concept of the rate of return received on individual investments. (The survey questions asked specifically about profit as a percentage of sales, but this qualification was likely ignored or not understood by many respondents.) Moreover, the public probably also used an entirely different concept of profits that included pay and other benefits accruing to high level management. In standard corporate accounting these are considered "employee costs," and are never counted as profits. Unlike small businesses, with which the public was more familiar, where managers and owners are the same people, corporate accounting limits the concept of profit to earnings paid as dividends or retained for corporate use. For example, in 1989, Craig O. McCaw, chairman of McCaw Cellular Communications, was the highest paid of all U.S. corporate executives with $53.9 million in salary, bonuses, and stock options—even though in strict accounting terms his company earned no profits.

In summary, Chevron used a standard definition of profits in its advertisement, although the corporation chose to measure profits as a percentage of sales, a procedure that minimized their apparent profit rate. The public had a much looser sense of what should be included in profits, and misunderstood the accounting definition. On the other hand, the public was correct in the sense that profits are best measured as a proportion of what has been invested. The contrast between these two uses of the same concept is instructive about the need for caution when strict accounting terms are compared with everyday usage.

Total Profits The meaning of the term profits is ambiguous even in its technical use by economists. A recent debate about the amount of profits in the U.S. economy underscored the discrepancy between "accounting profits," the sum of corporate profits reported to stockholders, and the theoretical concept of profits preferred by economists that is estimated by the U.S. Commerce Department.

Between 1980 and 1986, these profit statistics differed considerably. Based on a sudden drop in *accounting* profits, former chief economist for U.S. Steel William H. Peterson argued that insufficient funds were available for reinvestment in modern plant and equipment. In response to Peterson, Colgate University economist Thomas Michl pointed to U.S. Commerce profit data, which he claimed to be more accurate because they are adjusted to include only business operations that occur because of changes in inventories or because of changes in procedures for depreciating assets. For 1986, the Commerce Department profit statistics showed nearly double the amount reported in accounting profits, reversing Peterson's measured 4 percent profit decline to a nearly 4 percent profit *increase* between 1980 and 1986.

This dispute between Peterson and Michl serves as a flag of caution to researchers using data on aggregate profits. Whether or not the adjustments made by the Commerce Department are correct depends on complex economic theory, and thus is beyond the scope of our discussion. But researchers should note that there are often different statistics for what appear to be the same underlying concepts. As in the dispute between Peterson and Michl, the choice of statistics is critical to research findings.

How Now Dow?

The Dow Jones Industrial Average (DJIA) is probably the most commonly reported of all economics or business statistics, but few viewers of the nightly news know either the meaning of the "Dow" or its limitations. The Dow Jones Industrial Average is simply the total stock prices of thirty representative stocks (corrected for the minor detail of stock splits and changes in the thirty representatives). For example, on June 26, 1989, the DJIA, or the "Dow," was 2511: the total stock price of General Motors, McDonalds, and twenty-eight other of the largest U.S. corporations (multiplied by a correcting factor of 0.659).

Stock market experts agree that the Dow is a poor gauge of the overall market. By simply adding each stock price, the Dow gives greater weight to higher-priced stocks. For example, IBM's stock price, approximately $100 during the late 1980s, counted more strongly in the Dow, exerting a strong 80-point downward pull in the Dow between 1987 and 1989. On the other hand, the Exxon Corporation had much less effect because its stock sold for about half as much per share, even though Exxon is comparable in size to IBM. An additional drawback to the Dow Jones Industrial Average is its coverage of only thirty companies. The choice of thirty stocks stems from the Dow's origin in 1884 as an easily calculated measure of overall stock activity. Today, with computers, it is possible to include many stock prices, and to weight them by corporate size. Stock indexes such as the New York Stock Exchange Index and the Standard and Poors Index use these more sophisticated techniques.

SUMMARY

The examples reviewed in this chapter suggest two common problems that apply to many business statistics.

First, because most business statistics come from data reported by corporations themselves, there are limits on how much information is available. As shown in the dispute over line-of-business reporting, corporations have not been willing to disclose additional information above what is already required by law. Consequently, researchers and government regulators must rely on imperfect statistics, which is sometimes a considerable handicap.

Second, on a more positive note, these corporate reports are subject to strict accounting procedures. It is true that investors sometimes complain about corporate attempts to hide unfavorable information, as in the case of misleading language in annual reports. But overall, researchers using business statistics are more fortunate than most data users in the sense that few other data sources are subject to such intensive review by outside experts, or to such well-established reporting criteria. The problem is that these strict accounting procedures can be misinterpreted. For example, accounting rules for depreciation are the source of problems in measuring asset values and profitability. Users of these statistics need to be aware that depreciation often is measured with an eye toward the corporation's tax liability, rather than with any concern for creating a consistent data base for research purposes.

In conclusion, business is probably the most completely documented field covered in this book, in terms of both the volume of data and their interpretation by experts. As with much other social science data, a telephone call to the appropriate corporate or government official often will clarify problems encountered with these numbers. Researchers also should not overlook public libraries, which often have extensive holdings of business publications, including many that are too expensive for an individual to buy.

CASE STUDY QUESTIONS

1. One of the arguments in favor of line-of-business disclosure is that it is needed to answer important research questions. Describe a research project that would require line-of-business information. Describe public policies that might be changed based on this research project.

2. Design an advertising campaign for a business that would make use of SIC data. Be specific about how many digits you need in the SIC.

3. The 1985 *Economic Report of the President* argues that measures of the concentration of corporate assets are "deceiving because it masks substantial turnover in the rank and identity of the largest firms. For example, of the 500 largest industrial firms [in 1955] . . . only 262 remained in the top 500 in 1980." Evaluate this claim.

4. On March 27, 1990, the Dow Jones Industrial Average was up by 1.08 percent while the New York Stock Exchange index was up 1.80 percent. Explain the difference.

5. Traditionally, economists have used the *Fortune 500* industrial corporations as the sample for investigating the relationship between profitability and differences in types of corporate ownership. What kinds of companies were omitted from this research effort? Why might these omissions bias the research results?

6. In a 1963 antitrust suit, the U.S. Supreme Court ruled against the merger of the Aluminum Company of America (Alcoa) with a much smaller aluminum company called Rome. The following market shares for Alcoa were cited in the case:

Aluminum bare conductor wire and cable: 27.8 percent
Aluminum and copper bare conductor wire and cable: 10.3 percent
Aluminum and copper bare and insulated wire and cable: 1.8 percent
(Rome's market share was 2 percent or less in all markets.)

Using these data, construct cases both for and against the merger. (The Supreme Court ruled against the merger.)

Chapter 11

Government

By this next-to-last chapter, readers should be convinced that few social statistics are to be taken at face value. Thus, it will come as no surprise that there is controversy about statistics concerning the operations of the U.S. government itself. And again, there is little debate about the sincerity of those who gather the data. In fact, many of the problems were first identified by government statisticians. This chapter reviews disputes about military spending, welfare spending, the U.S. deficit, and the money supply. Important policy decisions depend on how we measure each of these variables. In addition, a final section reviews problems raised in earlier chapters about inflation and currency exchange rate adjustments. Again, the difficulty for researchers is choosing the correct statistic from the many numbers published by the government.

DATA SOURCES

Data collected by the U.S. government on itself are readily available. Statistical publications are inexpensive; voluminous information is distributed to Federal Depository libraries, and federal agencies generally are receptive to direct inquiries.

U.S. Budget

Detailed analysis of spending and taxation is contained in the annual Budget of the United States Government, submitted by the president to

---

Where the Numbers Come from

Organizations	Data Sources	Key Publications
Office of Management and Budget Executive Office of the President	Proposed budget of the United States	*The Budget of the United States Government*
Social Security Administration U.S. Department of Health and Human Services	Social security and other program payments	*Social Security Bulletin; Public Assistance Statistics*
Bureau of Labor Statistics U.S. Department of Labor	Consumer Expenditure Survey and other BLS surveys	*Monthly Labor Review; Consumer Price Index, Detailed Report; Producer Price Indexes*
Bureau of Economic Analysis U.S. Department of Commerce	Deflators from National income and product accounts	*Survey of Current Business*

For summary information, see *Economic Report of the President.*

Congress in January, and then revised substantially during the year. It is a massive book with additional volumes of appendix, special analyses, and historical tables. Summary data are published in a more manageable "United States Budget in Brief," the annual *Economic Report of the President*, and the July issue of the U.S. Commerce Department's *Survey of Current Business* (see the box above). These data are published in "fiscal years." From 1844 until 1976, the fiscal year ran from July 1 to June 30; in 1976 it was changed to October 1 to September 30. Thus, fiscal year 1990 included October 1, 1989, through September 30, 1990. The slight differences from the calendar year are overlooked for most research purposes.

Money

The money supply is measured by the board of governors of the U.S. Federal Reserve. Both its short-term estimates and longer-term official figures are widely available in official government publications, with analysis in many business periodicals.

Prices

Most inflation data are collected by the U.S. Labor Department's Bureau of Labor Statistics for its own price indexes, numbers that also form a large part of the U.S. Commerce Department's inflation adjustments for GNP accounting. The Bureau of Labor Statistics surveys more than one million price quotations to compute consumer and producer price indexes for a large number of products and geographic regions. These data are widely publicized: up-to-date estimates are available on telephone recordings, while historical data are published in several government documents.

Currency values are determined by market exchanges around the world, and widely publicized in newspapers and business periodicals. Composite exchange rates measuring values relative to several currencies at one time are calculated by central banks, including the U.S. Federal Reserve and the Bank of England.

CONTROVERSIES

How Much for the Military?

Two fundamental questions arise in assessing military spending. First, what is the total level of U.S. military spending? And second, how does U.S. military spending compare with Soviet Union military spending? These questions affected policy debates both when military spending was rising, and when it was reduced.

The Military Budget   During the 1988 presidential campaign, candidate Jesse Jackson called for cuts in the more than $500 billion military budget—or about $5,000 per year for every U.S. household. In response, political columnist George F. Will charged Jackson with dishonesty because the official U.S. budget listed military spending for that year at less than $300 billion. The difference between Jackson and his critics was about what constitutes military spending. The traditional government budgets included only Defense Department spending, a number used as the level of "military" spending in most popular accounts. Jackson based his figure on an estimate of "military-related" items in the budget, including: agencies other than the Defense Department such as the Energy Department, which constructs nuclear weapons, and NASA, which launches spy satellites, about $10 billion in 1987; veterans' benefits administered by the Veterans' Administration costing over $30 billion in 1987; and interest paid on debt accrued during past wars, estimated at over $70 billion in 1987.

These corrections, totaling just over $100 billion, suggest that Jackson's $500 billion estimate for the military was probably too high, but it is arguably more realistic than the $300 billion figure used in most popular accounts. In fact, the Bush administration changed the accounting procedure in 1989 to include $10 billion for non–Defense Department agencies as part of military spending in the official budget. Some economists maintain that the veterans' expenses should be included as well, and perhaps also interest payments, although this adjustment involves uncertainties about how much of past debt was due to military expenditures. Researchers should realize that expanded definitions of military spending, however reasonable, are not standard practice, and thus subject to criticism, as experienced by candidate Jackson.

The Soviet Military Budget   The most widely used estimates of Soviet military spending are calculated by the U.S. Central Intelligence Agency (CIA). Although the underlying data and methods are classified secrets, the total estimate is widely publicized by the U.S. government. Overall this official CIA estimate of Soviet military spending rose from a range of 6–8 percent of Soviet GNP for 1965–76, to 15–17 percent of GNP for 1986. This apparent growth in Soviet military spending was an important argument used in favor of increased U.S. spending buildup during the 1980s. In his first State of the Union address, President Reagan asserted, "Since 1970, the Soviet Union has invested $300 billion more in its military forces than we have." And many of President Reagan's advisers agreed with former President Richard Nixon's assessment that an "intelligence blunder" caused

Soviet military spending to be estimated at only one-half of its actual level during the 1970s.

Because so much of the data are classified, independent researchers are unable to assess the CIA reports completely. Nonetheless, experts outside the CIA maintain that enough is known about the procedures to question the assertion of presidents Reagan and Nixon that Soviet spending had increased dramatically. Contrary to widespread belief, the changes in CIA estimates were corrections in the *proportion* of the Soviet economy committed to the military, not an actual increase in military might. The major reason for these adjustments was uncertainty about how to compare U.S. and Soviet military spending when each economy uses entirely different price systems. Soviet prices, most of which were set by the central government, often had no relation to U.S. prices, most of which are set by the marketplace. For example, Soviet soldiers who are drafted earn considerably less than U.S. soldiers who have been hired in a competitive labor market since 1973. The problems are even greater for military hardware, for which there are often no Soviet prices whatsoever because weapons are not bought or sold in any market. Even in the United States, many military hardware items are purchased in noncompetitive markets which, as recent scandals have revealed, can cause extraordinarily high prices. These costs make it difficult to assess the military's use of real resources—as opposed to its use of federal budget dollars.

In 1976, the CIA revised its estimates of Soviet spending to 11–13 percent of Soviet GNP, up from a previous 6–8 percent range. According to critics this change was incorrectly interpreted as an increase in Soviet military might, when in fact the CIA primarily altered the prices estimated for military goods. In other words, the Soviet military was estimated to comprise a larger portion of the economy, but not necessarily more or better military goods. Similar price corrections were made during the 1980s, again with little commentary in popular accounts about why the changes were made. In addition, a 1983 CIA adjustment for the first time included Soviet civil defense, space activities, and internal security forces, categories that previously had not been included as military spending. As noted above, these areas were not counted in the traditional U.S. military budgets with which the Soviet budget was often compared.

In 1989, when the Soviet Union and the United States discussed reductions in military spending, the CIA estimates were still used. For example, former Reagan administration adviser Richard Pipes argued for continued high levels of U.S. military spending on the grounds that the Soviets had lied about the level of their military budget—that is, compared to official CIA estimates. While it is true that in prior years official Soviet data were not taken seriously, they were revised upward nearly fourfold in 1989 by President Gorbachev, to about 9 percent of Soviet GNP, a figure close to the estimate put forward by CIA critics.

Implications   The major lesson from the debate about Soviet spending is the need for caution in interpreting "official" data on an issue as politically sensitive as military spending. As the debate between Jackson and his critics illustrated, there is no single "correct" number for what constitutes military spending. The differences between Soviet and U.S. price systems further exacerbate comparisons of military spending. Most researchers use U.S. prices for comparison purposes because these market prices more accurately measure the use of resources. But these prices may also be distorted by the noncompetitive nature of U.S. military contracting.

It is difficult for independent researchers to confirm CIA results that are based on classified information. Nonetheless, it is important to remember the potential problems in measuring Soviet spending. Unfortunately, most media coverage of Soviet spending makes no reference to these limitations. If the critics are correct, official estimates have greatly exaggerated the Soviet threat leading the United States into a possibly unnecessary arms race that has cost many hundreds of billions of dollars, and has endangered the entire earth. One could hardly make a more convincing case for the need for researchers to understand carefully the data that lie behind policy decisions.

How Much for Welfare?

In common usage, "welfare" means assistance to the poor, or, in more technical terms, "means-tested" transfer payments, that is, programs for which recipients must prove they are poor. But a broader definition of welfare includes social programs available to everyone, such as social security, publicly funded health care, and public education. Several recent policy debates depend on which definition is used.

Does Welfare Work?   Charles Murray's 1984 book, *Losing Ground*, claimed that greatly expanded government programs for the poor, beginning with the War on Poverty in 1965, actually made matters worse for the supposed beneficiaries. In Murray's view, poverty declined *until* the government introduced misguided programs that created disincentives for the poor to work and maintain stable families.

Critics pointed out that "social welfare" as measured by Murray included a number of programs, not all of which are designed to help the poor. For example, between 1970 and 1984, means-tested spending counted for only one-seventh of the rise in total transfer payments. Most of the rest of the rise was an increase in programs for the elderly, for whom poverty indeed was reduced. In this view, means-tested programs have always been so underfunded that it is no surprise that poverty for groups other than the elderly has not been significantly reduced.

Whichever policy advice one supports for the welfare system, the debate illustrates the need to specify carefully what constitutes welfare spending. Failure to do so seriously undermined the credibility of Murray's findings.

Welfare for Everyone?   By the broad definition of welfare as including all social programs, the United States spends over 10 percent of national output on welfare, or more than $500 billion in 1990, a statistic that is used both to criticize and to defend government spending.

In a widely quoted analysis, economist Gordon Tullock argued in 1981 that there was sufficient federal transfer money to give all poor families a yearly income of $48,000—*if* all the funds were distributed to the poor. Of course, much of the most expensive government programs go to nonpoor recipients, most importantly, social security and Medicare. In Tullock's view these programs specifically, and government intervention generally, do not help those in need of welfare, but instead transfer resources to politically powerful groups.

Other researchers use the expanded definition of welfare to argue in favor of government programs. In this view, welfare works best if it is available to everyone and does not stigmatize the poor. For example, social programs in Sweden were about triple their U.S. level in 1983 (as a percentage of the total economy), providing a wide range of benefits, including health care, child care, higher education, job training, and retirement pay. Such expensive programs were justified not as a handout to the needy, but as the right of every resident.

These two views on government transfers show the importance of connotation in a politically loaded word such as welfare. In Tullock's view, welfare spending is a transfer from one group to another, sometimes to those not in need, whereas advocates of the Swedish model see welfare spending as a means to secure widespread social benefits. Researchers need to be aware of these quite different meanings.

How Big Is the Deficit?

When U.S. budget deficits reached a level of more than $100 billion during most years of the 1980s, Congress and the president felt pressured to bring the budget into closer balance. Unfortunately, one of the results was that the actual state of the government's finances was disguised. Three types of deliberate manipulation were practiced.

Selling off Government Assets   Several times during the 1980s the Reagan administration improved the apparent budgetary balance by planning to sell U.S. government assets. The 1982 "Asset Management Program" called for the sale of federal property, including large blocks of public lands. The prospective sale of the government-owned freight railroad system, Conrail, was included as revenue for the 1986 budget, and then again in 1987 when the sale was blocked for 1986. Finally, the 1988 budget included projected revenues from the sale of debts owed the government, including farm and school loans, that were to be sold to private investors for collection.

Whatever the advantages or disadvantages of public ownership for these assets—for example, environmentalists fought bitterly against the sale of public land—the sale of government assets was criticized by accountants as a one-shot injection of revenue. The deficit would fall only once and reappear the following year. In the private sector there are strict rules to prevent companies from using the sale of assets to cover up deficits.

Shifting Targets   In 1985, the U.S. Congress passed the Gramm-Rudman-Hollings Act, a mandate for continuous reductions in the deficit and a balanced budget by 1991. The Congress and the president never failed to meet each year's goals—but they also failed to cut the deficit anywhere near the Gramm-Rudman-Hollings intentions. Instead, gimmickry provided the false appearance of fiscal responsibility.

One simple procedure was to shift the military payday and some farm-support programs back into the previous year's budget. Since only this year's budget needed to be certified under Gramm-Rudman-Hollings, there was no penalty for worsening the previous year's budget. Of course, the change did not save the government a penny.

A second form of financial fudging involved moving items in and out of the budget that came under Gramm-Rudman-Hollings guidelines. For many years the government kept some items "off budget." The principle was to separate ongoing government programs from special funds such as school loans for which expenditures and repayment may not be expected to balance in any given year. But because Gramm-Rudman-Hollings applied only to on-budget items, several expensive items such as the federal government's bailout of savings and loan institutions were kept off budget. This bookkeeping trick reduced the apparent deficit by about $35 billion in 1988. On the other hand, for many years, the Social Security Trust fund had been included "on budget," a convenience of accounting that created a $50 billion shift away from the red in 1989.

Implications Fortunately for researchers many of these budget shenanigans have been relatively small, at least relative to the more than $100 billion deficits. The exceptions are items added to the budget or placed off budget. As of 1990 the savings and loan bailout was estimated to cost as much as $500 billion, while the social security surpluses were expected to continue to grow, becoming larger than the entire $3 trillion debt during the next century. In most economists' estimations, even without changing the trend in government spending and taxation, the social security surplus soon would absorb all current and past deficits. However, some time in the twenty-first century increases in social security payments as the baby boomers retire will then turn the surplus into a deficit (see chapter 2 on this point). In addition, greater than expected off-budget items such as the savings and loan insurance program, or increased losses from student loans and home mortgages could add to the deficit. Researchers need to look at both official and off-budget items to understand the total financial picture of the U.S. government. Although this difference is often overlooked in popular accounts of the budget, and in congressional compliance with Gramm-Rudman-Hollings, both sets of data are available, most readily in the annual *Economic Report of the President*.

A Debt Monster?

The U.S. federal debt, topping $3 trillion in the 1990s, is a number guaranteed to shock. The debt clock in New York City's Times Square ticked off more than $1 million every minute for most of the 1980s, totaling about $30,000 in accumulated debt for every U.S. family. Many economists agree that the deficit is a serious problem and call for policies of more taxes or reduced spending to decrease the deficit. But a contrary position is put forward by a number of influential economists, including 1988 American Economic Association president Robert Eisner and best-selling author and economist Robert Heilbroner. In their view, the fiscal problem of the U.S. government may be too little, not too much, debt.

Eisner and Heilbroner recommend several accounting corrections to the traditional definition of the debt. For example, they maintain that government accounting overstates the debt because it does not decrease the value of the debt when inflation occurs. But the major adjustment advocated by Eisner and Heilbroner is to separate government investments from other government expenditures. Analogy is made to the private sector where borrowing for investment purposes is recognized as vitally necessary. If no one incurred debt for investment, our economy would collapse: there would be no home building, no telephone system, no railroads, no other projects that require long-term financing. Of course, not all borrowing is good. For example, the bank likely will frown on a loan for a vacation or other types of consumption. But loans for housing or new equipment for a business are more likely to be approved because debt is being used for what economists call capital. These expenditures should be financed through borrowing, or we would waste time accumulating funds to pay for investments that could have been generating new economic activity.

Because many government expenditures such as bridge and road building clearly qualify as investment, Eisner and Heilbroner argue they should not be counted as a harmful part of the deficit. For 1989, Eisner attributes about $70 billion in federal government expenditures to net investment, that is, total investment less what is needed to replace worn-out older investment. If we also include state and local expenditure for education, then, according to Eisner: "the entire government budget deficit would disappear. And with it would have to go the oft-repeated charge that our budget deficits mean we are reckless with our future."

Critics object to these revised numbers on several grounds. First, they point out that deficits became a major problem during the 1980s primarily because of increased military and social security spending, neither of which is an increase in investment. Eisner responds that earlier budgets, seemingly in balance, actually were in tremendous surplus because of undifferentiated investment expenditures. Thus, increases in expenditures during the 1980s, although for consumption purposes, simply brought the budget into closer balance, not the deficit measured in traditional accounts.

Second, critics challenge Eisner's assessment of what constitutes investment. For example, Charles L. Schultze, chief economic adviser to President Carter, measures far less net investment in the federal budget, only an estimated $7 billion in 1989. Eisner and Heilbroner agree that investment is tricky to measure, and suggest that the federal government might follow the corporate model and keep a separate capital budget. In fact, many local governments already do so. But other noted economists oppose extension of the concept to the federal government because politicians would be too likely to manipulate the process to spend money without collecting taxes. Brookings Institution economist Henry J. Aaron points out that there is no independent accounting authority as exists for private corporations to insure proper bookkeeping.

The choice of deficit numbers appears to be guided by political perspective. Those opposed to government spending tend to point to the traditional high deficit numbers, while Eisner and others who have long urged more public programs, use much lower deficit estimates. Researchers need to look at several ways of measuring the deficit, choosing the appropriate statistic depending on the research project. For example, in comparing the relative advantage of spending priorities between the public and private sectors, we need to separate investment from other expenditures. Without a widely accepted U.S. government capital budget, the task is difficult, but the presence of a government deficit is in itself insufficient reason to favor private-sector spending over public spending.

Taxes

It seems a simple matter to understand taxes. After all, tax rates are public knowledge, and there are complete government records about the amount and type of taxes collected. But two factors complicate recent analysis of the U.S. tax system: first, how to measure the "fairness" of tax cuts, and second, how to measure who actually bears the burden of the tax system.

Fair Tax Cuts?   During the early 1980s the income tax rate was reduced for every taxpayer. Proponents argued that the tax cut was fair since it reduced the tax *rate* by the same proportion for every tax bracket. In other words, the top tax rate fell from 50 percent to 38.5 percent, while a middle tax rate of 20 percent fell to 15.4 percent, both a 23 percent drop in the tax rate.* Critics pointed out that in dollar amounts, the proportional tax cuts favored high-income earners, translating into more than $4,000 in savings for a $60,000 earner, versus only $460 for a $20,000 earner.

The problem was defining a "fair" tax cut. The 23 percent drop in tax rates was fair in the sense that it preserved the relative proportions of the tax system: the $60,000 earner contined to pay about nine times as much tax as the $20,000 earner. But, if fair is interpreted to mean the same savings in dollars, or even the same savings as a proportion of income, then the 1981–83 tax cuts were unfair to low- and middle-income groups. According to subsequent revelations by David Stockman, head of the administration's Office of Management and Budget at the time, there was deliberate deception in the administration's characterization of the tax cuts. The "across-the-board" label was a "Trojan horse to bring down the top [tax] rate."

Capital Gains Tax Cuts   A similar debate took place during the late 1980s about the advisability of cutting the capital gains tax, that is, the tax on profitable sale of assets such as stock or property. Common sense suggested that the rich are more likely to have assets for sale, and thus would gain from the capital gains tax cuts. But a widely publicized study of Internal Revenue Service data by former Treasury Assistant Secretary Paul Craig Roberts found that taxpayers with income under $20,000 would benefit as much as those with income over $200,000. On this basis, the *Wall Street Journal* and several political

---

*One further complication, and source of unfairness according to critics, was the prior reduction of the top bracket from 70 percent to 50 percent, a more than 23 percent cut.

leaders maintained that the change in the capital gains tax would benefit the poor as much as it would help the rich.

Other researchers pointed out that these income classifications were based on "ordinary" income (although in some reports the qualification was missing). "Ordinary" income excludes capital gains, which one critic charged is like "justifying a tax break for investment bankers on the grounds that if you don't count their income from investment banking, investment banks don't make much money." In addition, Brookings Institution economist Joseph Pechman points out that many wealthy individuals are able to use tax shelters to show low or even negative incomes on their tax returns. By not counting low incomes caused exclusively by such "losses," Pechman finds that contrary to the *Wall Street Journal*'s claims, capital gains received by those with income under $20,000 is only one-third the capital gains received by the over-$200,000 income earners. Such evidence helped defeat the capital gains tax cut during the 1989 Congress.

The lesson for researchers in both these debates is to look closely at what is called "fair." One can construct a case for the definitions of fairness used to defend the income tax and capital gains tax cuts. But in both these cases, an average citizen likely would interpret fairness differently from how it was used by government defenders of the tax cuts.

Who Bears the Tax Burden? The overall distribution of taxes among income groups is measured by what economists call the progressivity of the tax system. Taxes are progressive if tax rates increase for higher income groups. (Tax rates are regressive if they fall as one moves up the income ladder.) The most frequently cited studies of U.S. taxes were conducted by Brookings Institution economist Joseph Pechman, who also investigated the capital gains tax as described above. Pechman's research illustrates the problems in measuring the tax rate for different income groups.

At the Brookings Institution, Pechman used a data set called the MERGE files, which combined Internal Revenue Service tax returns with Census Bureau data on the characteristics of households. (Because neither the Internal Revenue Service nor the Census Bureau allows individuals to be identified specifically, a computer program "matched" tax data with similar households from the Census Bureau; in large numbers the procedure approximates what would happen if both tax and census data were available for the same households.)

The major challenge to Pechman and other researchers using the MERGE files was determining the allocation of taxes that can be passed on to parties other than those from whom the tax is collected. Consider social security taxes. Most economists agree that workers bear the burden not only for the approximately 7.5 percent taken out of their paychecks, but also for the equivalent sum paid by employers that is likely passed on to workers as lower wages and salaries. Similar problems occur in assessing the impact of other taxes such as the sales tax, some of which may be absorbed by sellers, property taxes that may be passed on to renters, and corporate income taxes passed on to consumers in higher prices.

The 1986 Pechman study included eight variations of possible assumptions about the ultimate bearer of the tax burden. For example, one variant assumed that employees ultimately paid the employer portion of social security taxes, and that property and corporate taxes were paid by property owners and stockholders rather than being passed on to consumers. By these assumptions, the tax system was most progressive, ranging in 1980 from about 20 percent taxation for the poorest one-tenth of the population to about 27 percent for the top one-tenth. Other assumptions measured far less progressivity, or in some cases a regressive system in which the total tax rate is higher on the poor than on the rich. According to Pechman, these results show that "the tax system has very little effect on the distribution of income," and that the United States could increase the progressivity of the tax system "without punitive tax rates that will hurt economic incentives."

On the other side, supporters of President Reagan's 1980s tax cuts maintained that the tax system hurt incentives because tax rates were in fact far more progressive than Pechman had found. A persistent critic of Pechman's findings was Edgar K. Browning. In a 1976 study for the American Enterprise Institute, Browning and his colleagues measured considerable overall progressivity in the tax system, ranging from less than 12 percent for the lowest income group to more than 38 percent for the top income group.

One reason Browning measured more progressively was that he took into account the effect of transfer payments such as social security, Aid to Families with Dependent Children, and food stamps. Browning pointed out that including these programs, which are untaxed, causes the tax system to become more progressive because the poor receive income that is not taxed. In a 1986 debate with Browning,

Pechman accepted this revision, but rejected Browning's claim that the overall trend in tax system was toward progressivity. According to Pechman, gains from transfers to low-income earners were offset by increases in social security taxes. Moreover, reductions in taxes for high-income groups caused taxes for the top 1 percent to fall from 39.6 percent in 1966 to only 25.3 percent in 1985.

In textbooks and popular media articles, tax rates are often presented without any discussion of these controversies about how to measure the tax burden for different income groups. Some conclusions are not disputed, such as the progressivity of the federal personal income tax over the range of low to middle incomes and regressivity of the social security tax between middle- and high-income groups. But most other estimates require assumptions that change the effective tax rates. In assessing the state of the current tax system and in understanding the effect of new tax rates, researchers must pay careful attention to controversies about the underlying assumptions.

Measuring Money

In the United States, both measurement and policy making for financial affairs rests primarily with the Federal Reserve System, a quasi-independent branch of government. (Similar central banking organizations exist in most other countries.) The Federal Reserve, or Fed as it is more commonly known, runs its own statistical gathering operation, gathering data on national production (see chapter 7) and financial affairs, most importantly, measurement of the money supply.

What Is Money? Economists use the term "money" in a far more complex manner than everyday usage would suggest. As defined by economists, money includes not just the coins and currency commonly called money, but also bank deposits that exist only on bank accounting sheets. The measurement challenge is determining which bank accounts should count as money. At stake are important economic policies, as well as many research projects that require a measure of the money supply.

Federal Reserve publication of money data began during the 1940s, based on surveys of banking institutions. Today daily reporting from approximately 10,000 large banks is supplemented by less regular reporting from smaller banks. Beginning in 1960, these numbers have been published as "monetary aggregates." Since then, money supply statistics have been expanded and redefined to take into account the changing financial system, as well as changing economists' views about the most appropriate measure of money. As of 1990, the two major definitions were labeled simply M1 and M2 based on the ease with which funds can be spent, a criterion called liquidity. M1, about $750 billion in 1987, includes only coins, currency, and checking accounts, funds readily available for use, whereas M2, about $2,900 billion in 1987, includes these money supplies plus savings accounts and money market accounts, funds less likely to be spent in the near future on goods and services.

At times the Federal Reserve has used M1 and M2 as key policy targets. For example, during the early 1980s the Federal Reserve set quite restrictive goals for M1 and M2 in an attempt to lower the inflation rate. In theory it should have been possible to control inflation by increasing the money supply at a noninflationary rate. Economists are divided about the efficacy of this experiment: inflation was reduced, but at enormous cost in unemployment and lost production. There is general agreement, however, that measurement problems made it difficult to use the money supply as a policy target.

At almost precisely the same time that the Federal Reserve started to target the money supply, the relationship between the money supply measures and the overall economy became especially erratic. Because of bank deregulation initiated during the late 1970s, there was unprecedented movement of money into new types of bank and money market accounts. As a result, M1 and M2 fluctuated when funds moved between bank accounts, confounding attempts to use them as indicators of the inflationary pressures in the underlying economy. Most economists and financial analysts applauded the 1983 decision by the Federal Reserve to abandon its single-minded attention to money supply statistics, and to expand its targets to include a number of economic variables such as interest rates and the growth in economic production.

Missing Currency?   Do you have $1,000 in your pocket? Probably not, although more than this amount of U.S. coins and currency is in circulation for every U.S. adult. Not all of this cash belongs to individuals; some cash lies in vending machines, business cash registers, and banks. But economists believe these locations account for little of the currency excess. Instead much of the missing money is likely held by drug dealers and other members of the underground economy who hold on to large amounts of cash because of disclosure rules when these sums are deposited in banks. No one knows how much money can be accounted for in this way. A second location for the missing money is currency held by foreigners, in particular in Latin American and Eastern Europe where dollars are valued as a stable form of money. Again, economists can only guess how many dollars circulate in these countries.

A number of important issues are at stake in tracking this money. As described in chapter 7, the appropriate response to the underground economy depends on its size, often estimated by the value of unaccounted-for currency. Dollars that flow overseas create a temporary windfall for the United States because imported products can be bought without foreigners using the money to demand U.S. products. In the long run, if the process reverses, there could be a sudden inflation-causing flow of dollars back into the United States. Finally, for both the United States and recipients of dollars, the dollar flow makes it difficult for monetary authorities to measure and control the money supply.

In summary, the problems in measuring the money supply are both conceptual—what to include in the money supply?—as well as practical—where is the missing currency? The interpretation of money supply statistics is an ongoing controversy among economists. These disputes illustrate the lack of precision, even in a statistic that one might think could be measured accurately.

Inflation

One of the most common problems in social science research and policy making is how to adjust variables for the effect of inflation. Although inflation adjustments are readily available from U.S. government agencies, the correct use of these adjustments is critical for accurate research as well as for appropriate inflation indexing in many labor union contracts, the social security system, and the income tax.

The most commonly used inflation rates are measured by the rates of change in the U.S. Commerce Department's Personal Consumption Expenditure's deflator (PCE) and the Labor Department's Consumer Price Index (CPI). Usually these statistics move up and down together, measuring approximately the same rate of inflation. For example, the oil shortage inflation of the late 1970s caused the inflation rate measured in both the PCE and the CPI to nearly double, reaching 10.7 and 13.5 percent respectively in 1980. However, the difference between the two inflation rates is indicative of a fundamental problem that has caused bitter policy disputes about the best way to measure inflation.

The Cost of Housing   There are a number of technical reasons why it is difficult to measure inflation, but in recent years one factor alone, the rapid increase in the cost of housing, has been responsible for most of the variation between different inflation rates. Two different problems complicate the measurement of home prices. First, rising interest rates frequently cause consumers to postpone home buying. Does a price increase add to overall inflation if consumers stop buying the product? In other words, should inflation measure what consumers would have paid if they bought housing as frequently as they did before prices rose? Or should inflation measure the actual cost of living, even if products are no longer purchased because of inflation?

A second difficulty in accounting for rising home prices is the investment aspect of housing. Consumers are compensated for rising home prices by the prospect of selling the house at a yet higher price. In this case, should we count housing inflation as much as for other products such as food, where price increases cannot be recouped through subsequent sale?

During the early 1980s these problems with home prices caused a major overhaul in the commonly used measures of inflation. At that time critics charged that the CPI gave greater weight to home purchases than was actually occurring in the depressed housing market, and did not correct for the increasing asset value of housing. An exaggerated rate of inflation in the CPI allegedly caused too-generous pay increases in union contracts and social security payments. The PCE was recommended as a better measure of inflation because it was based on rental costs that were not as strongly affected by interest rates.

Officials at the Labor Department's Bureau of Labor Statistics experimented with new versions of the CPI, introducing a new CPI statistic in 1983 that measured housing costs by their rental equivalence, essentially estimating how much it would cost to rent homes that actually are purchased. In this way, the bureau hoped to smooth out the effect of fluctuating interest rates, and to leave out the investment component of housing expenses. The new statistic was widely adopted for research purposes and used for indexing the federal income tax, social security payments, and other government programs.

In the years immediately after the new CPI was introduced, the problem with measuring housing prices receded somewhat. Falling interest rates meant that there was less difference between the new rental equivalence and the old homeownership cost estimate. As a result, for most of the 1980s, the new CPI was only slightly different from the old CPI, and programs adjusted to the CPI were not greatly affected by the new method for measuring inflation.

Change the CPI, Reduce Poverty   In 1989, however, the U.S. Census Bureau proposed that the new CPI be used *retroactively* to adjust the poverty line. Since its introduction in 1965, the poverty line had been increased along with the rate of inflation as measured in the CPI (see chapter 8). The new CPI methodology caused only imperceptible changes in the measurement of poverty after 1983. But for the years prior to 1983, the new rental equivalence method measured far less inflation than the old CPI statistic. By applying this new method retroactively to the years 1967 through 1983, the poverty line would be reduced substantially. For example, the 1988 poverty line for a family of four would fall from $12,092 to $10,997. Overall, the 1988 poverty rate would drop from 13.1 percent to 11.6 percent. This change would have caused cutbacks in government programs such as food stamps, free school lunches, Medicaid, and Head Start, for which recipients must prove their poverty status.

The new method for measuring poverty was not adopted, in part because of protests against its inequities. The proposal underscores, however, the importance of how inflation is measured. In this case, about 3.5 million people would have been "lifted" out of poverty simply because of seemingly minor differences in the measurement of housing costs. Those involved in public programs, and researchers (see Box 11.1) need to understand the potential effects of alternative inflation statistics.

Currency Rates

Converting currency values between countries is a common social science problem, providing a challenge in the interpretation of data from

---

Box 11.1. **CPI or PCE: Watch Out!**

When economists Bennett Harrison and Barry Bluestone published research showing an increase in low-pay jobs during the late 1970s and early 1980s (see chapter 8), critics charged that the results depended on use of the old CPI, a deliberate deception according to one newspaper account. Nonspecialist readers who probably had never heard of the different inflation indexes were regaled with the advantages of the PCE and the new CPI. Eventually Bluestone and Harrison were able to affirm their main findings. Recalculation using the new CPI, and other research using the PCE, measured a predominance of low-pay jobs. In the meantime, however, their credibility and policy advice were called into question. Congress's Joint Economic Committee, sponsors of Bluestone and Harrison's original study, instructed future researchers to use both the CPI and the PCE. Such caution is warranted for studies of income and other money amounts measured over time. A repeated lesson in this book has been the need for researchers to demonstrate the robustness of results under different assumptions.

---

different countries. Many comparisons depend critically on how prices are converted to a common currency.

The Problem of Many Currencies   Newspaper and magazine financial pages show the daily ups and downs of world currencies relative to one another. For example, on February 28, 1990, the U.S. dollar was up slightly against the Japanese yen, but down relative to the Canadian dollar. But many research projects require a statistic for the *overall* movement in the dollar. Common sense suggests that in measuring the value of the U.S. dollar we should count currency changes more for top trading partners such as Japan and Canada, than changes relative to Swedish or Spanish currencies, with whom the United States does less trade. In fact, just such "trade-weighted indexes" are calculated by the U.S. Federal Reserve Bank and the Bank of England. But differences in the methods for calculating these indexes cause research and policy-making confusion.

During the 1980s, the most commonly cited index was the Federal Reserve Board weighted value based on trade with ten countries: Germany, France, the United Kingdom, Belgium, Italy, Sweden, Spain, Switzerland, Canada, and Japan. This short list was sensible in 1972 when these countries accounted for most U.S. trade. But increasing trade with Korea, Mexico, Taiwan, and Brazil quickly made the index obsolete. When the dollar fell by 32 percent in 1985 and 1986 (based on the traditional index), U.S. imports should have declined because of higher prices for goods produced in other countries. Instead imports went up. The apparent paradox was explained in part by an *increase* in the value of the dollar relative to other countries not counted in the Federal Reserve index.

For some purposes, such as studying money management, the traditionally weighted index makes sense because international speculation occurs mostly between the ten major currencies. But for research on trade, as for example understanding the failure of trade deficit to fall in 1986, alternative trade-weighted indexes are needed such as one developed by an economist at the Dallas Federal Reserve Bank that includes all 131 countries trading with the United States. But even this more complete statistic will fail if it is not continually updated to take into account future changes in which countries trade with which others.

The Problem of Fluctuating Exchange Rates   After the 1973 introduction of floating exchange rates for most of the world's currencies, researchers faced an ongoing problem comparing well-being between countries. When the dollar is rising, as it did for many years during the 1980s, other countries appear to be much worse off. For example, during the early 1980s Germans appeared to be losing income as measured in dollars, although by other measures the German economy was doing well.

The problem is that comparative prices can be whipsawed by fast-changing exchange rates, at the same time that the volume of goods and services is unchanged. In order to focus on actual production, as opposed to comparative price changes, economists recommend a statistic called "Purchasing Power Parity," calculated by the Organization for Economic Cooperation and Development (OECD). Using this method, 1984 well-being was 32 percent higher in Germany than measured by currency exchange rates.

Popular accounts and some research continue to use traditional exchange rates for international price comparisons. In studying trade and travel, this is usually the correct approach. But when comparing living standards, it is preferable to use the less well known estimates for actual purchasing power. Otherwise, comparisons will be distorted in favor of the United States when the dollar rises, and in the opposite direction when the dollar falls.

The Problem of Unofficial Exchange Rates   A final problem in currency conversion is the existence of unofficial or black-market exchange rates. In a dramatic case, during the 1989 economic dislocation in East Germany, black market rates were more than ten times as high as official rates. Comparisons of East and West German production varied by a several-fold factor, depending how one compromised between these vastly different exchange rates. More market-oriented economies in Eastern Europe will ease this statistical conundrum; indeed, one motivation for introducing market prices is to facilitate trade with other countries. But in any situation where currency exchange controls exist, as for example in many Latin American countries, there may be unofficial money exchange. Research that looks at only the official rate may not accurately measure the actual price differences between countries.

Implications   Correcting prices for the effects of inflation and different currency values is a problem in research on a wide range of issues. Cost data on health, housing, and crime, as well as economic data on incomes, businesses, and government, usually must be adjusted for inflation if different time periods are compared, or for currency values if different countries are compared. The controversies described here serve as an introduction to these adjustments, and as a caution to their use. The overall lesson is that researchers should investigate alternative measures of inflation and currency value that would demonstrate how results change when different adjustments are used. Alternatively, if one measure of inflation or currency value is considered to be more accurate, then its use should be carefully justified.

SUMMARY

Data covered in this chapter have the advantage of accuracy in the sense that the numbers come from complete counts rather than surveys. Even inflation measures that do rely on survey data are derived from such massive samples that sampling error is not an issue. Instead, the problem for researchers is choosing which numbers to use. In the case of government budgets, inflation rates, and currency values, there is a choice between conflicting official statistics. For military spending and the deficit, official data are challenged by alternative data based on quite different accounting techniques. Finally, "welfare spending" and "fair taxes" have been shown to generate different statistics and opposite conclusions depending on how the terms are defined.

As this chapter demonstrates, "official government data" are not the only data available, nor always the most appropriate. But when an alternative statistic is used, explicit discussion of the choice is necessary. Jesse Jackson's use of alternative measures for military spending, for example, although quite reasonable, was easily criticized because he did not explain his use of nonstandard data. Another solution is to test research hypotheses based on varying assumptions. Especially in the case of inflation adjustment, research results are far more convincing if they do not change significantly when alternative statistics are used.

CASE STUDY QUESTIONS

1. The proportion of the U.S. money supply in $100 bills increased from 42 percent in 1982 to 49 percent in 1989. What might explain this change?

2. Studies of taxes often focus on federal taxes. But state and local taxes often take a bigger bite out of income, in particular for low-income groups. Estimate the regressive or progressive effect of state and local taxes where you live.

3. Some advocates of continued increases in U.S. military spending in 1990 argued that the Soviet Union spent 16 percent of its national economy on the military, more than double the proportion spent by the United States. How might this comparison overstate the difference in spending?

4. The proportion of the U.S. budget designated as investment depends critically on whether military spending is counted as investment or as consumption. Which components of military spending might be counted correctly as productive investment?

5. The CPI's methodology has changed over time, for example, in 1983 to count housing differently, and in 1987 to take into account different product purchases. But these changes are not used to revise *past* official estimates for the CPI. Why would such changes cause a legal and administrative nightmare?

	Old (1972–73)	New (1982–84)
Housing	38.1%	42.9%
Food	19.0%	16.2%
Fuel and utilities	7.5%	7.9%
Medical care	6.9%	5.4%

6. In 1987 the Consumer Price Index was revised to take into account changing household spending patterns, measured for 1982–84, replacing the old patterns based on a 1972–73 survey. Some of the spending patterns are listed above.

a) Can you suggest reasons why these categories shifted in importance?

b) Explain the surprisingly downward trend in the medical care proportion of spending. (Hint: Overall, many medical costs are paid by government, and employer-sponsored medical insurance is not counted as a consumer expense.)

c) How might spending patterns differ for the elderly? How could this difference cause social security increases based on the CPI to be too high or too low?

Chapter 12

Conclusions

Students of statistics soon learn that there is a dazzling array of mathematical techniques for analyzing data, testing hypotheses, and estimating the probability of error. However, the controversies reviewed in this book suggest that students and practitioners alike need to look more closely at the limitations of the data to which the sophisticated techniques are applied. Repeatedly the origin of policy disputes can be traced to questions about the underlying data: Why are some data reported as fact to the exclusion of other equally reputable data? Why are only certain data collected? Why are the data organized into particular categories? And why do the data so often generate apparently conflicting statistics? In order to answer these questions, it is convenient to divide the controversies discussed in the previous chapters into five major groups: headline makers; truth by repetition; missing statistics; the "social" in statistics; and mathematical concepts.

HEADLINE MAKERS

A few of the controversies involve egregious examples of misused statistics, the extreme of Disraeli's lies, damn lies, and statistics. In this category were statistics on the marriageability of older women, the rise of "youth" crime, the number of missing children, the number of undocumented immigrants, and the income of divorced women. In each case, the controversies were started by eye-catching popular articles that carried alarming messages, although not ones supported by careful examination of the underlying data. Moreover, each example exploited fear: older women will not marry; youth today are out of control; our children are likely to be abducted; and the United States is inundated with immigrants. Such reinforcement of stereotypical views is a tempting trap for newspapers and magazine writers who are looking for provocative headlines. Because articles that told the opposite side were published in academic journals, but not in the popular media, most readers learned only the original misleading statistics.

Part of the reason why the countervailing statistics received little attention was that those who might have publicized them were relatively powerless. In other words, the subjects of the articles, middle-aged women, children, and immigrants, had little access to the media that might have distributed alternative information. This situation of uncorrected statistical falsehood stands in contrast to disputed statistics involving corporate profits and wealthy individuals which prompted widely disseminated corrections to the original, ostensibly faulty, numbers. In general, we are likely to learn about disputed data when the issue involves the rich and powerful more often than when the controversies concern data involving the poor and powerless.

TRUTH BY REPETITION

A second group of statistical controversies were not actually incorrect, only misleading. The examples are numerous, and include: the personal savings rate, the number of homeless people, the illiteracy rate, GNP for poor countries, average family income, the Dow Jones Industrial Average, the *Fortune 500*, the size of the population one hundred years from now, productivity rates, and the cancer survival rate. In addition, there were statistics for which short-term changes were mistaken for long-term trends. Such examples included: quarterly estimates of GNP, monthly trade statistics, yearly crime rates, monthly unemployment rates, and yearly educational attainment statistics.

These statistics were cited in popular and academic articles even though experts warned about their misleading characteristics. Readers may consult discussion in previous chapters for the reasons why these statistics are misleading. The question remains: why were the discredited statistics still used? The answer appears to be a similar situation to the problem with sensationalist statistics: the numbers tell a good story. It was far easier to lament the decline in personal savings and a rising crime rate, or celebrate increased cancer survival rates and increased GNP, than to investigate the more complicated, but truthful, interpretation of these statistics. In an ironic twist, misleading statistics such as the Dow Jones averages and *Fortune 500* list have become important simply because they are perceived as important. Thus, the stock market responds to the Dow Jones, even though it is a poor measure of the overall stock market. And corporations take note of their status in the *Fortune 500*, even though accountants know it can be a misleading measure of corporate success.

This split between what the experts know and common usage of statistics has contributed to oversimplified analysis of policy issues. For example, in the study of illiteracy and of homelessness, popular accounts and even some research efforts focused on an attempt to reduce the social problem to a single number, thereby shifting discussion away from critical issues. There was more public debate about the precise illiteracy rate than about the more fundamental issue of what kind of literacy is necessary to function adequately in the United States. Similarly, there was a bitter dispute about the number of homeless people, without much understanding that homelessness was a transitory phase for a much larger number of individuals facing the problem of housing displacement. And finally, many popular media articles raised doubts about the future of social security based on the anticipated increase in the ratio of social security recipients to the working population. Although this statistic likely is correct, reports of it conveniently ignored an offsetting decline in the number of young people which will keep the ratio of dependents below its level during the 1960s and 1970s. In this case, oversimplification may have caused unnecessary concern about the current structure of the social security system and premature changes in its financing.

A second problem with oversimplification was the tendency to bias statistical reporting in favor of existing institutional arrangements. If complex analysis is sidestepped, then those who disseminate statistics can choose the simplification that benefits their interests. For example, in the field of cancer research, experts understand the limitation of survival rate statistics. Yet there is evidence that those who benefited from existing research budgets were willing to use oversimplified survival rate statistics to lobby for additional research funds on ways to extend cancer survival at the expense of funding research on cancer prevention.

In the field of crime prevention, it is widely recognized that the predominant measures of crime overemphasize some crimes while overlooking others. But official reports on crime, usually put out by the same agencies that operate the criminal justice system, typically ignore these caveats that might question their funding priorities. Similarly, key economic variables such as GNP and unemployment are reported by government officials in a manner that supports the success of their economic policies, even though professional economists are well aware of the limitations to these statistics.

The lesson for researchers again is to be skeptical. Statistics that gain credence because of repeated use may not be so well regarded by experts who know the limitations of the underlying data.

WHAT'S MISSING?

For some controversies the problem was simply the absence of appropriate statistics altogether. Researchers face a near dead end in trying to study the extent of white-collar crime. For the study of individual wealth there are some sources of data, but as illustrated by the controversy about the interpretation of Federal Reserve Board survey data, these statistics are quite incomplete. Similarly, only partial information is available on corporate management, corporate ownership, and line-of-business reporting. All of these cases involve data about those with power, and it does not require a conspiracy theory to argue that these individuals and groups are unwilling to participate in data-collection efforts in part out of a desire to protect their own status. From their perspective, little would be gained by sharing data on their position; on the contrary, social statistics might be used to argue that limits should be placed on their status.

The absence of other statistics can be traced to political conflict. During the 1980s, a number of statistical series were dropped by the U.S. government, including line-of-business reporting for diversified corporations, spendable weekly earnings as a measure of typical income, unemployment rates for New York City and Los Angeles, data on "small" strikes involving few workers, and education data on school busing and gender discrimination in teaching. The choice of which statistics were dropped seems to have been an obvious attempt to restrict research that took a certain point of view, in this case statistics that were embarrassing to the administration in power at the time.

From the other end of the economic and status ladder, the poor and the powerless are subject to considerable data-collection efforts. There are numerous studies of poverty, government income maintenance programs, the homeless, and the unemployed, especially in comparison to the handful of studies of wealth and high incomes. The ability of the powerful to avoid statistical efforts raises the question of what interest the poor or middle-income groups have in complying with data collection. The controversies described in this book suggest that the numbers are beneficial for these groups. An accurate measure of the poverty rate can be used to argue for more poverty programs; a complete picture of housing inadequacy (not just homelessness) can be used to argue for new housing programs; a complete count of unemployment can be used to argue in favor of new jobs programs. Of course, alternative statistics have been used to argue against each of these programs. But on balance better numbers weigh in favor of those without other resources to present their case.

WHAT'S "SOCIAL" IN SOCIAL SCIENCE STATISTICS

The third and by far largest category reviewed in this book involves controversies in which there were at least two apparently contradictory statistics. Here the situation is more complex than the problem of trendy headlines, misleading statistics, or missing statistics. For most controversies the numbers are not simply wrong or absent. Instead, apparently conflicting statistics occur because of the different ways in which the underlying data were organized into categories. This critical step of conceptualization is often overlooked even though it is fundamental to all subsequent use of data.

Racial classification is an obvious case in which there has been little recognition in research projects of the social construction of the categories. In retrospect, we can easily see the arbitrary and racist character of the 1790 U.S. Census three-fifths apportionment allocation for each black slave and the subsequent pseudo-scientific classification based on "quadroons" and "octoroons." But the current use of self-classification still reflects the older racist standard in the sense that partial black background usually means the individual is considered black. As a rebuttal to scientific racism, it is important to remember the social, not genetic, basis of the black and white racial categories.

The classification of Hispanics and Asians further demonstrates the arbitrary choice of which groups will be counted as separate "races" and the problems in defining the boundaries between these groups. As in the black-white dichotomy, the classification began from a white perspective in which all Hispanics and all Asians were grouped together, even though many individuals in the groups did not recognize such classification, typically preferring a country-of-origin label. Because of successful political efforts by Hispanic and Asian groups, these designations have changed with almost every census, which has been an inconvenience for research covering different time periods, but is nonetheless an important reminder of the social origins of race and ethnic designations.

For other controversies there were similar, if less dramatic, problems in classifying the underlying data. In studying crime, for example, researchers must define which crimes will be counted as crime before there can be any consideration of the crime rate, the causes of crime, or the effectiveness of responses to crime. Most importantly, the manner in which white-collar crime is treated—or ignored—in official statistics causes entirely different analysis of who commits crimes and the efficacy of current allocation of resources to deal with crime. Specifically, if white-collar crime is counted, then much more crime is associated with high-income and high-status groups, and police resources aimed at white-collar crime are lacking compared with the amount spent to deal with traditionally defined crimes.

Many of the other statistical controversies were based on conceptual problems in economic theory. The clearest examples came from GNP statistics for which there are debates about how to account for pollution, resource depletion, the underground economy, and nonmarket production. Similarly, conceptual problems arose in accounting for housing: is it a consumption expense, or an investment? Tax incidence required a number of theoretical assumptions about the ability of employers, landlords, and producers to pass the costs of taxes along to other groups. The measurement of the money supply involved complex issues of which types of assets serve as money. And the choice of categories affected the measurement of housing affordability, the overall price index, and the size of U.S. budget deficits.

It is beyond the scope of this book to resolve any of these controversies in economic theory. Yet it is important for researchers to realize the degree to which economists dispute some of the most fundamental numbers used to describe the U.S. economy. The questionable accuracy of economic data may be humbling to economists, but is often suggested within the profession as a necessary corrective to the advanced state of economic mathematical techniques. Without certainty about the underlying data, the most sophisticated economic model cannot be put to practical use.

THE MATHEMATICS OF SOCIAL SCIENCE STATISTICS

The issue of conceptualization occurred for some statistics that one might consider free of theoretical decisions about social categories. Controversy about the inflation rate, for example, might be mistaken simply for a mathematical issue about how to take into account the effect of many products with changing prices. But this issue, called the "index number problem" by statisticians, in fact involves choices about how much each product will be counted in the inflation index. For example, different weights attached to different housing costs caused considerable variation in the official inflation rate during the early 1980s. The measurement of housing quality also was an index number problem based on a choice between different indicators of housing quality. Which of the housing problems were chosen—rats, leaking roofs, and so on—affected the measures of the trend in overall quality. Estimates for the level of Soviet military spending, the measurement of currency rates in different countries, and the measurement of productivity for an economy with a changing product mix also involved similar indexing problems for which there was no single correct solution.

A second mathematical issue that required conceptual decisions was the choice between absolute and relative statistics. In order to measure the extent of poverty, researchers must choose between various poverty lines, some of which are constant, or nearly so, in terms of the standard of living they represent, while others measure poverty as relative to current living standards, even if those standards have increased in terms of buying power. The debate about the trend in infant mortality also hinged on the distinction between absolute and relative change. Compared to high levels of the past, U.S. infant mortality has declined, an absolute improvement. But on a relative basis compared to other countries, U.S. infant mortality is a singular measure of health care failure.

The issue of means and medians was critical for two statistical disputes discussed in this book: longevity for cancer patients and income. These dissimilar social issues share the common problem of an asymmetric distribution in which there is a large cluster in the low end (short survival, low incomes), and a few individuals at the high end (long survival, high incomes). The resulting difference between the mean and median requires researchers to pay careful attention to which measure is appropriate for a particular project.

Finally, the mathematical problem of projecting future statistics from current data was a controversial issue in several fields. Attempts to predict future crime incidence, the marriage rate of older women, and the future birth rate all suffered from the common problem of conservative assumptions in which current social conditions were assumed to continue. Too often these predictions carry the weight of mathematical certainty, when in fact society may change—indeed one purpose of social statistics can be to demonstrate precisely the need for those changes.

In summary, the mathematical complexities of social statistics also involve the problem of conceptualization. Thus, mathematical techniques—index numbers, means, medians, absolute and relative measures—all require the researcher to make choices about theoretical categories. Because of the complexities involved in learning the mathematical techniques, it is easy to overlook these underlying assumptions about how to organize the data, but they are critical for understanding precisely what is being measured and why there often are conflicting statistics for the same social issue.

WHAT'S A RESEARCHER TO DO?

The five major problems with social statistics—headline makers, error by repetition, missing statistics, lack of attention to social categories, and mathematical complications—all point to one remedy: data literacy. By better understanding the data that are used to create social statistics, we will be better equipped to understand complex social issues.

Ironically, the starting point for a critical view of the data may be an appreciation of the extensive data available to us. Many readers likely will share the amazement I felt in preparing this book at the sheer volume of U.S. social statistics. In addition to the well-known U.S. Census and Current Population Survey, there are large-scale U.S. surveys of housing, education, crime, crime victims, health, small business, large business, and a variety of demographic characteristics. Although some areas, such as health, enjoy larger and more complete surveys than, for example, education, nonetheless researchers in every field are confronted with ever-growing quantities of data, much of which is published by the government without further expert analysis. For social science students there is little prospect that they will run out of numbers to examine; the challenge is to use them correctly.

A second step toward data literacy is an appreciation of why we have so much data. Without political pressure, little of the vast U.S. data resources would have been collected. For example, the U.S. Census, which we may now take for granted, was not undertaken to provide a data set for researchers. Instead, the men who drafted the U.S. Constitution realized that the new democratic features of the government required statistics to determine the proportional representation from each state. Several methods were considered, including property values, before the concept of representation based on population was adopted (that is, except for slaves who were counted as three-fifths of a person). Thus, although women, children, alien residents, and slaves could not vote, representational apportionment still required a complete population count.

Political pressure during the Progressive Era on the dangers of U.S. workplaces provided the pressure for the first U.S. Bureau of Labor Statistics investigation and publication of workplace health and safety. In 1930, political leaders, who wanted statistical evidence of the severity of the depression, campaigned for better employment statistics in the census. Continued political lobbying led to the post–World War II Current Population Survey and its emphasis on employment statistics. In business statistics as well, it took pressure from those concerned about the power of large corporations to generate data used for antitrust enforcement as well as general research on the structure of markets in the U.S. economy.

These examples underscore the social nature of social science statistics. A society chooses what to measure—or better stated, groups within society struggle about what will be measured. The decisions to count all residents in the census, to document workplace hazards, to survey unemployment in great detail, and to measure how corporations dominate certain industries are all evidence that groups traditionally without power can use statistics as a resource to their advantage. On the other hand, the cutbacks in statistical efforts described above show how the numbers can be taken away as well. Overall, good statistics bring us closer to the truth, even when that truth undermines the authority of those in power.

A third step toward data literacy is an appreciation of the people behind the numbers. Among those who have traditionally fought for more and better social statistics are the men and women who collect and analyze the numbers for federal, state, and local governments. One might be tempted to respond that these individuals benefit personally from increased statistical collection. That is: the more numbers, the more jobs. But anyone who has consulted government statisticians is unlikely to take such a cynical view. The jobs are not well paid, the work is often tedious, and the rewards in terms of recognition are slim—that is, unless a statistician makes an error.

Most of all, many of these individuals are eager to talk about the numbers to which they have dedicated their work lives. Certainly no one is better prepared to discuss problems in the data, and quite often it is government statisticians who warn outside users about the limits of the statistics for research and policy purposes. In other words, for the most part, government statisticians are not blind to errors in the numbers they carefully generate, but instead these government workers tend to be advocates of careful scholarship and appropriate use of statistics.

Researchers can make use of this vital source of knowledge. There are many helpful reference works published by government statistical agencies, and it is often possible to consult directly with the government officials responsible for a particular data series. Unfortunately, the budget cutbacks of the 1980s hit hardest at the regional level, but there are still some offices for U.S. federal agencies outside of Washington, D.C. State and local statistical information services vary greatly in quality, but in some locations, they equal federal authorities in terms of data collection and public access.

Data literacy is critical for playing the Data Game. By understanding what data are available, how they came to be collected, and who is responsible for their dissemination, we can begin to use social statistics to understand the society in which we live. Statistics alone will not provide a roadmap to a better world; they can only set a framework for our powers of analysis. But the more data literate we are, the more power we have to create a world of our own choosing.

Notes

Chapter 2: Demography

DATA SOURCES

U.S. Census

History of U.S. Census in Patricia Cohen, *A Calculating People* (Chicago: University of Chicago Press, 1982); Margo J. Anderson, *The American Census: A Social History* (New Haven, Conn.: Yale University Press, 1988); current U.S. Census methods in Bryant Robey, "Two Hundred Years and Counting: The 1990 Census," *Population Bulletin 44* (April 1989); Hazard census data in U.S. Bureau of the Census, *Census of Population*, "General Social and Economic Characteristics, Part 19," PC80-1-C19 Kentucky (Washington, D.C.: U.S. Government Printing Office, 1983), p. 45.

Vital Statistics

Marriage and divorce statistics described in Nancy D. Pearch, *Data Systems of the National Center for Health Statistics*, Vital and Health Statistics, Series I; no. 16 (Washington, D.C.: U.S. Government Printing Office, 1981), p. 4; Donald J. Bogue, *Population of the United States* (New York: Free Press, 1985), pp. 165, 194–95; Larry L. Bumpass and James A. Sweet, *American Families and Households* (New York: Russell Sage Foundation, 1987), chaps. 2 and 5; data sample in National Center for Health Statistics, *Vital Statistics of the United States, 1987*, vol. 1, Natality, PHS-89-1100 (Washington, D.C.: U.S. Government Printing Office, 1989), p. 118.

CONTROVERSIES

The Population Undercount

In-person enumeration in Robey, *Two Hundred Years*, pp. 10–14. Undercount controversy in "Census Subject to Possible Correction," *Population Today 17*, 9

(September 1989):3ff; Dudley Kirk, "Pol Demography," *Society 18* (January–February 1981):22–25; "Census Mired in Dispute over Counting the Hidden," *Los Angeles Times*, March 15, 1989, p. 1; Reynolds Farley and Walter R. Allen, *The Color Line and the Quality of Life in America* (New York: Oxford University Press, 1987), pp. 420–38; cost to New York City in "Census Mired in Dispute," p. 19. Lawsuit in ibid. and "Accord on Census May Bring Change in Minority Data," *New York Times*, July 18, 1989, p. A-1. "Decision was politically motivated," and "Commerce canned the project," in "Plan to Assess Census Undercounting Dropped," *Science 239* (January 9, 1988), 456; Farley and Allen, *The Color Line*, pp. 424–25.

Box 2.1 Undercount in History

Jefferson to Washington in Robey, "Two Hundred Years," p. 35; 1870 census in Anderson, *American Census*, p. 89.

Undocumented Immigrants

Lawsuit in Frank D. Bean and Rodolfo O. de la Garza, "Illegal Aliens and Census Counts," *Society* (March/April 1988):48–53; "Lawsuit Challenges Census on Illegal Aliens," *New York Times*, February 18, 1988, p. A-16. "Army of Russian troops," in "Census Is for Citizens Only," *Glendale News-Press*, June 2, 1989. Estimation problems in Daniel Levine, Kenneth Hill, and Robert Warren, *Immigration Statistics: A Story of Neglect* (Washington, D.C.: National Academy Press, 1985), p. 88; Charles B. Keely, "Illegal Migration," *Scientific American 246* (March 1982): 41–42; "Immigration Law Complicates Census Planning," *Los Angeles Times*, May 11, 1987, I, p. 4.

Baby Boom

Ben J. Wattenberg, *The Birth Dearth* (New York: Pharus Books, 1987). "Is it possible . . . ?" in Tony Kaye, "The Birth Dearth," *New Republic*, January 19, 1987, pp. 20–23. Front cover news magazine coverage of book in "Are We Having Enough Babies?" *U.S. News and World Report*, January 22, 1987, pp. 56–63. Criticism of Wattenberg in Kaye, "The Birth Dearth," and Jonathan Lieberson, "Too Many People?" *New York Review of Books*, June 26, 1986, pp. 36–42. Problems of prediction in "Census Bureau Demographer's Unqualified Prediction," *New York Times*, February 5, 1989, p. 30; 1945 estimate in Kaye, "The Birth Dearth," p. 21. Keyfitz in Nathan Keyfitz, "The Social and Political Context of Population Forecasting," in William Alonso and Paul Starr, eds., *The Politics of Numbers* (New York: Russell Sage Foundation, 1987), pp. 256–58.

Will You Still Feed Me?

Example of projections in "What Will Happen When the Baby Boom Retires?" *USA Today Magazine of the American Scene*, August 1986, p. 15. Paul Craig Roberts in "Social Security Has Become a Giant Pyramid Scheme," *Business Week*, October 10, 1988, p. 28. Michael Boskin in *Too Many Promises: The*

Uncertain Future of Social Security (Homewood, Ill: Dow-Jones Irwin, 1986). Bernstein in Merton C. Bernstein and Joan Brodshaug Bernstein, *Social Security: The System That Works* (New York: Basic Books, 1988), p. 72. Ackerman in *Hazardous to Our Wealth* (Boston: South End Press, 1984), p. 121. On federal expenditures for social security, see Phillip Longman, *Born to Pay* (Boston: Houghton Mifflin, 1987), pp. 8–10. "We must consider . . . ," ibid., p. 9. On confusing demographics with politics, see John Myles, "The Trillion Dollar Misunderstanding," *Working Papers for a New Society*, July/August 1981, pp. 23–31.

Race and Ethnicity

Who Is Black?   History of Census questions in Ira S. Lowry, *The Science and Politics of Ethnic Enumeration* (Santa Monica, Calif.: Rand Corp., 1980), pp. 8–9; and William Petersen, "Politics and the Measurement of Ethnicity," in Alonso and Starr, *The Politics of Numbers*, pp. 208–209.

Box 2.2. Black Insanity, An Argument for Slavery

Patricia Cohen, *A Calculating People* (Chicago: University of Chicago Press, 1982), pp. 194–204; see also Anderson, *American Census*, pp. 29–31.

Who Is Asian?   History of Asian enumeration in Lowry, *The Science and Politics*, pp. 7–10. Problem answers in "Simpler 1990 Census Form Upsets Asian-Americans," *Los Angeles Times*, April 12, 1988, I, p. 3; "Concerns Raised on the '90 Census," *New York Times*, April 17, 1988, p. 31; "Census Won't List Various Asian Groups," *Wall Street Journal*, May 23, 1988, p. 19. Limited space in census in "Scrambling to Be Counted in Census," *New York Times*, December 3, 1989, p. A-17.

Who Is Hispanic?   Change in census method in Joan Moore and Harry Pachon, *Hispanics in the United States* (Englewood Cliffs, N.J.: Prentice-Hall, 1985), p. 3; see also Nancy A. Denton and Douglas S. Massey, "Racial Identity among Caribbean Hispanics," *American Sociological Review 54* (October 1989); 790–94. Respondent confusion in Lowry, *The Science and Politics*, p. 13. Los Angeles City Council in "L.A. Cases Seek Hispanic Gain," *New York Times*, July 10, 1989, p. A-15.

Box 2.3. Ethnicity and Race

Hispanics and race in Denton and Massey, "Racial Identity," pp. 790–808.

Implications   History of concept of race in J.C. King, *The Biology of Race* (Berkeley: University of California Press, 1981); see also Stephen J. Gould, *The Mismeasure of Man* (New York: W.W. Norton, 1981); and Ashley Montagu, *Man's Most Dangerous Myth: The Fallacy of Race* (New York: Oxford University Press, 1974).

Households and Families

Changing household characteristics in Nancy Folbre, *A Field Guide to the U.S. Economy* (New York: Pantheon Books, 1987), p. 3.9; and "Living Arrangements and Marital Status of Households and Families,'' *Family Economics Review 2*, 3, 1989, p. 16. Jencks in Christopher Jencks, "The Politics of Income Measurement," in Alonso and Starr, *The Politics of Numbers*, pp. 92–105.

Box 2.4. Head of Household

Householder change in Sweet and Bumpass, *American Families*, pp. 336–37.

Box 2.5. Individuals Living Alone

Data calculated from ibid., pp. 344, 376. Debate over post-1987 change in "New Data Show Fewer People Living Alone," *Wall Street Journal*, August 18, 1987, p. 35.

"Oh No, I Forgot to Get Married!"

"Too late," in *Newsweek*, June 2, 1986, p. 54. Bennett-Bloom-Craig study described in Thomas Exter, "How to Figure Your Chances of Getting Married," *American Demographics* (June 1987):50–52; later published in Neil G. Bennett, David E. Bloom, and Patricia H. Craig, "The Divergence of Black and White Marriage Patterns" *American Journal of Sociology 95*, 3 (November 1989): 692–722. Christensen in Bryce J. Christensen, "The Costly Retreat from Marriage," *Public Interest 91* (Spring 1988): 62–64. Census Bureau study in Jeanne E. Moorman, "The History and Future of the Relationship between Education and Marriage," March 1987, Marriage and Family Statistics Branch, U.S. Bureau of the Census; summarized in Exter, *How to Figure*. Comparison of two studies in ibid. and Susan Faludi, "The Marriage Trap," *Ms.* (July–August 1987):61ff. Comments on final Harvard-Yale article in "Study of Marriage Patterns Revised Omitting Impact of Women's Careers," *New York Times*, November 11, 1989, p. A-9.

Divorce

Problems with divorce data in Sweet and Bumpass, *American Families*, chap. 5; Bogue, *Population of the United States*, pp. 194–97. Mens' versus womens' responses in Sweet and Bumpass, *American Families*, p. 210. Separation without divorce in "Two-thirds of Marriages Will Fail, Study Says," *Los Angeles Times*, March 13, 1989, p. A-6. Data on trend in Arthur J. Norton and Jeanne E. Moorman, "Current Trends in Marriage and Divorce among American Women," *Journal of Marriage and the Family 49* (February 1987):3–14, and "Two-thirds of Marriages Will Fail." Harris in "One in Two? Not True," *Time,* July 13, 1987, p. 21; see also "Portrait of Divorce in America," *Newsweek*, February 2, 1987, p. 78. "It would be foolish," in "Two-thirds of Marriages Will Fail." Harris in "One in Two?" Census Bureau researchers in "Current Trends," p. 12; Martin and Bumpass in "Two-thirds of Marriages Will Fail."

CASE STUDY QUESTIONS

1. Harold Orlans, "The Politics of Minority Statistics," *Society 26* (May–June 1989):25.

2. Bumpass and Sweet in "Living Together," *Society 25*, 5 (July–August 1988): 3; and Koray Tanfer, "Patterns of Premarital Cohabitation among Never-Married Women in the United States," *Journal of Marriage and the Family 49* (August 1987):483–97.

3. Sweet and Bumpass, *American Families*, p. 210.

4. "Deciding What Counts in 1990," *Los Angeles Times*, March 14, 1989, p. 1; "Scrambling to be Counted," p. A-17.

5. Margo J. Anderson, *The American Census: A Social History* (New Haven: Yale University Press, 1988), pp. 144–49.

6. Sweet and Bumpass, *American Families*, p. 38.

7. Peggy Lovell Webster and Jeffrey W. Dwyer, "The Cost of Being Nonwhite in Brazil," *Social Science Research 72*, 2 (January 1988):136; and Carl N. Degler, *Neither Black Nor White* (New York: Macmillan, 1971). On the Caribbean, see "Racial Identity among Caribbean Hispanics," pp. 791–93.

Chapter 3: Housing

DATA SOURCES

U.S. Census

History of housing surveys in John S. Adams, *Housing America in the 1980s* (New York: Russell Sage Foundation, 1987), pp. 4, 29–30; see also Joseph W. Duncan and William C. Shelton, *Revolution in United States Government Statistics* (Washington, D.C.: U.S. Government Printing Office, 1978), p. 39. On census form, see Bryant Robey, "Two Hundred Years and Counting: The 1990 Census," *Population Bulletin 44*, 1 (April 1989):15–24. For advice on using census housing data, see U.S. Conference of Mayors, "Assessing Elderly Housing" (Washington, D.C.: American Association of Retired Persons, 1986). Data sample in Bureau of the Census, U.S. Department of Commerce, *1980 Census of Housing*, HC80-3-2, "Subject Reports: Mobile Homes," p. 8. On New Orleans, ibid., pp. 531–32.

American Housing Survey

History in Adams, *Housing America in the 1980s*, pp. 33–36. Data sample in U.S. Department of Housing and Urban Development, *American Housing Survey 1984*, H-170-84-85, p. 4.

Box 3.1. U.S. Census versus AHS

Differences described in Adams, *Housing America in the 1980s*, pp. 34–37.

Other Census Surveys

On housing starts, see Norman Frumkin, *Guide to Economic Indicators* (Armonk, N.Y.: M. E. Sharpe, 1990), pp. 127–31. On economic surveys, see U.S. Department of Commerce, Bureau of the Census, "Characteristics of New Housing:

1986," Construction Reports C25–186–13, p. 63. Data sample in U.S. Department of Commerce, *Current Construction Report*, October 1988, p. 16; and U.S. Department of Commerce, "Characteristics of New Housing," p. 17.

Other Price Data

Shelter index in U.S. Department of Labor, Bureau of Labor Statistics, *Handbook of Labor Statistics* (Washington, D.C.: U.S. Government Printing Office, 1988), pp. 166–67.

CONTROVERSIES

Housing Quality

Data in John C. Weicher, "Private Production: Has the Rising Tide Lifted All Boats?" in Peter D. Salins, ed., *Housing America's Poor* (Chapel Hill: University of North Carolina Press, 1987), p. 46. Dilapidated in Peter D. Salins, "America's Permanent Housing Problem," in Salins, *Housing America's Poor*, pp. 2–4. AHS quality measures in William C. Apgar, Jr., "The Leaky Boat: A Housing Problem Remains," in Salins, *Housing America's Poor*, pp. 67–89. Leaky roofs, rats in ibid., p. 69. Moving target in Salins, "America's Permanent," pp. 2–9. "One reason," in ibid., p. 2.

Is There an Affordability Crisis?

Experts on 25 percent in Adams, *Housing America in the 1980s*, p. 114. Spending data in Chester Hartman, "The Housing Crisis in Brief," in *America's Housing Crisis* (Boston: Routledge and Kegan Paul, 1983), pp. 17–18. Debate in ibid., pp. 17–25, and John I. Gilderbloom, "Trends in the Affordability of Rental Housing: 1970 to 1983," *Social Science Research 70*, 4 (July 1986):301. Price index in U.S. Department of Commerce, "Characteristics of New Housing: 1986," Construction Reports C25-86-13 (Washington, D.C.: U.S. Government Printing Office, 1987), p. 55. Affordability index in "The Housing 'Affordability' Index," *Changing Times 37*, 8 (August 1983):8. "We just can't" in Ben Wattenberg, *The Good News Is the Bad News Is Wrong* (New York: Simon and Schuster, 1984), p. 201. Brookes in "Surprise! Home Buyers Are Better Off Now," *Wall Street Journal*, October 17, 1988, p. A-22; 1988 prices in "Southland home costs soar again," *Los Angeles Times*, February 15, 1989, p. IV-2. Housing squeeze in James D. Wright, "Address Unknown: Homelessness in Contemporary America," *Society 26*, 4 (September–October 1989):52–53.

Government in the Housing Market

Rent control advocate in Michael Mandel, "A Real Look at Rent Control," *Dollars and Sense*, January–February 1986, pp. 8–17. Eleven percent in Cushing N. Dolbeare, "The Low-Income Housing Crisis," in Hartman, *America's Housing Crisis*, p. 39. Bad effects of public housing in John C. Weicher, "Private Production: Has the Rising Tide Lifted All Boats?" in Salins, *Housing America's Poor*, pp. 58–59. Rent control anathema in many conservative analyses, see for example, B. Bruce-Briggs, "Rent Control Must Go," *New York Times Magazine*, April 18, 1976, pp. 19–31. Filtering in Weicher, "Private Production," pp. 53–63. Criticism in Michael E. Stone, "Housing and the Economic Crisis," in Hartman, *America's Housing Crisis*, pp. 99–150.

The Homeless

HUD estimate discussed in Jon Erickson and Charles Wilhelm, *Housing the Homeless* (New Brunswick, N.J.: Center for Urban Policy Research, 1986), pp. 146–48. Communities estimate discussed in ibid., p. 129. Comparison in ibid., pp. 146–47. Freeman in Thomas J. Main, "What We Know about the Homeless," *Commentary*, May 1988, pp. 27–28. Never pin down in Wright, "Address Unknown," pp. 52–53. Rand Corporation study in ibid., p. 48. Doubling up in ibid., and Neighborhood Reinvestment Corporation in "18 Million Homeless Seen by 2003," *Washington Post*, June 3, 1987, p. A-8.

Geographic Units

Origins of 'tracts' in Duncan and Shelton, *Revolution*, p. 209; defined in Robey, "Two Hundred Years," p. 25. Definition of urban in James L. Newman, *Population Patterns, Dynamics and Prospects* (Englewood Cliffs, N.J.: Prentice-Hall, 1984), pp. 50–51. MSAs described in Adams, *Housing America in the 1980s*, pp. 31–32, 39. Standard Consolidated Areas described in ibid., p. 39.

Segregation

"Our Nation," National Advisory Commission on Civil Disorders, *Report* (Washington, D.C.: U.S. Government Printing Office, 1968), p. 1. Nixon administration blocked in "Middle-Class Black Housing Still Largely Segregated," *Washington Post*, December 30, 1987, p. A-4. On historical trend, see Reynolds Farley and Walter R. Allen, *The Color Line and the Quality of Life in America* (New York: Oxford University Press, 1987), pp. 139–57; see also Christine H. Rossell, "Does School Desegregation Policy Stimulate Residential Integration?" *Urban Education 21*, 4 (January 1987):403. Suburban movement in John R. Logan and Mark Schneider, "Racial Segregation and Racial Change in American Suburbs," *American Journal of Sociology 89* (January 1984):46–57. Overall trend in Douglas S. Massey and Nancy Denton, "Trends in the Residential Segregation of Blacks, Hispanics and Asians: 1970–1980," *American Sociological Review 52* (December 1987):802–25. "Most blacks" in ibid., p. 823. On segregation indexes, see Michael J. White, "Segregation and Diversity Measures in Population Distribution," *Population Index 52*, 2 (Summer 1986):198–221.

Is Seattle the Best Place to Live?

Ratings in Richard Boyer and David Savageau, *Places Rated Almanac* (New York: Prentice-Hall, 1989), pp. 392–400. Sophisticated approach in G.C. Blomquist, M.C. Berger, and J.P. Hoehn, "New Estimates of Quality of Life in Urban Areas," *American Economic Review 78*, 1 (March 1988):89–107.

CASE STUDY QUESTIONS

1. Apgar,"The Leaky Boat," p. 73.
2. Adams, *Housing America in the 1980s*, p. 44.
3. "New Home Sales Post 9.6% Rise," *New York Times*, January 4, 1990, p. C-1.
4. Brookes, "Surprise Home Buyers."
5. "Orange County Tops U.S.," *Los Angeles Times*, August 12, 1988, p. 22.
6. Constance Holden, "Counting the Homeless," *Science 234* (October 17, 1986):282.

Chapter 4: Health

DATA SOURCES

NCHS in Nancy D. Pearce, *Data Systems of the National Center for Health Statistics*; "Percent of persons 18 years of age and over who ate breakfast"; on Current Population Survey, see chapter 9; other government surveys in National Center for Health Statistics, U.S. Department of Health and Human Services, *Facts at Your Fingertips* (Washington, D.C.: U.S. Government Printing Office, May 1981). Headaches in ibid., p. 67. WHO data in World Health Organization, *World Health Statistics Annual*, 1988, pp. 389, 696.

CONTROVERSIES

Infant Mortality

As a health indicator in C. Arden Miller, "Infant Mortality in the U.S.," *Scientific American 253* (July 1985):31–37. Soviet Union in "Getting Russia Well Again," *The Economist*, November 21, 1987, pp. 51–52. Historical data in Miller, "Infant Mortality in the U.S." pp. 31–32. 1988 data in "Health Data Show Wide Gap," *New York Times*, March 23, 1990, p. A-17. Children's Defense Fund in "Slowing Drop in Infant Death Rate Fuels Debate," *Wall Street Journal*, July 23, 1985, p. 60. Schwartz in "Infant Death Rate Fell Again—Did You Hear?" *Wall Street Journal*, April 24, 1985, p. 30. For defense of U.S. health care system, see also Harvey Sapolsky, "The Numbers Are Awry on Infant Mortality," *Business Week*, August 15, 1988, p. 18. United States versus other countries in Miller, "Infant Mortality in the U.S." Swedish provinces in D. Rotstein, *The Paradox of Modern Medicine* (Cambridge, Mass.: MIT Press, 1967), pp. 24–25. Heterogeneous population in Harry Schwartz, *The Case for Modern Medicine* (New York: David McKay, 1972), p. 47. Data for whites and blacks in "Slowing Drop in Infant Death Rate." Studies of reasons in Joel C. Kleinman and Samuel S. Kessel, "Racial Differences in Low Birth Weight," *New England Journal of Medicine 317* (September 17, 1987):749–53; and Jann L. Murray and Merton Bernfeld, "The Differential Effect of Prenatal Care," *New England Journal of Medicine 319* (November 24, 1988):1385–91. Infants saved in "Infant Mortality among Black Americans," *Journal of the American Medical Association 257* (February 6, 1987):599.

Box 4.1. Abortion

Guttmacher data in *New York Times,* March 13, 1985, p. A-1; August 25, 1987, p. A-13; October 6, 1988, p. B-18.

Are We Living Longer?

Life expectancy in "Life Expectancy Remains at Record Level," *Statistical Bulletin 70*, 3 (July–September 1989):26–30. "Death Rate for Blacks Still High," *New York Times,* September 27, 1989, p. A-14; see also "A Disturbing Decline in Black Life Expectancy," *Business Week,* February 27, 1989. Unreliable rates for extreme elderly in Ira Rosenwaike, Nurit Yaffe, and Phillip C. Sagi, "The Recent Decline in Mortality of the Extreme Aged," *American Journal of Public Health 70* (October 1980):1074–80. Who lies in Kenneth C.W. Kammeyer and Helen L. Ginn, *An Introduction to Population* (Chicago: Dorsey Press, 1986), p. 71. Stephen Jay Gould, "The Median Isn't the Message," *Discover,* June 1985, pp. 40–42. U.S. mean life expectancy in Andrew Hacker, *U.S.: A Statistical Portrait* (New York: Viking, 1983), p. 65; Thomas McKeown, *The Role of Medicine: Dream, Mirage or Nemesis* (Princeton, N.J.: Princeton University Press, 1979). Debate summarized in John B. McKinlay and Sonja M. McKinlay, "The Questionable Contribution of Medical Measures to the Decline of Mortality in the United States in the Twentieth Century," *Health and Society* (Summer 1977):405–28; see also Kenneth C.W. Kammeyer and Helen L. Ginn, *An Introduction to Population* (Chicago: Dursey Press, 1986), pp. 142–51. Extrapolation in John M. Owen and James W. Vaupel, "An Exercise in Life Expectancy," *American Demographics*, November 1985, pp. 37–39. Walford in Roy L. Walford, *Maximum Life Span* (New York: W.W. Norton, 1983). Optimistic appraisal also in Theodore J. Gordon, "Medical Breakthroughs," *The Futurist,* January–February 1987, pp. 15–17.

Box 4.2. The Oldest Person on Earth

Roy L. Walford, *Maximum Life Span* (New York: W.W. Norton, 1983), pp. 12–15.

Cancer

"Same kind of . . . " in Ralph W. Moss, *The Cancer Syndrome* (New York: Grove Press, 1980), p. 16; see also Richard M. Nixon, "Acting against Cancer," *Saturday Evening Post*, July/August 1986, pp. 67–69. Halving U.S. mortality rate in J.C. Bailar III and Elaine M. Smith, "Progress against Cancer?" *New England Journal of Medicine 314*, 19 (May 8, 1986):1226. NCI versus critics in "Cancer: Illusory Progress?" *Scientific American,* June 1987, p. 29; "Cancer Stats Attacked as Misleading," *Science News 131* (April 25, 1987), p. 260; "Cancer Stats: Gains and Losses," *Science News 130* (December 13, 1986), p. 372; "Who's Got Cancer's Number," *U.S. News and World Report*, December 15, 1986, p. 76; "Battling Cancer: Figures Can Say Anything," *U.S. News and World Report*, May 19, 1986; James E. Enstrom and Donald F. Austin, "Interpreting Cancer Survival Rates," *Science 195* (March 4, 1977):847–51. Cancer research funding in "Outspoken and Impatient Scientist Takes Charge of War on Cancer," *New York Times*, February 7, 1989,

p. B-7. Breast cancer detection in Bailar and Smith, "Progress against Cancer?" pp. 1229–30. Prostate cancer detection in ibid., p. 1230. Research use of incidence rates in ibid., p. 1228.

Box 4.3. Likelihood of Breast Cancer

Richard R. Love, "The Risk of Breast Cancer in American Women," *Journal of the American Medical Association 257* (March 20, 1987):1470.

AIDS

AIDS cases in U.S. Department of Health and Human Services, Centers for Disease Control, *Morbidity and Mortality Weekly Report*, January 27, 1989, p. 39. AIDS estimates in "Pick a Number," *The Economist*, February 18, 1989, p. 24; "AIDS Counts," *Scientific American*, April 1989, p. 17.

Is Slower Safer?

Drop in 1974 fatalities in "Official Report Says: Speed Doesn't Kill," *Consumers' Research,* December 1986, p. 30. Predicted increase in fatalities in "Does Speed Kill?" *Newsweek*, July 21, 1986, p. 16; and 1987 increase in fatalities in ibid., Burnley in "65 MPH. Not Costing Lives," *New York Times*, May 4, 1988, p. A-18. Critics' answer in "U.S. Issues Fatality Data on 65 MPH.," *New York Times*, May 7, 1988, p. 36. Varying speeds in "Official Report Says," p. 29 and "Speeding, Coordination, and the 55-MPH Limit." Comments by Peter Asch, David T. Levy, Richard Fowles, Peter D. Loeb, Donald W. Snyder, and Charles A. Lave in *American Economic Review 79*, 4 (September 1989):913–31.

Benefit-Cost Analysis

For description of benefit-cost analysis, see James T. Campen, *Benefit, Cost and Beyond* (Cambridge, Mass.: Ballinger, 1986), or any of many textbooks such as Edward M. Gramlich, *Benefit-Cost Analysis of Government Programs* (Englewood Cliffs, N.J.: Prentice-Hall, 1981). Criticisms of value of human life in Mark Green and Norman Waitzman, "Cost, Benefit, and Class," *Working Papers for a New Society*, May/June 1980, pp. 39–51. $300,000 to $8,000,000 in "What Is the Audited Value of Life," *New York Times*, October 26, 1984, p. 24. $128 in Green and Waitzman, "Cost, Benefit and Class," p. 43. $400,000 in "What Is the Audited Value of Life." Construction workers in ibid., Mark Green in Green and Waitzman, "Cost, Benefit and Class," pp. 48–49. Advocates of risk assessment in Mary Douglas and Aaron Wildavsky, *Risk and Culture: The Selection of Technical and Environmental Dangers* (Berkeley: University of California Press, 1982); see also Council of Economic Advisers, *Economic Report of the President 1987* (Washington, D.C.: U.S. Government Printing Office, 1987), pp. 179–207; Henry Fairlie, "Fear of Living," *The New Republic*, January 23, 1989, pp. 16–18. Criticism of risk assessment in William R. Freudenburg, "Perceived Risk, Real Risk: Social Science and the Art of Probabilistic Risk Assessment," *Science 242* (October 7, 1988):44–49; and Langdon Winner, "On Not Hitting the Tar-Baby: Risk Assessment and Conservatism," in Mary Gibson, *To Breathe Freely* (Totowa, N.J.: Rowman and Allanheld, 1985), pp. 269–84. Lawn mowers versus nuclear power in ibid., p. 277. Chernobyl in "Life's Risks: Balancing

Fear against Reality of Statistics," *New York Times*, May 8, 1989, p. A-1; "Genuinely puzzling" in Winner, "On Not Hitting the Tar-Baby," p. 275. William R. Freudenberg in "Perceived Risk," p. 47. Summary of the problem in *Benefit, Cost and Beyond*, pp. 52–55. Langdon Winner in "On Not Hitting," pp. 280–82.

Box 4.4. Cost of Tamper-proof Closures

Paul W. MacAvoy, "FDA Regulation—At What Price?" *New York Times*, November 21, 1982, p. III-3.

CASE STUDY QUESTIONS

1. Richard J. David, "Did Low Birthweight among US Blacks Really Increase?" *American Journal of Public Health 76* (April 1986):380–84.

2. R.D. Retherford, G.M. Mirza, M. Irfan, and I. Alam, "The Decline That Wasn't" *Population Today*, November 1989, pp. 6–9.

3. "Death Rate for Blacks Still High," *New York Times*, September 27, 1989, p. A-14; see also "A Disturbing Decline in Black Life Expectancy," *Business Week*, February 27, 1989.

4. Utah in Myron Johnston, "Young and Alive," *American Demographics*, December 1986, p. 7. Cirrhosis of the liver in Victor Fuchs, *Who Shall Live?* (New York: Basic Books, 1974), pp. 52–54.

5. "Babies' Seats Are Air Safety Issue," *New York Times*, August 18, 1985, Sec. IV, p. 23; and "Tighter Safety Rules Planned for Young Children in Planes," *New York Times*, November 4, 1989, p. A-7.

Chapter 5: Education

DATA SOURCES

Description of NCES data in U.S. Department of Education, National Center for Education Statistics, *Digest of Education Statistics* (U.S. Government Printing Office, 1987), pp. 321–34; Census Bureau data in ibid., pp. 334–35. Other surveys in ibid., pp. 339–42.

CONTROVERSIES

Poor Data

Summary of NCES problems in Charles Cooke, Alan Ginsburg, and Marshall Smith, "The Sorry State of Education Statisics," *Education Digest 51*, 4 (December 1985):28–30. "Agency's Statistics Challenged," *New York Times*, March 11, 1986, p. C-1; "Statistics Gap in Education," *Washington Post*, May 3, 1986, p. A-25; and Anne C. Lewis, "New Data Collection System Raises New Questions," *Phi Delta Kappan*, June 1986, pp. 699–700. Achievement measurement discussed in John B. Carroll, "The National Assessments in Reading: Are We Misreading the Findings?" *Phi Delta Kappan*, February 1987, pp. 424–30.

High School Dropouts

New York City data in "Education: Koch Calls Schools Improved," *New York Times*, September 2, 1985, p. 23; "Dropouts: Data Maze," *New York Times*, March 4, 1987, p. B-24; "Regans Office Says New York City May Undercount Its Dropouts," *New York Times*, June 6, 1987, p. B-3 and "By Any Measure, Too Many Dropouts," *New York Times*, March 9, 1987, p. A-14. Other cities in "High Dropout Rate Contradicts Official Report," *Christian Science Monitor*, February 28, 1986, p. 3. Summary of measures in Russell W. Rumberger, "High School Dropouts: A Review of Issues and Evidence," *Review of Educational Research 57*, 2 (Summer 1987):101–121; see also G. Natriello, A.M. Pallas, and E.L. McDill, "Taking Stock: Renewing Our Research Agenda on the Causes and Consequences of Dropping Out," *Teachers College Record 87* (1986):430–40. Census Bureau trend in "Report Finds Fewer Dropouts," *New York Times*, April 2, 1987, p. B-10. "General identification," in Margaret D. LeCompte and Stephen D. Goebel, "Can Bad Data Produce Good Program Planning?" *Education and Urban Society 19*, 3 (May 1987):263.

Illiteracy

0.5 percent in "Losing the War of Letters," *Time*, May 5, 1986, p. 68. 33 percent and 60 million functional illiterates in Jonathan Kozol, *Illiterate America* (New York: Doubleday, 1985), p. 4. Census Bureau study publicity in "Losing the War of Letters." Critics in "Specialists Attack Report on U.S. Illiteracy Rate," *Washington Post*, May 3, 1986, p. A-6. Educational Testing Service in Carroll, "The National Assessments." Literacy funding in Kozol, *Illiterate America*, p. 5; and "Illiteracy Seen as Threat to U.S. Economic Edge," *New York Times*, September 7, 1988, p. A-23.

Black Educational Progress

Progress in Reynolds Farley and Walter R. Allen, *The Color Line and the Quality of Life in America* (New York: Oxford University Press, 1987), p. 190. Quality of schools in ibid., pp. 203–208. Harrison and Gorhman in "Even College Degrees Might Not Lift Blacks out of Poverty," *Business Week*, February 5, 1990, p. 18. Reversal of gains in "Mid- and Low-Income Minorities in Decline on College Rolls," *New York Times*, January 15, 1990, p. A-11 and "Survey Shows Blacks Lag in Finishing College," *New York Times*, December 3, 1987, p. A-23. Black men in "Experts Foresee a Social Gap between Sexes among Blacks," *New York Times*, February 5, 1989, p. A-1. Wilson in ibid. Recent progress in "Intense College Recruiting Drives Lift Black Enrollment to a Record," *New York Times*, April 15, 1990, p. A-1.

School Desegregation: What Has Happened?

Orfield resignation in "Adviser to U.S. Desegregation Study Quits," *New York Times*, October 30, 1985, p. A-12; and Ellen K. Coughlin, "When Research Comes up against Politics," *Chronicle of Higher Education*, November 27, 1985,

p. 7. Commission report in "Desegregation Plans Said to Improve Race Balance," *New York Times*, May 20, 1987, p. A-27. Orfield study in "Blacks Holding Ground, Hispanics Losing in Desegregation," *Phi Delta Kappan*, January 1987, p. 406. Welch debate in Finis Welch, "A Reconsideration of the Impact of School Desegregation Programs on Public School Enrollment of White Students, 1968–76," *Sociology of Education 60* (October 1987):215–21. Response in Franklin D. Wilson, "A Reply to Finis Welch," *Sociology of Education 60* (October 1987):222–23; see also Christine H. Rossell, "Does School Desegregation Policy Stimulate Residential Integration: A Critique of the Research," *Urban Education 21*, 4 (January 1987):403–20. Wilson in "A Reply," p. 223.

Teacher Shortage?

Debate in C. Emily Feistritzer, *Teacher Crisis: Myth or Reality* (Washington, D.C.: National Center for Education Information, 1986). "Seriously considered," in ibid., p. 7. "Nowhere near" in "Controversial Report Says Teacher Supply Keeping Pace with Demand," *Phi Delta Kappan*, February 1987, p. 481. "Massive hiring," in ibid. Increasingly female, fewer minorities in Feistritzer, *Teacher Crisis*, p. 91.

Class Size

Debate on class size in *Phi Delta Kappan*, December 1980, pp. 239–44. Subsequent experiments in Helen Pate Bain and C.M. Achilles, "Interesting Developments on Class Size," *Phi Delta Kappan*, May 1986, pp. 662–65. Summary of problems in Margaret D. LeCompte and Stephen D. Goebel, "Can Bad Data Produce Good Program Planning?" *Education and Urban Society 19*, 3 (May 1987):250–68.

CASE STUDY QUESTIONS

1. Michael G. Bruce, "Higher Education: Taking Our Bearings," *Phi Delta Kappan*, November 1987, pp. 239–40; and Edward M. White and Ruediger Ahrens, "European vs. American Higher Education," *Change*, September/October 1989, pp. 53–55.
2. "The Misleading Concept of 'Average,' " *New York Times,* July 12, 1989, p. B-7.
3. "Making the Grade," *American Demographics*, May 1987, p. 8.
4. Cooke, Ginsburg, and Smith, "The Sorry State of Education Statistics," p. 29.

Chapter 6: Crime

DATA SOURCES

Uniform Crime Reports

UCR described in Federal Bureau of Investigation, U.S. Department of Justice, *Uniform Crime Reporting Handbook* (Washington, D.C.: U.S. Government Printing Office, 1984); and Federal Bureau of Investigation, U.S. Department of Justice, *Crime in the United States 1987* (Washington, D.C.: U.S. Government Printing Office, 1988), pp. 1–5. Muncie data in ibid., p. 78.

Box 6.1. The Crime Index

Crime clock in *Crime in the United States*, p. 6. Crime statistics in ibid., p. 41.

National Crime Survey

National Crime Survey described in Bureau of Justice Statistics, U.S. Department of Justice, *Criminal Victimization in the United States 1985* (Washington, D.C.: U.S. Department of Justice, 1987), pp. 1–2; reporting to police by income in ibid., p. 79.

CONTROVERSIES

How Accurate Are Crime Statistics?

Comparison of UCR and National Crime Survey in J.F. Sheley, *America's Crime Problem* (Belmont, Calif.: Wadsworth, 1985), pp. 75–99; Albert Biderman, "Surveys of Population Samples for Estimating Crime Incidence," *Annals of the American Academy of Political Science*, November 1967, pp. 16–33; Jan M. Chaiken and Marcia R. Chaiken, "Crime Rates and the Active Criminal," in J.Q. Wilson, ed., *Crime and Public Policy* (San Francisco: Institute for Contemporary Studies, 1983), pp. 12–25. UCR misrepresentation of crime in New York City in Marvin E. Wolfgang, "Uniform Crime Reports: A Critical Reappraisal," in Bruce J. Cohen, ed., *Crime in America* (Itasco, Ill.: F.E. Peacock, 1985), p. 41; in Washington, D.C., in James P. Levine, Michael C. Musheno, and Dennis J. Palumbo, *Criminal Justice in America* (New York: John Wiley and Sons, 1986), p. 99; in Indianapolis, in Harold E. Pepinsky and Paul Jesilow, *Myths That Cause Crime* (Cabin John, Md.: Seven Locks Press, 1985), p. 28. Problems with National Crime Survey in Stephen E. Brown and Thomas W. Wooley, "The National Crime Survey Program: Problems in Sample Selection and Data Analysis," *Social Science Quarterly 66* (March 1985):186–93. Debate about 1980 crime rates in "U.S. Study Group's Proposals Assailed by Council on Crime," *New York Times*, September 10, 1981, p. B-10.

Box 6.2. Rape

"How Justice Department Collected the Data for Its Rape Study," *New York Times*, May 24, 1985, p. A-24; "Reporting Rape," *New York Times*, April 21, 1987, p. 22.

Box 6.3. A Worldwide Problem?

Currie, *Confronting Crime*, pp. 24–35. Detroit murder rate in "Children Killing Children," *Washington Post* December 4, 1986, p. A-1. American men die, in Currie, *Confronting Crime*, p. 25.

Will You Be a Crime Victim?

Bureau of Justice Statistics, U.S. Department of Justice, *Technical Report*, "Lifetime Likelihood of Victimization," March 1987; "83% to Be Victims of Crime Violence," *New York Times*, March 9, 1987, p. A-13.

Are Criminals Getting Younger—Or Older?

"Children Killing Children," *Washington Post*, December 4, 1986, p. A-1. Young people in groups in *Newsweek*, March 23, 1981, p. 80; George Sunderland, "Geriatric Crime Wave: The Great Debate," *Police Chief*, October 1982, pp. 40ff. Baby boom explanation for rise and fall in crime rate in "Behind Drop in U.S. Crime Rate, Experts Note Persisting Problems," *Christian Science Monitor*, April 2, 1985, p. 5; Alfred Blumstein and Jacqueline Cohen, "Characterizing Criminal Careers," *Science*, August 28, 1987, pp. 985–91.

Does Poverty Cause Crime?

Crime rate in Highland Park and Grosse Point in FBI, *Crime in the United States*, p. 84. C.S. Tittle et al. research in Charles R. Tittle, Wayne J. Villemez, and Douglas A. Smith, "The Myth of Social Class and Criminality: An Empirical Assessment of the Empirical Evidence," *American Sociological Review 43* (1978):643–56. Criticisms in Gary Kleck, "On the Use of Self-report Data to Determine the Class Distribution of Criminal and Delinquent Behavior," *American Sociological Review 47* (June 1982):427–33. "American youths of all backgrounds . . . " in Elliott Currie, *Confronting Crime: An American Challenge*, (N.Y.: Pantheon, 1985), p. 157. Behavioral Research Institute study in ibid., pp. 158–59; see also Richard McGahey, "Economic Conditions, Neighborhood Organization and Urban Crime," in M. Tonry and A. Reiss, Jr., eds., *Communities and Crime* (Chicago: University of Chicago Press, 1986), pp. 231–70.

Why Is the Black Crime Rate So High?

Crime rates by sex, age, and race in Bureau of Justice Statistics, U.S. Department of Justice, *Report to the Nation on Crime and Justice* (Washington, D.C.: U.S. Department of Justice, 1988), p. 31. Black prison population in Andrew Hacker, "Black Crime, White Racism," *New York Review of Books*, March 3, 1988, p. 36. Hacker in ibid., pp. 36–41. Wright in Bruce Wright, *Black Robes, White Justice* (New York: Carol Publishing, 1987). Currie in Currie, *Confronting Crime*, pp. 152–59. "Genuine social disaster," in ibid., p. 160.

Does Capital Punishment Deter Murder?

Isaac Ehrlich time series study in Isaac Ehrlich, "The Deterrent Effect of Capital Punishment: A Question of Life and Death," *American Economic Review*, June 1975, pp. 397–417. Use before Supreme Court in Richard M. McGahey, "Dr. Ehrlich's Magic Bullet: Economic Theory, Econometrics, and the Death Penalty," *Crime and Delinquency*, October 1980, p. 485. Criticisms of Ehrlich summarized in ibid., pp. 485–502; see also Jan Palmer, "Economic Analyses of the Deterrent Effect of Punishment: A Review," *Journal of Research in Crime and Deliquency*, January 1977, pp. 4–21; Peter Passell and John B. Taylor, "The Deterrent Effect of Capital Punishment: Another View," *American Economic Review*, June 1977, p. 445; and *Yale Law Journal* symposium, December 1975. Isaac Ehrlich cross-sectional study in "Capital Punishment and Deterrence: Some Further Thoughts and Additional Evidence," *Journal of Political Economy*, August 1977, pp. 741–88. Criticisms in McGahey, *Dr. Ehrlich's Magic Bullet*, pp. 496–98; Franklin E. Zimring and Gordon Hawkins, *Capital Punishment and the American Agenda* (New York: Cambridge University Press, 1987), pp. 178–84. Very small deterence in ibid., pp. 180–81. "There has been no spate of articles . . . " in McGahey, *Dr. Ehrlich's Magic Bullet*, p. 501.

Box 6.4. Missing Children—How Serious a Problem?

On missing children, Peter Schneider, "Lost Innocents: The Myth of Missing Children," *Harper's*, February 1987, pp. 47–53; Ellen Goodman, "Missing Children: Facts and Fears," *Washington Post*, July 10, 1985, p. A-19.

What about White-Collar Crime?

Sutherland on white-collar crime in *White Collar Crime* (New York: Dryden Press, 1949). FBI white-collar crime data in "U.S. Reports 18% Rise in '85 in White-Collar Convictions," *New York Times*, September 29, 1987, p. A-24. Broader definition of white-collar crime in Marshall B. Clinard and Peter C. Yeager, *Corporate Crime* (New York: Free Press, 1980); Russell Mokhiber, *Corporate Crime and Violence: Big Business Power and the Abuse of Public Trust* (San Francisco: Sierra Club Books, 1988); "Staying out of Prison Takes a Lot of Class," *Dollars and Sense*, no. 21 (November 1976); Pepinsky and Jesilow, *Myths That Cause Crime*, pp. 58–65. Green on white-collar crime in Mark Green and John F. Berry, "White-Collar Crime is Big Business," *The Nation*, June 8, 1985, pp. 689ff. "Stealing $200 Billion the Respectable Way," *U.S. News and World Report*, May 20, 1985, pp. 83–86. Other estimates in J.W. Coleman, *The Criminal Elite* (New York: St. Martins Press: 1985), pp. 2–11; Rieman on white-collar crime in Pepinsky and Jesilow, *Myths That Cause Crime*, p. 33.

CASE STUDY QUESTIONS

1. Data from U.S. Justice Department, *Crime in the United States*, p. 41.
2. See references on accuracy of UCR and National Crime Survey.
3. See Albert Biderman and Albert J. Reiss, Jr., "On Exploring the 'Dark Figure' of Crime," *Annals of the American Academy of Political Science*, November 1967, pp. 1–15; and Gordon P. Waldo, *Measurement Issues in Criminal Justice* (New York: Sage Publications, 1983).
4. See, "Sharp Decline in Crime Rates," *Washington Post*, October 26, 1986, p. A-4.
5. See Philip J. Cook, "The Case of the Missing Victims: Gunshot Woundings in the National Crime Survey," *Journal of Quantitative Criminology 1*, 1 (1985):91–102.

6. "The Plague of Crime," *Newsweek*, March 23, 1981, p. 46. The same week *Time* called it "The Curse of Violent Crime," *Time*, March 23, 1981, p. 17. Data from Bureau of Justice Statistics, U.S. Department of Justice, *Sourcebook of Criminal Justice Statistics, 1986*, p. 180, and *Crime in the United States*, p. 41.

Chapter 7: The National Economy

DATA SOURCES

U.S. Commerce Department

History of national income and produce accounts summarized in Joseph W. Duncan and William C. Shelton, *Revolution in United States Government Statistics* (Washington, D.C.: U.S. Government Printing Office, 1978), pp. 74–107, and Mark Perlman, "Political Purpose and the National Accounts," in W. Alonso and P. Starr, *The Politics of Numbers* (New York: Russell Sage Foundation, 1987), pp. 135–51. GNP data in U.S. Department of Commerce, *Survey of Current Business*, February 1986, p. 18. Summary of NIPA in "National Income and Product Accounts Estimates," *Survey of Current Business*, January 1988, pp. 11–13. Official accounting methods in Bureau of Economic Analysis, U.S. Department of Commerce, "GNP: An Overview of Source Data and Estimating Methods," BEA-MP-4 (Washington, D.C.: U.S. Government Printing Office, September 1987). Data sample in Council of Economic Advisers, *Economic Report of the President*, 1990, p. 294. Census of manufacturing described in Bureau of the Census, U.S. Department of Commerce, "1982 Census of Manufactures, Publications Order Form," MC82-1, August 1984, and Statistical Policy Division, Office of Management and Budget, *Statistical Services of the U.S. Government* (Washington, D.C.: U.S. Government Printing Office, 1975), pp. 125–43. Data sample in Bureau of the Census, U.S. Department of Commerce, *1982 Census of Manufactures*, "Industry Series, Newspapers, Periodicals, Books and Miscellaneous Publishing," MC82-I-27A, p. 26. Trade statistics described in U.S. Department of Commerce, *Understanding U.S. Foreign Trade Data* (Washington, D.C.: U.S. Government Printing Office, August 1985). Data sample in U.S. Bureau of the Census, *U.S. Imports for Consumption and General Imports*, Report FT246/Annual 1987 (Washington, D.C.: U.S. Government Printing Office, 1988), pp. 1–37.

Box 7.1. The People behind the Numbers

Women's dress shoes in U.S. Department of Commerce, "Tanning; Industrial Leather Goods; and Shoes," *1982 Census of Manufactures*, MC82-1-31A (Washington, D.C.: U.S. Government Printing Office, 1982), p. 31. Manufacturing employment in U.S. Department of Labor, *Employment and Earnings 36*, 10 (October 1989):77. GNP data in Council of Economic Advisers, *Economic Report of the President 1988* (Washington, D.C.: U.S. Government Printing Office, 1988), p. 250.

U.S. Labor Department

Productivity measures described in Bureau of Labor Statistics, U.S. Department of Labor, *Handbook of Labor Statistics* (Washington, D.C.: U.S. Government

Printing Office, 1985), pp. 226–27. Data sample in Lawrence J. Fulco, "U.S. Productivity Growth since 1982," *Monthly Labor Review*, December 1986, p. 18.

U.S. Federal Reserve Board

U.S. Federal Reserve Board, "Introduction to Flow of Funds," 1980; "Recent Developments in Economic Statistics at the Federal Reserve: Part 1," *Business Economics*, October 1988, pp. 47–52; and Norman Frumkin, *Tracking America's Economy* (Armonk, N.Y.: M.E. Sharpe, 1987), pp. 114–35. Data sample in Board of Governors, Federal Reserve System, *Federal Reserve Bulletin 75*, 8 (August 1989):A43.

Private Sector

On credit-reporting agencies, see chapter 11. On Bureau of Economic Analysis, see Duncan and Shelton, *Revolution in United States Government Statistics*, p. 107. Data sample in U.S. Small Business Administration, *State of Small Business* (Washington, D.C.: U.S. Government Printing Office, 1987), p. 25.

CONTROVERSIES

Which GNP?

Flash data discontinued in "GNP Flash Estimate to be Dropped," *Washington Post*, January 28, 1986, p. E-1. On GNP secrecy, see Allan H. Young, "Evaluation of GNP Estimates," *Survey of Current Business*, August 1987, p. 36, and "Sealed Lips, Locked Safes," *Business Week*, May 23, 1988, pp. 96–101. On GNP revisions, see "Evaluation of GNP Estimates"; see also Bureau of Economic Analysis, "The Use of National Income and Product Accounts," Staff Paper 43 (Washington, D.C.: U.S. Government Printing Office, January 1986); and "Critics Say U.S. Economic Picture Is Blurred by Reliance on Bad Data," *Wall Street Journal*, January 10, 1986, p. 19. On 1984 error, see "Imprecise Beacons of Truth," *Financial World*, March 18, 1986, pp. 112–13. Change in growth rate 1982–86 in Council of Economic Advisers, *Economic Report of the President 1990* (Washington, D.C.: U.S. Government Printing Office, 1990), p. 282. For example of mistake in using unrevised data, see "Discounting 'Strong' Rates," *Wall Street Journal*, September 1, 1987, p. 31; and comments on Warren T. Brooks, "Hiding a Boom in a Statistical Bust," *Wall Street Journal*, August 6, 1987, p. 24.

Box 7.2. Been Down So Long It Looks Like Up

On GNP real growth rates, see *Economic Report of the President 1988*, p. 251. "Been down so long," from Richard Fariña, *Been Down So Long It Looks Like Up* (New York: Random House, 1966).

Box 7.3. Forecasting

Moore in "Economists Missing the Mark," *New York Times*, December 12, 1984, p. D-1. Economic indicators described in Norman Frumkin, *Guide to Economic*

Indicators (Armonk, N.Y.: M.E. Sharpe, 1990), pp. 163–72. Criticism in Lacy Hunt, "An Antiquated Irrelevant Index," *Wall Street Journal*, March 29, 1988, p. 30; "A Better Entrail," *The Economist*, February 10, 1990, p. 65.

Problems with GNP

Kuznets's role is discussed in Duncan and Shelton, eds., *Revolution in United States Government Statistics*, p. 77. Critics of growth: Ezra J. Mishan, *The Costs of Economic Growth* (New York: Praeger, 1967); Kenneth Boulding, *Economics of Pollution* (New York: New York University Press, 1971). Measure of economic welfare in William Nordhaus and James Tobin, "Is Growth Obsolete?" in National Bureau for Economic Research, *Fiftieth Anniversary Colloquium V* (New York: Columbia University Press, 1972). On BEA nonacceptance of welfare measures, see "The Use of National Income and Product Accounts," p. 25. Alternative measures of welfare in Robert Eisner, "Extended Accounts for National Income and Product," *Journal of Economic Literature 26*, 4 (December 1988):1611–84. Repetto in Robert Repetto, "Nature's Resources as Productive Assets," *Challenge*, September–October 1989, pp. 16–20. Underground economy in Carol S. Carson, "The Underground Economy: An Introduction," *Survey of Current Business 64* (May 1984):21–27 and (July 1984):106–18. GNP estimates in Peter M. Gutmann, "The Subterranean Economy," *Financial Analysts Journal*, November–December 1977, pp. 26ff; Edgar Feige, "How Big is the Irregular Economy?" *Challenge*, November–December 1979, pp. 5–13; Philip Mattera, *Off the Books: The Rise of the Underground Economy* (London: Pluto Press, 1985). Already counted in GNP in Edward F. Denison, "Is U.S. Growth Understated Because of the Underground Economy?" *Review of Economics and Income and Wealth*, March 1982, pp. 1–16. Unemployment and income data accuracy in Richard J. McDonald, "The 'Underground Economy' and BLS Statistical Data," *Monthly Labor Review*, January 1984, pp. 4–16. Housework estimates in Robert Eisner, "Extended Accounts," pp. 1673–74. Effect on research in Robert Eisner, "The Total Incomes System of Accounts," *Survey of Current Business*, January 1985, pp. 32–34.

Intercountry Comparisons

World Bank in International Bank for Reconstruction and Development/The World Bank, *World Development Report* (New York: Oxford University Press, 1989), pp. 159, 164. Rostow in W.W. Rostow, *Politics and the Stages of Growth* (London: Cambridge University Press, 1971). For another example of GNP use, see Hollis Chenery and Moises Syrquin, *Patterns of Development* (London: Oxford University Press, 1975). World Bank loans in Raymond Vernon, "The Politics of Comparative Economic Statistics," in Starr, *The Politics of Statistics*, pp. 65–66.

Measuring Productivity

"U.S. Productivity in Crisis," *Newsweek*, September 8, 1980, pp. 53ff. Magdoff in "The Economist's New Clothes," *The Nation*, March 27, 1982, pp. 355ff.

Issue debated in Samuel Bowles, David M. Gordon, and Thomas E. Weisskopf, "At the Heart of Economic Decline," *The Nation*, July 10–17, 1982, and Harry Magdoff, "A Statistical Fiction," *The Nation*, July 10–17, 1982, pp. 44–48. Methodology summarized in U.S. Department of Labor, Bureau of Labor Statistics, *Handbook of Labor Statistics* (Washington, D.C.: U.S. Government Printing Office, 1988), chap. 10 and 11.

Importance of choice of years in Molly McUsic, "U.S. Manufacturing: Any Cause for Alarm?" *New England Economic Review*, January–February 1987, pp. 9–10. Misrepresentative choice of years in U.S. Chamber of Commerce, *Supply Side Economics* (Washington, D.C.: U.S. Government Printing Office, 1981), slide 10. Data showing increase in Council of Economic Advisers, *Economic Report of the President* (Washington, D.C.: U.S. Government Printing Office., 1988), p. 301.

Service-sector problems are readily admitted by the BLS; see for example: Jerome A. Mark, "Problems Encountered in Measuring Single- and Multifactor Productivity," *Monthly Labor Review*, December 1986, pp. 3–11; Jerome A. Mark, "Measuring Productivity in Service Industries," *Monthly Labor Review*, June 1982, pp. 3–8; and Ronald E. Kutscher and Jerome A. Mark, "The Service-producing Sector: Some Common Perceptions Reviewed," *Monthly Labor Review*, April 1983, pp. 21–24; see also "(Mis)measuring Productivity," *Dollars and Sense*, November 1988, p. 18. On government productivity, see Donald M. Fisk, "Measuring Productivity in State and Local Government," Bulletin 2166, U.S. Department of Labor, Bureau of Labor Statistics (Washington, D.C.: U.S. Government Printing Office, January 1984).

Changing products in Mark, "Problems Encountered," pp. 4–6. Solow in Mancur Olson, "The Productivity Slowdown, the Oil Shocks, and the Real Cycle," *Journal of Economic Perspectives 2*, 4 (Fall 1988):45; Mishel in Lawrence R. Mishel, "The Late Great Debate on Deindustrialization," *Challenge*, January–February 1989, pp. 35–43; see also Lawrence Mishel, *Manufacturing Numbers: How Inaccurate Statistics Conceal U.S. Industrial Decline* (Washington, D.C.: Economic Policy Institute, 1988), and *Survey of Current Business* (Summer 1988). On construction productivity, see Martin Neil Baily and Margaret M. Blair, "Productivity and American Management," in M. Baily et al., eds., *American Living Standards* (Washington, D.C.: The Brookings Institution, 1988), pp. 185–86; and Rosanne Cole, "Reviving the Federal Statistical System: A View from Industry," *American Economic Review 80*, 2 (May 1990):334.

The Savings Rate

Joint Economic Committee in "Low Savings Rate Seen as Main U.S. Problem," *Los Angeles Times*, April 19, 1989, I, p. 12. Savings data in *Economic Report of the President 1988*, p. 278. Federal Reserve data in Frank de Leeuw, "Conflicting Measures of Private Savings," *Survey of Current Business*, November 1984, p. 17. Business saving in Susan Lee and Tatiana Pouschine, "Are We a Nation of Spendthrifts?" *Forbes*, December 16, 1985, pp. 128–34; see also Lou Ferleger and Jay R. Mandle, "The Saving Shortfall," *Challenge*, March–April 1989, pp. 57–59; "There is no evidence," in "The American Savings Slump," *U.S. News and World Report*, March 25, 1985, p. 64; Robert Kuttner, "Let's Not Get All Worked Up Again over Savings," *Business Week*, April 2, 1990, p. 18.

International Statistics

Summary of problem in Robert E. Lipsey, "Reviving the Federal Statistical System: International Aspects," *American Economic Review 80*, 2 (May 1990):337–40. On problems with short-term data, see Edwin A. Finn, Jr., "Of Apples, Oranges and Toyotas," *Forbes*, January 26, 1987, pp. 34–35; Taiwan and Japanese gold in "Trade Reports Sometimes Not What They Seem," *Los Angeles Times*, July 4, 1988, IV, p. 1. On uncounted exports see "Measuring the Service Economy," *New York Times*, October 27, 1985, p. F-4 and "In a Maze of Numbers," *The Economist*, August 20, 1988, pp. 61–62; Freeman in "Measuring the Service Economy." Foreign production in William G. Shepard and Dexter Hutchins, "There's No Trade Deficit, Sam!" *Financial World*, February 23, 1988, pp. 28–35.

CASE STUDY QUESTIONS

1. See Norman J. Glickman and Douglas P. Woodward, *The New Competitors: How Foreign Investors Are Changing the U.S. Economy* (New York: Basic Books, 1989); "Readers Report," *Business Week*, March 12, 1990, pp. 16–17.
2. Robert Eisner, "The Total Incomes System of Accounts," *Survey of Current Business*, January 1985, p. 33.
3. See Donald M. Fisk, "Measuring Productivity in State and Local Government," Bulletin 2166, U.S. Department of Labor, Bureau of Labor Statistics (Washington, D.C.: U.S. Government Printing Office, January 1984).
4. Marilyn Waring, *If Women Counted: A New Feminist Economics* (New York: Harper and Row, 1988).
5. See Kevin F. McCrohan and James D. Smith, "A Consumer Expenditure Approach to Estimating the Size of the Underground Economy," *Journal of Marketing 50* (April 1986):48–60.

Chapter 8: Wealth, Income, and Poverty

DATA SOURCES

Wealth

Federal Reserve wealth survey in U.S. Federal Reserve Board, "1986 Survey of Consumer Finances." Summarized in Robert B. Avery and Arthur B. Kennickell, "Rich Rewards," *American Demographics*, June 1989, pp. 19–22. Data sample in ibid., p. 20. Census Bureau wealth survey in U.S. Department of Commerce, "Household Wealth and Asset Ownership: 1984," Current Population Reports, Series P–70, no. 7, summarized in Joe Schwartz, "Americans' Nest Eggs," *American Demographics*, December 1986, pp. 52–53. Survey described in nineteenth-century census described in Joseph W. Duncan and William C. Shelton, *Revolution in United States Government Statistics* (Washington, D.C.: U.S. Government Printing Office, 1978), p. 5. Data sample in Courtney Slater and Christopher Crane, "The Net Worth of Americans," *American Demographics*, July 1986, p. 5. Indirect estimates in James D. Smith and Stephen D. Franklin, "The Concentration of Personal Wealth," *American Economic Review 64*, 4 (May 1974):162–67; James D. Smith, "Recent Trends in the

Distribution of Wealth in the U.S.: Data, Research Problems, and Prospects,'' in Edward N. Wolff, ed., *International Comparisons of the Distribution of Household Wealth* (Oxford: Clarendon, 1987), pp. 72–89. Methods summarized in Lars Osberg, *Economic Inequality in the United States* (Armonk, N.Y.: M.E. Sharpe, 1984), pp. 38–45. Data sample in Edward W. Wolff and Marcia Marley, "Introduction and Overview," in Wolff, *International Comparisons*, p. 1.

Income

U.S. Census data described in chapter 2. Data sample in U.S. Bureau of the Census, *State and Metropolitan Area Data Book* (Washington, D.C.: U.S. Government Printing Office, 1986), Table 2, p. XLIV. CPS described in chapter 9. For critical commentary on CPS methodology, see Christopher Jencks, "The Politics of Income Measurement," in William Alonso and Paul Starr, eds., *The Politics of Numbers* (New York: Russell Sage Foundation, 1987), pp. 83–131. Data sample in *State and Metropolitan Area Data Book*, Table 2, p. XLIV. Data sample in U.S. Labor Department, *Employment and Earnings*, May 1985, p. 93. PSID summarized in Greg J. Duncan, *Years of Poverty, Years of Plenty* (Ann Arbor: Institute for Social Research, University of Michigan, 1984). PSID compared with other sources in Christopher Jencks, *Who Gets Ahead: The Determinants of Economic Success in America* (New York: Basic Books, 1979), pp. 274–75.

CONTROVERSIES

Are the Rich Getting Richer?

Federal reserve studies in *Federal Reserve Bulletin*, December 1984 and March 1986. JEC study in Smith and Franklin, "The Concentration of Wealth in the United States." Controversy in "Scandal at the Fed?" *Dollars and Sense*, April 1987, pp. 10–22.

What Is Wealth?

Wealth data in Robert B. Avery and Arthur B. Kennickell, "Rich Rewards," *American Demographics*, June 1989, p. 20. Census Bureau data in Avery and Kennickell, "Rich Rewards," pp. 19–22. Financial net worth in "Where's the Wealth?" *Dollars and Sense*, April 1985, pp. 8–17. Retirement wealth in Martin Feldstein, "Social Security, Induced Retirement, and Aggregate Capital Accumulation," *Journal of Political Economy 82* (September 1974):905–26, and "Perceived Wealth in Bonds and Social Security: A Comment," *Journal of Political Economy 84* (April 1976):331–36; Edward N. Wolff, "Pensions and Social Security in the U.S.," in Wolff, *International Comparisons*; and " 'Superstar' Feldstein and His Little Mistake," *Dollars and Sense*, December 1980, pp. 8–9.

Box 8.1. Mean, Median, and Mode

1980 data and discussion of U.S. Census Bureau use of mean and median in Jencks, "The Politics of Income Measurement," pp. 86–88.

Who Is the Richest?

Discovery of Vogel in "The 400 Richest People in America," *Forbes*, October 26, 1987, p. 106. Crown discrepancy in "Billionaires," *Fortune*, October 12, 1987, p. 120, and "The 400 Richest People," pp. 116–17. Discussion of problems in measuring wealth in "What Lies behind the Numbers," *Fortune*, p. 129; and "The 400 Richest People," p. 112.

Are We Better Off?

Income per person data advocated in John E. Schwarz and Thomas J. Volgy, "The Myth of America's Economic Decline," *Harvard Business Review*, September–October 1985, pp. 101–102; Jerry Flint, "How Are We Doing?" *Forbes*, July 13, 1987, p. 94; and Charles Murray, *Losing Ground* (New York: Basic Books, 1984). Debate about data in Courtenay Slater, "Dollars That Count," *American Demographics*, January 1986, pp. 4–7. Spendable earnings data debate in Paul O. Flaim, "The Spendable Earnings Series: Has It Outlived Its Usefulness?" *Monthly Labor Review*, January 1982, pp. 3–9; Thomas E. Weisskopf, "Use of Hourly Earnings Proposed to Revive Spendable Earnings Series," *Monthly Labor Review*, November 1984, pp. 38–43; Paul O. Flaim, "Proposed Spending Earnings Series Retains Basic Faults of Earlier One," *Monthly Labor Review*, November 1984, pp. 43–44. Family income data in U.S. Bureau of the Census, "Money Income of Households, Families and Persons in the United States," Series P–60. Limitations of data in Jencks, "The Politics of Income Measurement." Data in U.S. Census Bureau, *Statistical Abstract* (Washington, D.C.: U.S. Government Printing Office, 1989), p. 445.

Box 8.2. Economic Consequences of Divorce

L. Weitzman, *The Divorce Revolution* (New York: Free Press, 1985); S.D. Hoffman and G.J. Duncan, "What *Are* the Economic Consequences of Divorce?" *Demography 25*, 4 (November 1988):641–45.

Good Jobs, Bad Jobs

Debate in Bennett Harrison and Barry Bluestone, *The Great U-Turn: Corporate Restructuring and the Polarizing of America* (New York: Basic Books, 1988); and Barry Bluestone and Bennett Harrison, "The Generation of Low Wage Employment, 1963–86," *American Economic Review,* May 1988, pp. 124–28; Warren T. Brookes, "Low Pay Jobs: The Big Lie," *Wall Street Journal,* March 25, 1987, p. 1-B; Marvin H. Kosters and Murray N. Ross, "A Shrinking Middle Class?" *The Public Interest 90* (Winter 1980):3–27.

What Is Poverty?

Political shaping of poverty line in Martin Rein, "Problems in the Definition and Measurement of Poverty," in *Poverty in America* (Ann Arbor: University of Michigan Press, 1968), p. 125; "The Hand That Shaped America's Poverty

Line as the Realistic Index," *New York Times*, August 4, 1989, p. A-12; Orshansky method described in Leonard Beeghley, "The Measurement of Poverty," *Social Problems 31*, 3 (February 1984):322–33. Debate about poverty measures summarized in Isabel V. Sawhill, "Poverty in the U.S.: Why Is It So Persistent?" *Journal of Economic Literature 26*, 3 (September 1988):1073–85. Poverty line is too low argued in Osberg, *Economic Inequality*, pp. 63–73 and Harrell R. Rodgers, Jr., "Hiding versus Ending Poverty," *Politics and Society 8*, 2 (1978):253–66; and Patricia Ruggles, "The Poverty Line—Too Low for the 90s," *New York Times*, April 26, 1990, p. A-23. Poverty line is too high argued in Rose Friedman, *Poverty: Definitions and Perspectives* (Washington, D.C.: American Enterprise Institute, 1965); June O'Neill,"Poverty: Programs and Policies," in Annelise Anderson and Dennis Bark, eds., *Thinking about America* (Stanford, Calif.: Hoover Institute, 1988); Gordon Tullock, *Economics of Income Redistribution* (Boston: Kluwer-Nijhoff, 1983), p. 2. Benefit programs and poverty line in "Poverty Estimates Lowered by Inclusion of Noncash Benefits," *Monthly Labor Review*, May 1984, pp. 46–47; Anderson in Beeghley, "The Measurement of Poverty," p. 331. Criticisms of market value approach in ibid., and "Defining Away the Poor," *Dollars and Sense*, January/February 1987, p. 9.

Do the Poor Stay Poor?

PSID results described in Sawhill, "Poverty in the U.S.," p. 1080. Conservative view in Mark Lilla, "Why the 'Income Distribution' Is So Misleading," *The Public Interest 77* (Fall 1984):68, and Charles Murray, *Losing Ground: American Social Policy 1950–1980* (New York: Basic Books, 1984). Liberal intepretation of PSID in Mary Jo Bane, "Household Composition and Poverty," in Sheldon H. Danziger and Daniel H. Weinberg, eds., *Fighting Poverty: What Works and What Doesn't* (Cambridge, Mass.: Harvard University Press, 1986), pp. 209–31.

CASE STUDY QUESTIONS

1. Osberg, *Economic Inequality*, p. 25.
2. "Income Distribution," *Dollars and Sense*, February 1983, pp. 6–7.
3. Robert B. Hill, "The Black Middle Class Defined," *Ebony*, August 1987, p. 30; Andrew Brimmer, "Income and Wealth," *Ebony*, August 1987, p. 46; see also Gerald Jaynes and Robin Williams, *A Common Destiny: Blacks and American Society* (Washington, D.C.: National Academy Press, 1989).
4. Poor families headed by women in Bane, "Household Composition and Poverty," p. 217.
5. Jencks, "The Politics of Income Measurement," pp. 92–105.
6. Suzanne M. Bianchi and Daphne Spain, *American Women in Transition* (New York: Russell Sage Foundation, 1986), pp. 170–73; Nancy F. Rytina, "Comparing Annual and Weekly Earnings from the Current Population Survey," *Monthly Labor Review 106* (April 1983):32–36; Randy Albelda, "Women's Income Not up to Par," *Dollars and Sense*, July/August 1988, pp. 6–8.

Chapter 9: Labor Statistics

DATA SOURCES

U.S. Bureau of Labor Statistics

A short summary of BLS data is U.S. Department of Labor, *Workers, Jobs, and Statistics* (Washington, D.C.: U.S. Government Printing Office; 1983). Detailed official descriptions in U.S. Department of Labor, *BLS Handbook of Methods*, vol. 1 (Washington, D.C.: U.S. Government Printing Office; 1982). Other descriptions in Norman Frumkin, *Tracking America's Economy* (Armonk, N.Y.: M. E. Sharpe, 1987), chap. 5; Albert T. Sommers and Lucie R. Blau, *The U.S. Economy Demystified* (Lexington, Mass.: D.C. Heath, 1988), pp. 78–80. Data sample in U.S. Labor Department, *Employment and Earnings*, May 1985, p. 20.

U.S. Census Bureau

On U.S. Census, see notes to chapter 2. Data sample in Bureau of the Census, U.S. Department of Commerce, *1980 Census of Population*, "Occupation by Industry," PC80-2-7C (Washington, D.C.: U.S. Government Printing Office, May 1984), pp. 148–49. On economic census, see U.S. Department of Commerce, Bureau of the Census, *Guide to the 1982 Economic Censuses and Related Statistics* (Washington, D.C.: U.S. Government Printing Office, 1984). Data sample in Bureau of the Census, U.S. Department of Commerce, *1982 Census of Governments*, "Compendium of Public Employment," GC82(3)-2 (Washington, D.C.: U.S. Government Printing Office, November 1984), p. 182.

CONTROVERSIES

Unemployment

Measuring unemployment during the Great Depression, see William T. Moye and Joseph Goldberg, *The First Hundred Years of the Bureau of Labor Statistics* (Washington, D.C.: U.S. Government Printing Office, 1985), pp. 125–77; Margo J. Anderson, *The American Census: A Social History* (New Haven, Conn.: Yale University Press, 1988), pp. 162–89. "The tide of employment" in Moye and Goldberg, *The First Hundred Years*, p. 130. History of Current Population Survey in John E. Bregger, "The Current Population Survey: A Historical Perspective and BLS's Role," *Monthly Labor Review*, June 1984, pp. 8–14.

Unemployment underestimate debate discussed in David M. Gordon, *Problems in Political Economy* (Lexington, Mass.: D.C. Heath, 1977), pp. 70–75; and "Undercounting the Unemployed," *Dollars and Sense*, October 1986, pp. 18–19. BLS unemployment measures described in *BLS Handbook of Methods*, chap. 1; Norman Frumkin, *Tracking America's Economy* (Armonk, N.Y.: M.E. Sharpe, 1987), chap. 5. History of unemployment measure in Moye and Goldberg, *The First Hundred Years*, pp. 237–43; Brookings Institution study described in "Undercounting the Unemployed," p. 1.

Overcount in Peter Gutmann, "Statistical Illusions, Mistaken Policies, *Challenge*, November–December 1979, p. 17. Response to Gutmann in Richard J.

McDonald, "The 'Underground Economy' and BLS Statistical Data," *Monthly Labor Review*, January 1984, pp. 11–15. On natural rate of unemployment debate, see for example, Paul A. Samuelson and William D. Nordhaus, *Economics* (New York: McGraw-Hill, 1989), pp. 296–301.

Alternative measures in Alexander Keyssar, *Out of Work: The First Century of Unemployment in Massachusetts* (New York: Cambridge University Press, 1986). New U.S. jobs in John E. Schwarz and Thomas J. Volgy, "The Myth of America's Decline," *Harvard Business Review*, September–October 1985, p. 101. Reagan on 5 million new jobs in *New York Times*, September 8, 1984, p. A-1. Bush on 30 million jobs in *New York Times*, August 19, 1988, p. A-1; backed away from in *New York Times*, August 24, 1988, p. A-1.

Box 9.1. Fewer Statistics; Less Money

"L.A. Sues Labor Dept. over Counting Jobs," *Los Angeles Times*, April 9, 1988, p. II-1.

Better Jobs?

Occupational data described in John Thompson, "BLS Job Cross-Classification System Relates Information from Six Sources," *Monthly Labor Review*, November 1981, pp. 40–44. Edwards's classification scheme in Alba Edwards, *Comparative Occupational Statistics for the United States* (Washington, D.C.: U.S. Bureau of the Census, 1943), pp. 175–76, and H. Anderson, *Occupational Trends in the United States* (Stanford, Calif.: Stanford University Press; 1940), p. 40. Criticisms in Margo Anderson Conk, *The United States Census and the New Jersey Urban Occupational Structure, 1870–1940* (Ann Arbor, Mich.: UMI Research Press, 1980), and Harry Braverman, *Labor and Monopoly Capital* (New York: Monthly Review Press, 1974), pp. 429–32. White collars in Peter M. Blau and Otis D. Duncan, *The American Occupational Structure* (New York: Wiley, 1967). Replicated in David L. Featherman and Robert M. Hauser, *Opportunity and Change* (New York: Academic Press, 1978). For summary of complex analysis based on occupational structures, see Dennis Gilbert and Joseph Kahl, *The American Class Structure* (Homewood, Ill.: Dorsey, 1982), chaps. 3 and 6. Criticism of white-collar, blue-collar distinction in Patrick H. Horan, "Is Status Attainment Research Atheoretical?" *American Sociological Review 43* (August 1978):534–41, and Sidney M. Willhelm, "Opportunities Are Diminishing," *Society*, March–April 1979, pp. 11–17. On 1980 reclassification, see Nancy F. Rytina and Suzanne M. Bianchi, "Occupational Reclassification and Changes in Distribution by Gender," *Monthly Labor Review*, March 1984, pp. 11–16.

Union Membership

Union membership data described in Michael Goldfeld, *The Decline of Organized Labor in the United States* (Chicago: University of Chicago Press, 1987), pp. 8–25; Edward C. Kokkelenberg and Donna R. Sockell, "Union Membership in the United States, 1973–1981," *Industrial and Labor Relations Review 38* (July 4, 1985):497–533; Henry S. Farber, "The Recent Decline of Unionization in the United States," *Science*, November 13, 1987, pp. 915–20. Strike data described in U.S. Department of Labor, Bureau of Labor Statistics, *Monthly Labor Review*, January 1987, p. 78.

Is the Workplace Safe?

History of BLS safety and health investigations in Moye and Goldberg, *The First Hundred Years*, pp. 58–61, 99–101, 132–33, 251–53. Safety and health data under OSHA described in Harvey J. Hilaski, "Understanding Statistics on Occupational Illnesses," *Monthly Labor Review*, March 1981, pp. 25–29. Debate about effectiveness of OSHA in Kenneth B. Noble, "For OSHA Balance Is Hard to Find," *New York Times*, January 10, 1988, p. E-5.

International Labor Statistics

International labor statistics described in *BLS Handbook of Methods*, chap. 16; International Labor Office, *World Labor Report*. Definitions of labor force and unemployment in Patrick J. McMahon, "An International Comparison of Labor Force Participation," *Monthly Labor Review*, May 1986, pp. 3–12; Joyanna Moy, "An Analysis of Unemployment and Other Labor Market Indicators in 10 Countries," *Monthly Labor Review*, April 1988, "Appendix: Revisions in Comparative Statistics," pp. 48–50. BLS comparable data in *Economic Report of the President* and *Handbook of Labor Statistics*. Bush on job creation in *New York Times*, August 19, 1988, p. A-1; backed away from in *New York Times*, August 24, 1988, p. A-1. European workforce in McMahon, "An International Comparison of Labor Force Participation."

CASE STUDY QUESTIONS

1. Ben J. Wattenberg, *The Good News Is the Bad News Is Wrong* (New York: Simon and Schuster, 1984), pp. 231–33.
2. Establishment job data compared in "Dueling Figures Hint at a Slowdown in Job Growth," *Business Week*, September 26, 1988, p. 28. Analysis of divergent series in Paul O. Flaim, "How Many New Jobs since 1982? Data from Two Surveys Differ," *Monthly Labor Review*, August 1989, pp. 10–15.
3. Council of Economic Advisers, *Economic Report of the President 1990* (Washington, D.C.: U.S. Government Printing Office, 1990), p. 340.
4. Debate about improvement in women's job status in Francine D. Blau and Marianne A. Ferber, *The Economics of Women, Men and Work* (Englewood Cliffs, N.J.: Prentice-Hall, 1986), pp. 228–79; Suzanne M. Bianchi and Daphne Spain, *American Women in Transition* (New York: Russell Sage Foundation, 1986), pp. 159–68.
5. Women in Japanese labor force in International Labor Office, *World Labor Report 1* (Geneva: International Labor Office; 1984), p. 54.

Chapter 10: Business Statistics

DATA SOURCES

On number and types of businesses, see principles of economics textbooks, for example, Campbell R. McConnell, *Economics* (New York: McGraw-Hill, 1987), pp. 113–19.

Public Corporations

On SEC, see Adolph G. Lurie, *How to Read Annual Reports—Intelligently* (Englewood Cliffs, N.J.: Prentice-Hall, 1984). List of companies reporting in U.S. Securities and Exchange Commission, "Companies Required to File Annual Reports" (Washington, D.C.: U.S. Government Printing Office, 1988). How to read annual reports in Fred C. Armstrong, *The Business of Economics* (St. Paul, Minn.: West Publishing, 1986), pp. 137–43. Annual reports criticized in "Curious about the Crash? Don't Read Your Annual Report," *Business Week*, April 11, 1988, p. 66. Data sample in General Motors 1988 Annual Report, pp. 2–3. Business handbooks include Moody's, Standard and Poors, Dun and Bradstreet publications, and Ward's Business Directory. Data sample in *Fortune*, April 24, 1989, p. 354, and *The Business Week Top 1,000*, Special 1989 Issue, p. 166.

Privately Held Corporations

Ranking and discussion of methods in "The Joy of Private Capital," *Forbes*, December 12, 1988, pp. 178–80. Comparative size of public corporations in "The Biggest Blowout Ever," *Fortune*, April 24, 1989, p. 347. See also *MacMillan Directory of Leading Private Companies* (Wilmette, Ill.: National Register Publishing Co.). Helpful resource is Gordon T. Law, Jr., and Michael E. Reilly, *A Guide to Information on Closely Held Corporations* (Buffalo: New York State School of Industrial and Labor Relations, 1986).

Small Businesses

Number and revenue in U.S. Small Business Administration, *The State of Small Business 1987* (Washington, D.C.: U.S. Government Printing Office, 1987), p. 17. Data sample in Dun's Marketing Services, *Million Dollar Directory 1989* (Parsippany, N.J.: Dun's Marketing Services, Inc.) p. 2886.

Aggregate Statistics

Small Business Data Source described in U.S. Small Business Administration, "Handbook of Small Business Data" (Washington, D.C.: U.S. Government Printing Office, 1983). Data sample in U.S. Small Business Administration, *State of Small Business 1987*, p. 283.

CONTROVERSIES

Who Is the Biggest of Them All?

Debate on use of *Fortune* sales data in letter to the editor by M.A. Adelman, *Fortune*, September 1955, p. 20; and F.M. Scherer, *Industrial Market Structure and Economic Performance*, 2d rev. ed. (Boston: Houghton Mifflin, 1980), p. 47. Sara Lee in "The Fortune 500," *Fortune*, April 24, 1989, p. 354. Changes in list in "A New Era of Rapid Rise and Run," *Fortune*, April 24, 1989, p. 77. On problems of asset measurement in accounting textbooks, see for example, Belverd

E. Needles, Jr., Henry R. Anderson, and James C. Caldwell, *Principles of Accounting* (Boston: Houghton-Mifflin, 1987), pp. 493–565. Market value method defended in *The Business Week Top 1,000*, Special 1989 Issue, pp. 14–20. Comparison of all size measurements in S.S. Shalit and U. Sankar, "The Measurement of Firm Size," *Review of Economics and Statistics 59* (August 1977):290–98.

Box 10.1. Which Is Larger?

For use of list, see for example, Robert J. Carbaugh, *International Economics* (Cambridge, Mass.: Winthrop Publishers, 1980), p. 219. Current data in *Fortune 500*, April 28, 1986, p. 1982, and *The Economist, The World in Figures* (Boston: G.K. Hall, 1989), p. 9.

Box 10.2. Top of the World

Data and discussion in "Who's Sitting on Top of the World," *Business Week*, July 18, 1988, pp. 137–38; see also "Ranking the Leaders," *Wall Street Journal*, September 29, 1986, p. 17.

Are the Big Too Big?

On history of antitrust, see Steven C. Salop, "Symposium on Mergers and Antitrust," *Journal of Economic Perspectives 1*, 2 (Fall 1987):3–12; and Paul A. Samuelson and William D. Nordhaus, *Economics* (New York: McGraw-Hill, 1989), pp. 619–24. Market share use in F. M. Scherer and David Ross, *Industrial Market Structure and Economic Performance*, 3d rev. ed. (Boston: Houghton Mifflin, 1990), pp. 72–96, 184–85. Critique of use of market share in Betty Bock, *Concentration, Oligopoly, and Profit* (New York: The Conference Board, 1972). HHI index described in Salop, "Symposium," p. 7 and "Herfindahl Index," *The New Palgrave: A Dictionary of Economics*, vol. 2 (New York: Stockton Press, 1987), p. 639. 1980s policy debated in *Journal of Economic Perspectives 1*, 2 (Fall 1987):3–54. Problems in defining market in Franklin M. Fisher, "Horizontal Mergers: Triage and Treatment," *Journal of Economic Perspectives 1*, 2 (Fall 1987), p. 26. Pabst and Blatz in Scherer, *Industrial Market Structure*, 2d rev. ed., p. 557. Northwest and Republic in Fisher, "Horizontal Mergers: Triage and Treatment," pp. 32–35. Glass bottles in Scherer and Ross, *Industrial Market Structure*, 3d rev. ed., pp. 180–86. 1980s trend in ibid., p. 191. IBM in ibid., pp. 459–62. History of antitrust enforcement in Richard G. Lipsey, Peter O. Steiner, and Douglas D. Purvis, *Economics* (New York: Harper and Row, 1987), p. 294. University of Chicago influence described in Stephen A. Rhoades, "The Decline and Possible Resurrection of Antitrust Policy toward Mergers," *Antitrust Law and Economic Review 17*, 4 (1985):49–55. Shepard in William G. Shepherd, "Causes of Increased Competition in the U.S. Economy 1939–1980," *Review of Economics and Statistics*, November 1982, pp. 613–26, and William G. Shepherd, "Bust the Reagan Trustbusters," *Fortune*, August 4, 1986, pp. 225–27.

Box 10.3. The Herfindahl-Hirschman Index

Scherer and Ross, *Industrial Market Structure*, 3d rev. ed., pp. 72–73, 185.

The Urge to Merge—Are the Big Getting Bigger?

R.J. Reynolds-Nabisco buyout described in Bryan Burrough and John Helyar, *Barbarians at the Gate: The Fall of RJR Nabisco* (New York: Harper and Row, 1990). Trend in Scherer and Ross, *Industrial Market Structure*, 3d rev. ed., pp. 153–59. Early research in Adolf Berle and Gardiner Means, *The Modern Corporation and Private Property* (New York: Harcourt-Brace, 1968). Defense of takeovers in Council of Economic Advisers, *Economic Report of the President 1985* (Washington, D.C.: U.S. Government Printing Office, 1985), pp. 187–216. Increasing trend in manufacturing concentration in Samuelson and Nordhaus, *Economics* (1985), p. 622; Scherer and Ross, *Industrial Market Structure*, 3d rev. ed., pp. 59–61. In favor of merger controls, in Walter Adams and James W. Brock, *The Bigness Complex* (New York: Pantheon, 1986). See also symposium on takeovers, *Journal of Economic Perspectives 2*, 1 (Winter 1988).

Box 10.4. Standard Industrial Classification

On specific codes, see Dun's Marketing Services, "Standard Industrial Classification Statistics." Use of codes in Scherer, *Industrial Market Structure*, 2d rev. ed., pp. 59–60, and Scherer and Ross, *Industrial Market Structure*, 3d rev. ed., p. 74. On problems with SIC, see Rosanne Cole, "Reviving the Federal Statistical System: A View from Industry," *American Economic Review 80*, 2 (May 1990):333–34.

Line-of-Business Reporting

Favor disclosure in Frederic M. Scherer, "Segmental Financial Reporting," in Harvey J. Goldschmid, ed., *Business Disclosure: Government's Need to Know* (New York: Columbia University Center for Law and Economic Studies, 1979), pp. 3–57. Opposing disclosure in George J. Bentson, "The FTC's Line of Business Program," in Goldschmid, *Business Disclosure*, pp. 58–140. Resolution in Scherer and Ross, *Industrial Market Structure*, 3d rev. ed., p. 419.

Box 10.5. Who Owns the Corporation?

Vic Reinemer, "Corporate Ownership and Control: A Public Policy View," in Goldschmid, *Business Disclosure*, pp. 142–75; Scherer and Ross, *Industrial Market Structure*, 3d rev. ed., pp. 42–44.

How Much Profit?

Chevron in "Chevron Energy Report," *New York Times*, November 18, 1980, p. A-20; see also Richard C. Gerstenberg (former Chair, General Motors), "The Profit System and America's Growth," *New York Times*, March 4, 1974, p. 29. Public estimate in James D. Gwartney and Richard Stroup, *Economics* (San Diego: Harcourt Brace Jovanovich, 1987), p. 493. On accounting losses accompanying high executive salaries, see "Pay Stubs of the Rich and Corporate," *Business Week*, May 7, 1990, p. 59. Accounting profits described in accounting textbooks; see for example, Needles, Anderson, and Caldwell, *Principles of*

Accounting, pp. 98–116. On interest payments, see "Are True Profits Falling or Rising?" *New York Times*, January 15, 1990, p. C-2. Adjusted data described in "Corporate Profits: Reading between the Bottom Lines," *Business Week*, June 15, 1987, pp. 102–104. Debate about use of data in William H. Peterson, "Putting an End to Adversarial Unionism," *New York Times*, July 26, 1987, p. C-2; and letter to the editor from Thomas R. Michl, *New York Times*, August 23, 1987, p. F-16.

How Now Dow

Dow described in Gary E. Clayton and Martin Gerhard Giesbrecht, *Everyday Statistics* (New York: McGraw-Hill, 1990), pp. 105–109. IBM and Exxon in "Dow 2500: Then and Now," *The Independent Investor 5*, 14 (July 26, 1989).

CASE STUDY QUESTIONS

1. Frederic M. Scherer, "Segmental Financial Reporting," in Goldschmid, *Business Disclosure*, pp. 3–57.
2. See discussion and references on SIC above.
3. Council of Economic Advisers, *Economic Report of the President 1985* (Washington, D.C.: U.S. Government Printing Office, 1985), p. 200.
4. *New York Times*, March 28, 1990, p. C-11.
5. Scherer, *Industrial Market Structure*, 2d rev. ed., pp. 39–41.
6. Ibid., p. 552–53.

Chapter 11: Government

DATA SOURCES

U.S. budgets in *Budget of the United States Government* (Washington, D.C.: U.S. Government Printing Office). Budget process described in Joseph J. Minarik, *Making America's Budget Policy* (Armonk, N.Y.: M.E. Sharpe, 1989). U.S. Federal Reserve statistics described in "Recent Developments in Economic Statistics at the Federal Reserve: Part 2," *Business Economics*, July 1989, pp. 40–47, and Norman Frumkin, *Tracking America's Economy* (Armonk, N.Y.: M.E. Sharpe, 1987), chap. 17. Consumer and producer price indexes described in Bureau of Labor Statistics, U.S. Department of Labor, *Handbook of Labor Statistics* (Washington, D.C.: U.S. Government Printing Office, 1985), pp. 346–49. Commerce Department inflation adjustments in Allan H. Young, "Alternate Measures of Real GNP," *Survey of Current Business*, April 1989, pp. 27–34. On currency adjustments, see "Index of Weighted Average Exchange Values of the U.S. Dollar: Revisions," *Federal Reserve Bulletin*, August 1978, p. 700.

CONTROVERSIES

How Much for the Military?

Jackson in "Jackson Thrives on Double Standards," *Los Angeles Times*, January 29, 1988, p. II:7. Budget revisions in "Undercounting Military Spending," *Dollars and Sense*, September 1987. See also "Bush Aides Issue Changes for Reagan's 1990 Budget," *New York Times*, February 14, 1989, p. A-12. Soviet budget in Franklyn D. Holzman, "Politics and Guesswork," *International Security 14*, 2 (Fall 1989):101–31, and Arthur Macy Cox, "The CIA's Tragic Error," *New York Review of Books*, November 6, 1980, pp. 21–24. Pipes in "The Russians Are Still Coming," *New York Times*, October 9, 1989, p. A-15.

How Much for Welfare?

Murray in Charles Murray, *Losing Ground: American Social Policy 1950–1980* (New York: Basic Books, 1984). Critics in Christopher Jencks, "How Poor Are the Poor?" *New York Review of Books*, May 9, 1985, pp. 40–49. One-seventh in Sol Levitan, "The Evolving Welfare System," *Society 23*, 2 (January 2, 1986):5. U.S. spending in "Comparing Social Paychecks," *Dollars and Sense*, October 1989, p. 23. Tullock in Gordon Tullock, *Economics of Income Redistribution* (Boston: Kluwer-Nijhoff, 1983), p. 2. Sweden in "Comparing Social Paychecks."

How Big Is the Deficit?

"Asset management" in "Plan to Sell Surplus Property to Lower Deficit Hits Snags," *New York Times*, May 29, 1984, p. I-11. Conrail in "Uncle Sam's Loan Sale," *Business Week*, January 26, 1987, pp. 41–42. Shifting payday and off budget in John Miller, "Washington's Magic Act," *Dollars and Sense*, January–February 1990, pp. 9–11; and "The Bottom Line: Gramm-Rudman Isn't Working," *Business Week*, April 10, 1989, p. 36. On social security surplus, see "Budget: Dilemma Is How to Spend Surpluses," *Los Angeles Times*, May 22, 1988, p. A-1.

A Debt Monster?

Eisner position summarized in Robert Eisner, "The Federal Deficit: How Does It Matter?" *Science 237* (September 25, 1987):1577–82. Heilbroner summarized in Robert Heilbroner and Peter Bernstein, *The Debt and the Deficit* (New York: W.W. Norton, 1989). Capital accounting discussed in ibid., pp. 95–97 and Robert Eisner, "The Total Incomes System of Accounts," *Survey of Current Business*, January 1985, pp. 24–34. "The entire government . . . " in Robert Eisner, "Budget Deficits: Rhetoric and Reality," *Journal of Economic Perspectives 3*, 2 (Spring 1989):75. Criticism and other approaches in "Symposium," *Journal of Economic Perspectives 3*, 2 (Spring 1989). See also Letters, *New York Times*, March 12, 1989, IV, p. E-24. Schultze in Charles L. Schultze, "Of Wolves, Termites, and Pussycats: Or, Why We Should Worry about the Budget Deficit," *Brookings Review* (Summer 1989):26–33; Aaron in Letters, *New York Times*, March 12, 1989, IV, p. E-24. See also "Dual Federal Budgets Could Mislead," *Wall Street Journal*, December 16, 1986, p. 35. Heilbroner on public projects in Heilbroner and Bernstein, *The Debt*, pp. 106–109.

Taxes

On 1980s tax cut, see Frank Ackerman, *Hazardous to Our Wealth: Economic Policies in the 1980s* (Boston: South End Press, 1984), pp. 33–48. Stockman in

William Greider, "The Education of David Stockman," *Atlantic*, December 1981, pp. 46–47. On capital gains, see Paul Craig Roberts, "Ditch the Capital-Gains Tax Once and for All," *Business Week*, April 3, 1989, p. 21; "Review and Outlook," *Wall Street Journal*, July 25, 1989, p. A-18, and July 28, 1989, p. A-10; Joseph A. Pechman, "Letters to the Editor," *Wall Street Journal*, August 1, 1989, p. A-11; Robert S. McIntyre, "Tax Deform," *New Republic*, August 21, 1989, pp. 18–21. Tax burden in Joseph Pechman, *Who Paid the Taxes* (Washington, D.C.: Brookings Institution, 1985); and Edgar K. Browning and William R. Johnson, *The Distribution of the Tax Burden* (Washington, D.C.: American Enterprise Institute, 1979). Further debate in Edgar K. Browning, "Pechman's Tax Incidence Study: A Note on the Data," and Joseph A. Pechman, "Pechman's Tax Incidence Study: A Response," *American Economic Review 76*, 5 (December 1986):1214–19, and Joseph A. Pechman, "The Future of the Income Tax," *American Economic Review 80*, 1 (March 1990):1–20. See also Randy Albelda, "Let Them Pay Taxes," *Dollars and Sense*, April 1988, pp. 9–11.

Measuring Money

Federal Reserve and measurement of money supply in many economics textbooks; see for example, Paul A. Samuelson and William D. Nordhaus, *Economics* (New York: McGraw-Hill, 1989), chap. 11. Use of monetary targets summarized in Donald L. Kohn, "Policy Targets and Operating Procedures in the 1990s," *Federal Reserve Bulletin 76*, 1 (January 1990):1–7; and Robert J. Gordon, *Macroeconomics* (Glenview, Ill.: Scott, Foresman, 1990), pp. 454–58. On underground economy, see chap. 7. Overseas money in "$180 Billion in U.S. Currency Eludes Tally; Is it Abroad?" *New York Times*, February 20, 1990, p. C-1.

Inflation

CPI versus PCE in Jack E. Tripleti, "Reconciling the CPI and the PCE Deflator," *Monthly Labor Review*, September 1981, pp. 3–15. Data in Council of Economic Advisers, *Economic Report of the President 1988* (Washington, D.C.: U.S. Government Printing Office, 1988), pp. 255, 317. Housing issue in U.S. Department of Labor, "Changing the Homeownership Component of the Consumer Price Index to Rental Equivalence," *CPI Detailed Report* (Washington, D.C.: U.S. Government Printing Office, January 1983). Criticism in "Switching Yardsticks: A New Measure of Inflation," *Dollars and Sense*, December 1981, p. 9. On other products, see Robert J. Gordon, *The Measurement of Durable Good Prices* (Chicago: University of Chicago Press, 1990). New poverty rate in Ronald Kwan, "Playing with Numbers," *Dollars and Sense*, May 1990, pp. 20–21. On Harrison and Bluestone controversy, see chap. 8. Deliberate deception in Warren T. Brookes, "Low-Pay Jobs: The Big Lie," *Wall Street Journal*, March 25, 1987, p. 32. Example of use of PCE in Frank Levy, "Incomes, Families, and Living Standards," in Robert E. Litan et al., *American Living Standards* (Washington, D.C.: The Brookings Institution, 1988), pp. 108–53.

Currency Rates

U.S. dollar values in "Business Week Index," *Business Week,* March 12, 1990, p. 6. Trade-weighted indexes in "The Buck Stops Where?" *Dollars and Sense,* March 1987, pp. 20–21. German well-being in "Comparing Wealth as Money Fluctuates," *New York Times,* August 23, 1988, p. IV-3. Purchasing power parity in Derek Blades, "International Statistics: An OECD View," *Business Economics,* July 1986, p. 42. East German currency in "The West German Mark May Soon Rule the East," *Business Week,* November 27, 1989, p. 65.

CASE STUDY QUESTIONS

1. "$180 Billion in U.S. Currency Eludes Tally; Is It Abroad?" *New York Times,* February 20, 1990, p. C-1, and Phillip Mattera, *Off the Books* (London: Pluto Press, 1985), p. 44.

2. Randy Albelda, "Let Them Pay Taxes," *Dollars and Sense,* April 1988, pp. 9–11.

3. Soviet budget in Franklyn D. Holzman, "Politics and Guesswork," *International Security 14,* 2 (Fall 1989):101–31; Arthur Macy Cox, "CIA's Tragic Error," *The New York Review of Books,* November 6, 1980, pp. 21–24; "The Russians Are Still Coming," *New York Times,* October 9, 1989, p. A-15.

4. Robert Heilbroner and Peter Bernstein, *The Debt and the Deficit* (New York: W.W. Norton, 1989); Charles L. Schultze, "Of Wolves, Termites, and Pussycats: Or, Why We Should Worry about the Budget Deficit," *Brookings Review* (Summer 1989):26–33.

5. Robert J. Gordon, *Macroeconomics* (Glenview, Ill.: Scott, Foresman, 1990), pp. 53–54.

6. "The Changes behind the CPI's New Look," *Business Week,* March 2, 1987, p. 24; Charles Mason and Clifford Butler, "New Basket of Goods and Services Being Priced in Revised CPI," *Monthly Labor Review,* January 1987, pp. 3–22; Mary Lynn Schmidt, "Comparison of the Revised and Old CPI," *Monthly Labor Review,* November 1987, pp. 3–6.

Chapter 12: Conclusions

For analysis of social and economic statistics, see John Irvine, Ian Miles, and Jeff Evans, *Demystifying Social Statistics* (London: Pluto Press, 1981); William Alonso and Paul Starr, *The Politics of Numbers* (New York: Russell Sage Foundation, 1987); and Lou Ferleger, " 'Truth' from Numbers: Sorting Out Statistics," *Socialist Review 93,* 4 (May–August 1987):91–104. On assumptions used in government statistics, see Jerry Miron and Christina D. Romer, "Reviving the Federal Statistical System: The View from Academia," *American Economic Review 80,* 2 (May 1990):329–36. On choices for U.S. enfranchisement, see Margo J. Anderson, *The American Census: A Social History* (New Haven, Conn.: Yale University Press, 1988), pp. 11–12.

Index

About the Author

Mark H. Maier is Associate Professor of Economics at Glendale College, Glendale, California. He is the author of *City Unions: Managing Discontent in New York City* (Rutgers University Press, 1987). Dr. Maier received his Ph.D. in economics from the Graduate Faculty, New School for Social Research in 1980.